UNOBTRUSIVE
MEASURES

SAGE CLASSICS

———————•◆•———————

*T*he goal of the **Sage Classics Series** is to help bring new generations of social scientists and their students into a deeper, richer understanding of the roots of social science thinking by making important scholars' classic works available for today's readers. The Series will focus on those social science works that have the most relevance for impacting contemporary thought, issues, and policy—including increasing our understanding of the techniques, methods, and theories that have shaped the evolution of the social sciences to date.

The works chosen for the Series are cornerstones upon which modern social science has been built. Each volume includes an introduction by a preeminent leader in the discipline, and provides an historical context for the work while bringing it into today's world as it relates to issues of modern life and behavior. Moving into the future, opportunities for application of the findings are identified and references for further reading are provided.

It is our hope at Sage that the reissuance of these classics will preserve their place in history as having shaped the field of social science. And it is our wish that the Series, in its reader-friendly format, will be accessible to all in order to stimulate ongoing public interest in the social sciences as well as research and analysis by tomorrow's leaders.

Sage Classics 2

UNOBTRUSIVE MEASURES

Revised Edition

Eugene J. Webb • Donald T. Campbell
Richard D. Schwartz • Lee Sechrest

Sage Publications, Inc.
International Educational and Professional Publisher
Thousand Oaks ▪ London ▪ New Delhi

First Edition 1966 by Rand McNally College Publishing Company

For information:

Sage Publications, Inc.
2455 Teller Road
Thousand Oaks, California 91320
E-mail: order@sagepub.com

Sage Publications Ltd.
6 Bonhill Street
London EC2A 4PU
United Kingdom

Sage Publications India Pvt. Ltd.
M-32 Market
Greater Kailash I
New Delhi 110 048 India

Printed in the United States of America

ISBN: 0-7619-2011-0 (cloth)
ISBN: 0-7619-2012-9 (paperback)

This book is printed on acid-free paper.

00 01 02 03 04 05 06 7 6 5 4 3 2 1

Acquiring Editor:	C. Deborah Laughton
Editorial Assistant:	Eileen Carr
Production Editor:	Wendy Westgate
Editorial Assistant:	Patricia Zeman
Typesetter:	Lynn Miyata
Indexer:	Molly Hall
Cover Designer:	Michelle Lee

CONTENTS

————•◆•————

PREFACE TO THE
FIRST EDITION (1965)

————— •◆• —————

his monograph has had a series of working titles, and we
should identify them for the benefit of our friends who
shared early drafts. To some, this is *The Bullfighter's Beard*—
a provocative, if uncommunicative, title drawn from the observation that
toreros' beards are longer on the day of the fight than on any other day. No one
seems to know if the torero's beard really grows faster that day because of
anxiety or if he simply stands further away from the blade, shaking razor in
hand. Either way, there were not enough American aficionados to get the point,
so we added . . . *and Other Nonreactive Measures.*

This title lasted for a while, but the occasionally bizarre content of the
material shifted the working title to *Oddball Research, Oddball Measures,* and
the like. Most of our friends have known the manuscript under one of the
"oddball" labels, and it is only a fear of librarians that has caused us to drop it.
In this day of explicit indexing, we feared that the book would nestle on a shelf
between *Notes for the T Quarterback* and *Putting Hints for Beginning Golfers.* As
much as we might enjoy the company of an Arnold Palmer, we prefer it outside
the library. A widely circulated version used the nontitle *Other Measures.* The
list of titles we have specifically decided *not* to use is even longer and less
descriptively adequate.

In presenting these novel methods, we have purposely avoided consideration of the ethical issues which they raise. We have done so because we feel that this is a matter for separate consideration. Some readers will find none of the methods objectionable, others may find virtually all of them open to question. Each school is welcome to use this compilation to buttress its position—either to illustrate the harmless ingenuity of social scientists or to marshal a parade of horribles. Although the authors vary in moral boiling points, we are all between these positions. Some of the methods described strike us as possibly unethical; their inclusion is not intended as a warrant for their use. But we vary among ourselves in criteria and application. We do not feel able at this point to prepare a compelling ethical resolution of these complex issues. Nonetheless, we recognize the need of such a resolution and hope that our compilation will, among other things, stimulate and expedite thoughtful debate on these matters.

Perhaps the most extreme position on this matter has been stated by Edward Shils (1959). He asserts that all social science activity should be disciplined by careful attention to the problem of privacy. He would rule out any "observations of private behavior, however technically feasible, without the explicit and fully informed permission of the person to be approved." His concern on this issue would lead him to recommend that questionnaire and interview studies be sharply limited by ethical considerations. Among the practices he deplores are (a) the simulation of warmth by the interviewer to insure rapport and (b) giving the appearance of agreement of answers on controversial questions to encourage the expression of unpopular attitudes.

He would have the interviewer not only avoid such practices but also disclose, presumably in advance, his purpose in asking the question. This disclosure should include not only a statement of the researcher's "personal goal, e.g., to complete a thesis" but also his "cognitive intention." Groups or types of questions "ought to be justified by the explanation of what the answers will contribute to the clarification of the problem being investigated." Even the technique of participant observation seems to Shils "morally obnoxious . . . manipulation" unless the observer discloses at the outset his intention of conducting a social scientific investigation.

Most social scientists would find this position too extreme. If it were adopted, it would add enormously to the problems of reactivity with which this monograph is primarily concerned. Nevertheless, Shils's position specifies some of the dangers to the citizen and social science of an unconscionable invasion of privacy. Few would deny that social scientists can go too far in intruding on privacy. Recording deliberations in a jury room or hiding under beds to record pillow talk are techniques which have led to moral revulsion on the part of large numbers of professionals. Manipulations aimed at the arousal of anxiety or extreme aggression could conceivably produce lasting damage to the psychological health of experimental subjects.

What is needed is a set of criteria by which various research techniques can be appraised morally. Each of the social sciences has attempted to develop a code of ethics for guidance in these matters. So far, however, these have suffered from the absence of a careful analysis of the problem. We need a specification of the multiple interests potentially threatened by social science research: the privacy of the individual, his freedom from manipulation, the protection of the aura of trust on which the society depends, and, by no means least in importance, the good reputation of social science.

The multiple methods presented here may do more than raise these questions for discussion. They may provide alternatives by which ethical criteria can be met without impinging on important interests of the research subjects. Some of the methods described here, such as the use of archival records and trace measures, may serve to avoid the problems of invasion of privacy by permitting the researcher to gain valuable information without ever identifying the individual actors or in any way manipulating them. If ethical considerations lead us to avoid participant observation, interviews, or eavesdropping in given circumstances, the novel methods described in this monograph may be of value not only in improving and supplementing our information but also in permitting ethically scrupulous social scientists to do their work effectively and to sleep better at night.

We received notable aid from the following of our associates: Howard S. Becker, James H. Crouse, Kay C. Kujala, Irene E. Nolte, Michael L. Ray, Jerry R. Salancik, Carole R. Siegman, Gerald Solomon, and Susan H. Stocking. The acute eye and sensitive pen of Rand McNally's Lucia Boyden we bow before.

This study was supported in part by Project C-998, Contract 3-20-001, with the Media Research Branch, Office of Education, U.S. Department of Health, Education and Welfare, under provisions of Title VII of the National Defense Education Act.

Grateful acknowledgment is made to the following for permission to use copyrighted material: *American Journal of Psychology; Annual Review of Psychology;* Atheneum Publishers; Basic Books; Cambridge University Press; Criterion Books; Doubleday; Free Press of Glencoe and Macmillan; Harcourt, Brace and World; Holt, Rinehart and Winston; *Human Oganization* and the Society for Applied Anthropology; Little, Brown and Company; *Public Opinion Quarterly;* Oxford University Press; Simon & Schuster; *Speech Monographs* and the Speech Association of America; University of Chicago, Graduate School of Business; and Yale University Press.

The errors which have penetrated the perimeter of our friends we acknowledge. Surely every reader will think of studies which could have been included, yet were heinously omitted. If such studies are sent to the senior author, at Northwestern, an amended bibliography will be prepared and distributed— either in another edition of this book or separately.

—E. J. W.
—D. T. C.
—R. D. S.
—L. S.
Evanston, Illinois
June, 1965

INTRODUCTION TO
THE CLASSIC EDITION OF
UNOBTRUSIVE MEASURES

————•◆•————

*T*hirty-five years ago, we joined Gene Webb and Don Campbell in writing *Unobtrusive Measures*. We had a good time doing it, and many of our readers enjoyed it. Over the years, this book has been read by tens of thousands of undergraduate and graduate students. So was its successor, an expanded version of the original, published under the title *Nonreactive Measures in the Social Sciences* (Webb, Campbell, Schwartz, Sechrest, & Grove, 1981). Although we could measure their numbers, roughly at least, by citing sales and library circulation figures, those numbers would not necessarily tell us what we most want to know. Thirty-five years later, we ponder this question: Why does this book continue to be of interest?

Our explanation is that this book still serves a need, while saving its users from unnecessary pain. The need it has generally filled is to encourage its readers to do some creative thinking about how to find things out—and how to make systematic use of what they do find out. As we review the references to Webb et al., we reach the conclusion that it clarified a pervasive problem in social science research and that it proposed a plausible remedy. The problem is now well understood, but the remedy continues to be sought.

The problem was one of validity. Logical positivism had provided a faith that the social sciences could aspire to the kind of precision spectacularly attained in the natural sciences. It was a time when even naive operationism could gain a hearing, whereas more sophisticated epistemologies (ways of knowing) ruled the day. Rudolf Carnap (Ayer, 1959) and others of the Vienna School generalized the logico-deductive method so that it seemed to apply to every search for knowledge, provided it could pass the test described by Karl Popper (1959) as "falsifiability." Logical positivism soon began to show flaws. In the natural sciences, Werner Heisenberg (1927) had enunciated his famous uncertainty principle that in quantum mechanics the measure of one physical property makes another related property less accurately knowable. Thomas Kuhn (1962) demonstrated that even in physics, theories were maintained in the face of contrary evidence until and unless the existing "dominant paradigm" was eventually replaced.

In the social sciences, fallacious conclusions and failures of replicability shook the confidence of the truest of scientific true believers. A celebrated example was the discovery of the so-called Hawthorne Effect, whether it was real or not, in which productivity unexpectedly appeared to be related to motivation rather than level of lighting. Don Campbell encountered similar unexpected results in his study (with H. Laurence Ross) of the Connecticut speed crackdown that seemed to slow cars down through rigorous enforcement—but only until a pattern of evasion among drivers, police, and judges defeated the original intention. The other three authors had had similar experiences that raised questions for each of us about prevailing methodologies in social science (Campbell & Ross, 1968).

Against this background, we looked for a strategy that could help with the problem of validity in social science research. We were interested in new and underused methods, of course. We were intrigued in particular by the promise of quasi-experimental designs, as developed by Campbell and Stanley (1966), later to be elaborated by Cook and Campbell (1979). But this book did not prescribe a particular method or mode of analysis. It sought instead to invite innovation in the gathering and analysis of data. What was needed, we thought, was a new mind-set in planning and carrying out research in the social sciences. As the book took shape, that is what we tried to provide.

Two themes emerged: first, that multiple methods—properly used in combination—help to overcome threats to validity and, second, that there are many ways of gathering data beyond those in current, conventional use. Chapter 1 explains the threats to validity of single-method research and shows how in principle these threats can be reduced by the integrated use of multiple methods. Examples of unconventional methods are found throughout Chapters 2 through 6. Chapter 7, "A Final Note," in effect wishes well to researchers as they undertake to achieve more valid results.

We used all kinds of illustrations to loosen the bonds of methodological orthodoxy. At the time we wrote, each of the disciplines had fallen into a pattern wherein the proper research method tended to become *the* method of learning the truth. Anthropologists used ethnography, sociologists used surveys, psychologists filled their journals with laboratory experiments. All of us enjoyed swimming against these currents.

Years later, innovative methods have passed into the mainstream of social science research. Unobtrusive measures are so widely accepted that they are frequently used without reference to the book itself. Even so, the book continues to be cited. References to Webb et al. in the recent *Social Sciences Citation Index* come to 14 in the calendar year 1995, 10 in 1996, 18 in 1997, and 18 through September 1998. References are found in every field in which research is done on human behavior. Here are a few subjects, inferable from the titles: Jamaican children's representation of tourism (Gamradt, 1995), migration and life satisfaction in Eastern Canada (Goyder, 1995), gender identity at work (Ely, 1995), patient control in the hospice (Mesler, 1995), attitudes toward disabled people (Antonak & Livneh, 1995), community partnership in policy designs (Springer & Phillips, 1994), selling house brands (Anderson & Robertson, 1995), self-interest versus social identification in attitude formation (Boninger, Berent, & Krosnick, 1995), the Chinese democracy movement (Zuo & Benford, 1995), external consultants and client success (Gable, 1996), personal initiative in East and West Germany (Frese, Kring, Soose, & Zempel, 1996), impact of media coverage on child abuse reporting (McDevitt, 1996), special-needs children in adoptive families (Groze, 1996), evaluating drug prevention programs (Duryea & Nagel, 1995), race relations in organizations (Alderfer & Tucker, 1996), patriarchal ideology and wife assault (Sugarman & Frankel,

1996), supervision of nurses (Fowler, 1996), public participation in land plan-ning (Moote, McClaran, & Chickering, 1997), validity of mental health pa-tients' accounts of coercion (Lidz et al., 1997), local shopping in rural commu-nities (Miller & Kean, 1997), late-adult suicide (Bauer et al., 1997), community mobilization on an Indian reservation (McLean, 1997), renting rooms to homosexuals (Page, 1998), dream research outside the laboratory (Domhoff & Schneider, 1998), disruptive behavior in schools (Wright & Dusek, 1998), and so on.

The variety in this list indicates that the book has been widely used. Some of these uses combine the two themes of innovative measures and multiple methods, but that is relatively rare. Instead, the works citing *Unobtrusive Measures* often use only a portion of the general strategy. Even then, however, there is an awareness of the importance of the twin messages conveyed in the book: creatively measure, triangulate, and cross-validate. A few examples will illustrate.

A political scientist, Glenn R. Parker (1986) studied travel vouchers of members of the House of Representatives to determine whether their propen-sity to return to their home constituency increased or decreased as their seniority increases. His finding was that the visits increase, according to that single indicator. Yet in presenting the finding, he was aware that a single measure would not suffice. Accordingly, his article cites an earlier study by Richard Fenno (1978), which uses interviews with congressional staffers as a way of determining the same information. Given the congruence of the find-ings, Parker uses the Fenno findings as a second method that adds validity to the conclusion indicated by his own data.

James A. Wright and Jerome B. Dusek (1998) treat disciplinary referrals to the principal's office as an "unobtrusive, archival measure of student behaviors whose compilation is unlikely to result in reactivity effects (changes in behavior in reaction to observation) of either referring teachers or referred students." The authors go on to praise this measure as more efficient than "other more direct and time-intensive methods of behavioral assessment such as direct observation" (p. 140).

Robert Rosenthal and Peter D. Blanck (1993) discuss the problems of validity as they affect the use of social science evidence in court cases. An overly broad question can press research findings into uses for which the conclusions reached would be misleading. As an example, they would not infer that private schools *cause* better education merely from comparative test scores in the absence of randomization or other means of controlling for initial differences in student body. Absent such methods, they recommend that the question be narrowed to "whether performance differences exist" (p. 1211).

Michael Hennessey and Robert F. Saltz (1989) studied techniques for reducing alcohol intoxication in a U.S. Navy enlisted club, comparing the results with a comparable club in which the traditional pattern was sustained. Their study used multiple measures *and* multiple methods. Multiple measures were more economical than multiple methods. They also report analytic difficulties with multiple-method-derived data and some techniques they devised for resolving some of these difficulties.

Sociologists Jiping Zuo and Robert D. Benford (1995) write about the Chinese democracy movement in the period just prior to the violent confrontation of June 4, 1989, between students and the military in Tienanmen Square. Ms. Zuo was present in China for the four months during which the democracy movement reached its zenith. She gathered data using a variety of methods: participant observation, formal interviews, guided conversations, "unobtrusive conversational listening," plus "private letters, print and electronic news media accounts, computer bulletin boards, and published secondary sources" (p. 132). The use of these multiple methods, they contend, was needed to focus not only on "changes in the political opportunity structure but also on how these changes were interpreted and articulated such that activists' claims resonated with the experiences and cultural narratives of Chinese citizens" (p. 133).

Marit A. Berntson and Brian Ault (1998) also use multiple measures in studying the historic problem of reasons for joining the National Socialist German Workers Party in the period preceding Hitler's 1933 rise to power in Germany. Their principal data come from the essays of women who responded to a prize contest for essays on why they joined the Nazi Party—a contest reported by Theodore Abel (1966). Data on the men's responses had been reported by Abel and later analyzed in detail by Merkl (1975). Merkl uses multiple sources of data to supplement Abel's sources. The most recent use, by Berntson and Ault, specifically uses the concepts of *Unobtrusive Measures* to estimate the significance of lost archival data and to examine the validity of data from Abel by relating it to Nazi party records and demographic statistics—

thus meeting the criterion of what has come to be widely known as triangulation.

Of course, the use of multiple sources has always characterized the work of fine scholars working in data-rich settings in history and ethnography. Needed, however, when this book was written—and needed now—is the extension of multiple-methods thinking to research in the social sciences that systematically seek to develop valid generalizations. The temptation, as with the natural sciences, has been to rely heavily on a given precise method, replicated in diverse settings. It is here that the problems of validity multiply, and that is where this book sought—and seeks again—to make its contribution.

There is little we can add at this point to the formulation of the first chapter. Clearly, ingenuity is required if the social sciences are to fulfill their promise. Nor will individual creativity suffice. Threats to validity in the social sciences, as in all the sciences, never end. They are inevitable in the continuing search for knowledge. The effort to deal with them requires ingenuity, not just of the individual scholar but of the shared enterprise. To the extent that this book helps to guide the quest, we are glad to have had a hand in it as companions to our senior authors: Gene Webb and Don Campbell.

It seems appropriate to add a word of reminiscence and sentiment. How often in a professional lifetime does one get the chance to work closely with people who so fully combined *humor, humanity,* and *serious purpose?* We are grateful that we had that experience. We like to believe that the book embodies these characteristics. If so, that may help to explain why it continues to be a popular reference and why, with republication, it may become a well-worn volume in the libraries of those, professionals and others, who want to be reminded of unusual ways to find things out.

Our two coauthors combined in their distinctive ways those several qualities. Gene Webb was known to everyone as a man with a marvelous, light sense of humor. At the same time, he had some serious convictions—not only about social science but also about responsible journalism. The written word had for him a magical element, and his prose in much of Chapters 2 through 6 shows that touch of his. His sense of humor and his convictions combined in a habit he had of propagandizing for Irish unity. In the 1960s, stores selling typewriters would put on an exhibit so that customers could type something as a sample. Instead of typing the cliché "Now is the time for all good men to come to the aid of their country," Gene would regularly type, "The six northern counties must be returned." We never found out whether any Ulstermen read these messages, or if they did, how they reacted.

When he left Northwestern, Gene took a job at the business school at Stanford. His office was in a cluster of three offices. The other two were occupied in the late 1980s by two former U.S. cabinet officers: John Gardner, who was Secretary of Health, Education, and Welfare during the Carter administration, and George Schultz, who served in several cabinet posts under Ronald Reagan. Gene reveled in the fact that he could finally rest content with being the least distinguished among these particular colleagues.

As for Don Campbell, those who knew him invariably found in him an incredible degree of understanding. For Don, the enterprise was serious indeed. At 79, he was still going strong—giving a colloquium in Texas and heartening an insecure graduate student before flying back to Bethlehem for the major operation that led to his death. He was a man who liked to say he suffered fools gladly. Over the years, it became clear that all people were of interest to him, especially those engaged in the difficult tasks of social science. So the best interpretation of his statement is that all of us, in seeking the truth, are easily fooled—and that it is up to us to help each other in the effort to enhance our understanding. The corpus of his work, cited in American social science more frequently than that of any other U.S. scholar, represents a continuing contribution to the understanding of human behavior and society.

This book is only a fraction of Don Campbell's legacy. Several volumes are now in print that contain his collected works. But to this book, as well as to his other writings, he gave the kind of serious attention, broad scope, and profound analysis that made his work so fundamentally important for all who would strive, as in Cardinal Newman's epitaph, to go from "symbols and shadows to the truth."

Finally, a note on presentation for this edition of *Unobtrusive Measures*. We have left the text in its original form, except for references to works that were "in press" at the time. Where possible, the publication date for those references has been supplied. We have not changed the earlier usage in which the pronoun *he* served to indicate *he* or *she*. Nor have we changed the term *Negro* to *Black* or *African American*. On both of these significant stylistic matters—and on some minor copy questions as well—our interest in preserving the original text ultimately outweighed our concern for contemporary usage. We thank Stuart Klein, Syracuse University Law '99, and Michael Maroney, Syracuse University Law '00 for valuable research help. Margaret Smith did a fine job with secretarial assistance for this edition.

—Richard D. Schwartz
—Lee Sechrest

BIBLIOGRAPHY FOR THE INTRODUCTION

Abel, T. (1966). *The Nazi movement*. New York: Atherton.

Alderfer, C. P., & Tucker, R. C. (1996). A field experiment for studying race-relations embedded in organization. *Journal of Organizational Behavior, 17*, 43-57.

Anderson, E., & Robertson, T. S. (1995). Inducing multiline salespeople to adopt house brands. *Journal of Marketing, 59*(2), 16-31.

Antonak, R. F., & Livneh, H. (1995). Randomized-response technique: A review and proposed extension to disability attitude research. *Genetic Social and General Psychology Monographs, 121*, 97-145.

Ayer, A. J. (1959). *Logical positivism*. New York: Free Press.

Bauer, M. N., Leenaars, A. A., Berman, A. L., Jobes, D. A., Dixon, J. F., & Bibb, J. L. (1997). Late adulthood suicide: A life-span analysis of suicide notes. *Archives of Suicide Research, 3*(2), 91-108.

Berntson, M. A., & Ault, B. (1998). Gender and Nazism. *American Behavioral Scientist, 41,* 1193-1218.

Boninger, D. S., Berent, M. K., & Krosnick, J. A. (1995). Origins of attitude importance: Self-interest, social identification, and value relevance. *Journal of Personality and Social Psychology, 68,* 61-80.

Campbell, D. T., & Ross, H. L. (1968). Connecticut crackdown on speeding: Time series data in quasi-experimental analysis. *Law & Society Review, 3,* 33-53.

Campbell, D. T., & Stanley, J. C. (1966). *Experimental and quasi-experimental designs for research*. Chicago: Rand McNally.

Cook, T. D., & Campbell, D. T. (1979). *Quasi-experimentation: Design and analysis issues for field settings*. Chicago: Rand McNally.

Domhoff, G. W., & Schneider, A. (1998). New rationales and methods for quantitative dream research outside the laboratory. *Sleep, 21,* 398-404.

Duryea, E., & Nagel, L. (1995). Behavior assessment and cross-validation by surrogate measures in drug prevention research. *Journal of Drug Education, 25,* 335-342.

Ely, R. J. (1995). The power in demography: Women's social construction of gender identity at work. *Academy of Management Journal, 38,* 589-634.

Fenno, R. F., Jr. (1978). *Homestyle: House members in their districts*. Boston: Little, Brown.

Fowler, J. (1996). The organization of clinical supervision within the nursing profession: A review of the literature. *Journal of Advanced Nursing, 23,* 471-478.

Frese, M., Kring, W., Soose, A., & Zempel, J. (1996). Personal initiative at work: Differences between East and West Germany. *Academy of Management Journal, 39,* 37-63.

Gable, G. G. (1996). A multidimensional model of client success when engaging external consultants. *Management Science, 42,* 1175-1198.

Gamradt, J. (1995). Jamaican children's representations of tourism. *Annals of Tourism Research, 22,* 735-762.

Goyder, J. (1995). Migration and regional differences in life satisfaction in the anglophone provinces. *Canadian Journal of Sociology, 20,* 287-307.

Groze, V. (1996). A 1-year and 2-year follow-up of adoptive families and special needs children. *Children and Youth Services Review, 18,* 57-82.

Heisenberg, W. (1927). Ueber den anschaulichen Inhalt der quantentheoretischen Kinenatik und Mechanik. *Zeitschriftfur Physik, 43,* 172-198.

Hennessey, M., & Saltz, R. F. (1989). Adjusting for multimethod bias through selection modeling. *Evaluation Review, 13,* 380-399.

Kuhn, T. (1962). *The structure of scientific revolutions.* Chicago: University of Chicago Press.

Lidz, C. W., Mulvey, E. P., Hoge, S. K., Kirsch, B. L., Monahan, J., Bennett, N. S., Eisenberg, M., Gardner, W., & Roth, L. H. (1997). The validity of mental patients' accounts of coercion-related behaviors in the hospital admission process. *Law and Human Behavior, 21,* 361-376.

McDevitt, S. (1997). The impact of news media on child-abuse reporting. *Child Abuse & Neglect, 20,* 261-274.

McLean, S. (1997). A communication analysis of community mobilization on the Warm-Springs-Indian-Reservation. *Journal of Health Communication, 2*(2), 113-125.

Merkl, P. H. (1975). *Political violence under the swastika: 581 early Nazis.* Princeton, NJ: Princeton University Press.

Mesler, M. A. (1995). The philosophy and practice of patient control in hospice: The dynamics of autonomy versus paternalism. *Omega: Journal of Death and Dying, 30,* 173-189.

Miller, N. J., & Kean, R. C. (1997). Reciprocal exchange in rural communities: Consumers' inducement to inshop. *Psychology & Marketing, 14,* 637-661.

Moote, M. A., McClaran, M. P., & Chickering, D. K. (1997). Theory in practice: Applying participatory democracy theory to public land planning. *Environmental Management, 21,* 877-889.

Page, S. (1998). Accepting the gay person: Rental accommodation in the community. *Journal of Homosexuality, 36,* 31-39.

Parker, G. R. (1986). Is there a political life cycle in the House of Representatives? *Legislative Studies Quarterly, 11,* 375-392.

Popper, K. (1959). *The logic of scientific discovery.* New York: Basic Books.

Rosenthal, R., & Blanck, P. D. (1993). Science and ethics in conducting, analyzing, and reporting social science research: Implications for social scientists, judges, and lawyers. *Indiana Law Journal, 68,* 1209-1228.

Springer, J. F., & Phillips, J. L. (1994). Policy learning and evaluation design: Lessons from the community partnership demonstration program. *Journal of Community Psychology,* 117-139.

Sugarman, D. B., & Frankel, S. L. (1996). Patriarchal ideology and wife assault: A meta-analytic review. *Journal of Family Violence, 11,* 13-40.

Webb, E. J., Campbell, D. T., Schwartz, R. D., Sechrest, L., & Grove, J. B. (1981). *Nonreactive measures in the social sciences.* Boston: Houghton Mifflin.

Wright, J. A., & Dusek, J. B. (1998). Compiling school base rates for disruptive behaviors from student disciplinary referral data. *School Psychology Review, 27,* 138-147.

Zuo, J. P., & Benford, R. D. (1995). Mobilization processes and the 1989 Chinese Democracy Movement. *Sociological Quarterly, 36,* 131-156.

To the memory of Sir Francis Galton

ONE

APPROXIMATIONS TO KNOWLEDGE

————•◆•————

his survey directs attention to social science research data *not* obtained by interview or questionnaire. Some may think this exclusion does not leave much. It does. Many innovations in research method are to be found scattered throughout the social science literature. Their use, however, is unsystematic, their importance understated. Our review of this material is intended to broaden the social scientist's currently narrow range of utilized methodologies and to encourage creative and opportunistic exploitation of unique measurement possibilities.

Today, the dominant mass of social science research is based upon interviews and questionnaires. We lament this overdependence upon a single, fallible method. Interviews and questionnaires intrude as a foreign element into the social setting they would describe, they create as well as measure attitudes, they elicit atypical roles and responses, they are limited to those who are accessible and will cooperate, and the responses obtained are produced in part by dimensions of individual differences irrelevant to the topic at hand.

1

But the principal objection is that they are used alone. No research method is without bias. Interviews and questionnaires must be supplemented by methods testing the same social science variables but having *different* methodological weaknesses.

In sampling the range of alternative approaches, we examine their weaknesses, too. The flaws are serious and give insight into why we do depend so much upon the interview. But the issue is not choosing among individual methods. Rather, it is the necessity for a multiple operationism, a collection of methods combined to avoid sharing the same weaknesses. The goal of this monograph is not to replace the interview but to supplement and cross-validate it with measures that do not require the cooperation of a respondent and that do not themselves contaminate the response.

Here are some samples of the kinds of methods we will be surveying in Chapters 2 through 6 of this monograph:

- The floor tiles around the hatching-chick exhibit at Chicago's Museum of Science and Industry must be replaced every six weeks. Tiles in other parts of the museum need not be replaced for years. The selective erosion of tiles, indexed by the replacement rate, is a measure of the relative popularity of exhibits.

- The accretion rate is another measure. One investigator wanted to learn the level of whisky consumption in a town which was officially "dry." He did so by counting empty bottles in ashcans.

- The degree of fear induced by a ghost-story-telling session can be measured by noting the shrinking diameter of a circle of seated children.

- Chinese jade dealers have used the pupil dilation of their customers as a measure of the client's interest in particular stones, and Darwin in 1872 noted this same variable as an index of fear.

- Library withdrawals were used to demonstrate the effect of the introduction of television into a community. Fiction titles dropped, nonfiction titles were unaffected.

- The role of rate of interaction in managerial recruitment is shown by the overrepresentation of baseball managers who were infielders or catchers (high-interaction positions) during their playing days.

- Sir Francis Galton employed surveying hardware to estimate the bodily dimensions of African women whose language he did not speak.

- The child's interest in Christmas was demonstrated by distortions in the size of Santa Claus drawings.

- Racial attitudes in two colleges were compared by noting the degree of clustering of Negroes and whites in lecture halls.

These methods have been grouped into chapters by the characteristic of the data: physical traces, archives, observations.

Before making a detailed examination of such methods, it is well to present a closer argument for the use of multiple methods and to present a methodological framework within which both the traditional and the more novel methods can be evaluated.

The reader may skip directly to Sherlock Holmes and the opening of Chapter 2 if he elects, infer the criteria in a piece of detection himself, and then return for a validity check.

OPERATIONISM AND MULTIPLE OPERATIONS

The social sciences are just emerging from a period in which the precision of carefully specified operations was confused with operationism by definitional fiat—an effort now increasingly recognized as an unworkable model for science. We wish to retain and augment the precision without bowing to the fiat.

The mistaken belief in the operational definition of theoretical terms has permitted social scientists a complacent and self-defeating dependence upon single classes of measurement—usually the interview or questionnaire. Yet the operational implication of the inevitable theoretical complexity of every measure is exactly opposite; it calls for a multiple operationism, that is, for multiple measures which are hypothesized to share in the theoretically relevant components but have different patterns of irrelevant components (e.g., Campbell, 1960; Campbell & Fiske, 1959; Garner, 1954; Garner, Hake, & Eriksen, 1956; Humphreys, 1960).

Once a proposition has been confirmed by two or more independent measurement processes, the uncertainty of its interpretation is greatly reduced. The most persuasive evidence comes through a triangulation of measurement processes. If a proposition can survive the onslaught of a series of imperfect measures, with all their irrelevant error, confidence should be placed in it. Of course, this confidence is increased by minimizing error in each instrument and by a reasonable belief in the different and divergent effects of the sources of error.

A consideration of the laws of physics, as they are seen in that science's measuring instruments, demonstrates that no theoretical parameter is ever measured independently of other physical parameters and other physical laws. Thus, a typical galvanometer responds in its operational measurement of voltage not only according to the laws of electricity but also to the laws of gravitation, inertia, and friction. By reducing the mass of the galvanometer needle, by orienting the needle's motion at right angles to gravity, by setting the needle's axis in jeweled bearings, by counterweighting the needle point, and by other refinements, the instrument designer attempts to minimize the most important of the irrelevant physical forces for his measurement purposes. As a result, the galvanometer reading may reflect, *almost* purely, the single parameter of voltage (or amperage, etc.).

Yet from a theoretical point of view, the movement of the needle is always a complex product of many physical forces and laws. The adequacy with which the needle measures the conceptually defined variable is a matter for investigation; the operation itself is not the ultimate basis for defining the variable. Excellent illustrations of the specific imperfections of measuring instruments are provided by Wilson (1952).

Starting with this example from physics and the construction of meters, we can see that no meter ever perfectly measures a single theoretical parameter; all series of meter readings are imperfect estimates of the theoretical parameters they are intended to measure.

Truisms perhaps, yet they belie the mistaken concept of the "operational definition" of theoretical constructs which continues to be popular in the social sciences. The inappropriateness is accentuated in the social sciences because we have no measuring devices as carefully compensated to control all irrelevancies as is the galvanometer. There simply are no social science devices designed with so perfect a knowledge of all the major relevant sources of variation. In physics, the instruments we think of as "definitional" reflect magnificently successful theoretical achievements and themselves embody classical experiments in their very operation. In the social sciences, our measures lack such control. They tap multiple processes and sources of variance of which we are as yet unaware. At such a stage of development, the theoretical impurity and factorial complexity of every measure are not niceties for pedantic quibbling but are overwhelmingly and centrally relevant in all measurement applications which involve inference and generalization.

Efforts in the social sciences at multiple confirmation often yield disappointing and inconsistent results. Awkward to write up and difficult to publish, such results confirm the gravity of the problem and the risk of false confidence that comes with dependence upon single methods (Campbell, 1957; Campbell & Fiske, 1959; Campbell & McCormack, 1957; Cook & Selltiz, 1964; Kendall, 1963; Vidich & Shapiro, 1955). When multiple operations provide consistent results, the possibility of slippage between conceptual definition and operational specification is diminished greatly.

This is not to suggest that all components of a multimethod approach should be weighted equally. Prosser (1964) has observed: ". . . but there is still no man who would not accept dog tracks in the mud against the sworn, testimony of a hundred eye-witnesses that no dog had passed by" (p. 216). Components ideally should be weighted according to the amount of extraneous variation each is known to have and, taken in combination, according to their independence from similar sources of bias.

INTERPRETABLE COMPARISONS AND
PLAUSIBLE RIVAL HYPOTHESES

In this monograph, we deal with methods of measurement appropriate to a wide range of social science studies. Some of these studies are comparisons of a single group or unit at two or more points in time; others compare several groups or units at one time; others purport to measure but a single unit at a single point in time; and, to close the circle, some compare several groups at two or more points in time. In this discussion, we assume that the goal of the social scientist is always to achieve interpretable comparisons, and that the goal of methodology is to rule out those plausible rival hypotheses which make comparisons ambiguous and tentative.

Often it seems that absolute measurement *is* involved, and that a social instance is being described in its splendid isolation, not for comparative purposes. But a closer look shows that absolute, isolated measurement is meaningless. In all useful measurement, an implicit comparison exists when an explicit one is not visible. "Absolute" measurement is a convenient fiction and usually is nothing more than a shorthand summary in settings where plausible rival hypotheses are either unimportant or so few, specific, and well known as to be taken into account habitually. Thus, when we report a length "absolutely" in meters or feet, we immediately imply comparisons with numerous familiar objects of known length, as well as comparisons with a standard preserved in some Paris or Washington sanctuary.

If measurement is regarded always as a comparison, there are three classes of approaches which have come to be used in achieving interpretable comparisons. First, and most satisfactory, is experimental design. Through deliberate randomization, the *ceteris* of the pious *ceteris paribus* prayer can be made *paribus*. This may require randomization of respondents, occasions, or stimulus objects. In any event, the randomization strips of plausibility many of the otherwise available explanations of the difference in question. It is a sad truth that randomized experimental design is possible for only a portion of the settings in which social scientists make measurements and seek interpretable comparisons. The number of opportunities for its use may not be staggering, but, where possible, experimental design should by all means be exploited. Many more opportunities exist than are used.

Second, a quite different and historically isolated tradition of comparison is that of index numbers. Here, sources of variance known to be irrelevant are controlled by transformations of raw data and weighted aggregates. This is analogous to the compensated and counterbalanced meters of physical science which also control irrelevant sources of variance. The goal of this old and currently neglected social science tradition is to provide measures for meaningful comparisons across wide spans of time and social space. Real wages, intelligence quotients, and net reproductive rates are examples, but an effort in this direction is made even when a percentage, a per capita, or an annual rate is computed. Index numbers cannot be used uncritically because the imperfect knowledge of the laws invoked in any such measurement situation precludes computing any effective all-purpose measures.

Furthermore, the use of complex compensated indices in the assurance that they measure what they are devised for has in many instances proved quite misleading. A notable example is found in the definitional confusion surrounding the labor force concept (Jaffe & Stewart, 1951; Moore, 1953). Often a relationship established between an over-all index and external variables is found due to only one component of the index. Cronbach (1958) has described this problem well in his discussion of dyadic scores of interpersonal perception. In the older methodological literature, the problem is raised under the term *index correlations* (e.g., Campbell, 1955; Guilford, 1954; Stouffer, 1934).

Despite these limitations, the problem of index numbers, which once loomed large in sociology and economics, deserves to be reactivated and integrated into modern social science methodology. The tradition is relevant in two ways for the problems of this monograph. Many of the sources of data suggested here, particularly secondary records, require a transformation of the raw data if they are to be interpretable in any but truly experimental situations. Such transformations should be performed with the wisdom accumulated within the older tradition, as well as with a regard for the precautionary literature just cited. Properly done, such transformations often improve interpretability even if they fall far short of some ideal (cf. Bernstein, 1935).

A second value of the literature on index numbers lies in an examination of the types of irrelevant variation which the index computation sought to exclude. The construction of index numbers is usually a response to criticisms of less sophisticated indices. They thus embody a summary of the often unrecorded criticisms of prior measures. In the criticisms and the corrections are clues to implicit or explicit plausible rival interpretations of differences, the viable threats to valid interpretation.

Take so simple a measure as an index on unemployment or of retail sales. The gross number of the unemployed or the gross total dollar level of sales is useless if one wants to make comparisons within a single year. Some of the objections to the gross figures are reflected in the seasonal corrections applied to time-series data. If we look at only the last quarter of the year, we can see that the effect of weather must be considered. Systematically, winter depresses the number of employed construction workers, for example, and increases the unemployment level. Less systematically, spells of bad weather keep people in their homes and reduce the amount of retail shopping. Both periodic and aperiodic elements of the weather should be considered if one wants a more stable and interpretable measure of unemployment or sales. So, too, our custom of giving gifts at Christmas spurs December sales, as does the coinciding custom of Christmas bonuses to employees. All of these are accounted for, crudely, by a correction applied to the gross levels for either December or the final quarter of the year.

Some of these sources of invalidity are too specific to a single setting to be generalized usefully; others are too obvious to be catalogued. But some contribute to a general enumeration of recurrent threats to valid interpretation in social science measures.

The technical problems of index-number construction are heroic. "The index number should give *consistent* results for different base periods and also with its counterpart price or quantity index. No reasonably simple formula satisfies both of these consistency requirements" (Ekelblad, 1962, p. 726). The consistency problem is usually met by substituting a geometric mean for an arithmetic one, but then other problems arise. With complex indices of many components, there is the issue of getting an index that will yield consistent scores across all the different levels and times of the components.

In his important work on economic cycles, Hansen (1921) wrote, "Here is a heterogeneous group of statistical series all of which are related in a causal way, somehow or another, to the cycle of prosperity and depression" (p. 21). The search for a metric to relate these different components consistently, to be able to reverse factors without chaos, makes index construction a difficult task. But the payoff is great, and the best approximation to solving both the base-reversal and factor-reversal issues is a weighted aggregate with time-averaged weights. For good introductory statements of these and other index-number issues, see Ekelblad (1962), Yule and Kendall (1950), and Zeisel (1957). More detailed treatments can be found in Fisher (1923), Mills (1927), Mitchell (1921), and Mudgett (1951).

The third general approach to comparison may be called that of "plausible rival hypotheses." It is the most general and least formal of the three and is applicable to the other two. Given a comparison which a social scientist wishes to interpret, this approach asks what other plausible interpretations are allowed by the research setting and the measurement processes. The more of these, and the more plausible each is, the less validly interpretable is the comparison.

Platt (1964) and Hafner and Presswood (1965) have discussed this approach with a focus in the physical sciences.

A social scientist may reduce the number of plausible rival hypotheses in many ways. Experimental methods and adequate indices serve as useful devices for eliminating some rival interpretations. A checklist of commonly relevant threats to validity may point to other ways of limiting the number of viable alternative hypotheses. For some major threats, it is often possible to provide supplementary analyses or to assemble additional data which can rule out a source of possible invalidity.

Backstopping the individual scientist is the critical reaction of his fellow scientists. Where he misses plausible rival hypothesis, he can expect his colleagues to propose alternative interpretations. This resource is available even in disciplines which are not avowedly scientific. J. H. Wigmore (1937), a distinguished legal scholar, showed an awareness of the criteria of other plausible explanations of data:

> If the potential defect of Inductive Evidence is that the fact offered as the basis of the conclusion may be open to one or more other explanations or inferences, the failure to exclude a single other rational inference would be, from the standpoint of *Proof,* a fatal defect; and yet, if only that single other inference were open, there might still be an extremely high degree of probability for the Inference desired. . . . The provisional test, then, from the point of view valuing the Inference, would be something like this: *Does the evidentiary fact point to the desired conclusion . . . as the inference . . . most plausible or most natural out of the various ones that are conceivable?* (p. 25)

The culture of science seeks, however, to systematize the production of rival plausible hypotheses and to extend them to every generalization proposed. While this may be implicit in a field such as law, scientific epistemology requires that the original and competing hypotheses be explicitly and generally stated.

Such a commitment could lead to rampant uncertainty unless some criterion of plausibility was adopted before the rival hypothesis was taken as a serious alternative. Accordingly, each rival hypothesis is a threat only if we can give it the status of a law at least as creditable as the law we seek to demonstrate. If it falls short of that credibility, it is not thereby "plausible" and can be ignored.

In some logical sense, even in a "true" experimental comparison, an infinite number of potential laws could predict this result. We do not let this logical state of affairs prevent us from interpreting the results. Instead, uncertainty comes only from unexcluded hypotheses to which we, in the current state of our science, are willing to give the status of established laws: these are the plausible rival hypotheses. While the north-south orientation of planaria may have something to do with conditioning, no interview studies report on the directional orientation of interviewer and interviewee. And they should not.

For those plausible rival hypotheses to which we give the status of laws, the conditions under which they would explain our obtained result also imply specific outcomes for other sets of data. Tests in other settings, attempting to verify these laws, may enable us to rule them out. In a similar fashion, the theory we seek to test has many implications other than that involved in the specific comparison, and the exploration of these is likewise demanded. The more numerous and complex the manifestations of the law, the fewer singular plausible rival hypotheses are available, and the more parsimony favors the law under study.

Our longing is for data that prove and certify theory, but such is not to be our lot. Some comfort may come from the observation that this is not an existential predicament unique to social science. The replacement of Newtonian theory by relativity and quantum mechanics shows us that even the best of physical science experimentation probes theory rather than proves it. Modern philosophies of science as presented by Popper (1935, 1959, 1962), Quine (1953), Hanson (1958), Kuhn (1962), and Campbell (1965a, 1965b), make this point clear.

INTERNAL AND EXTERNAL VALIDITY

Before discussing a list of some common sources of invalidity, a distinction must be drawn between internal and external validity. *Internal validity* asks whether a difference exists at all in any given comparison. It asks whether or not an apparent difference can be explained away as some measurement artifact. For true experiments, this question is usually not salient, but even there, the happy vagaries of random sample selection occasionally delude one and spuriously produce the appearance of a difference where in fact none exists. For the rival hypothesis of chance, we fortunately have an elaborated theoretical model which evaluates its plausibility. A p-value describes the darkness of the ever present shadow of doubt. But for index-number comparisons not embedded in a formal experiment, and for the plausible-rival-hypothesis strategy more generally, the threats to internal validity—the argument that even the appearance of a difference is spurious—is a serious problem and the one that has first priority.

External validity is the problem of interpreting the difference, the problem of generalization. To what other populations, occasions, stimulus objects, and measures may the obtained results be applied? The distinction between internal and external validity can be illustrated in two uses of randomization. When the experimentalist in psychology randomly assigns a sample of persons into two or more experimental groups, he is concerned entirely with internal validity— with making it implausible that the luck of the draw produced the resulting differences. When a sociologist carefully randomizes the selection of respondents so that his sample represents a larger population, representativeness or external validity is involved.

The psychologist may be extremely confident that a difference is traceable to an experimental treatment, but whether it would hold up with another set of subjects or in a different setting may be quite equivocal. He has achieved internal validity by his random assignment but not addressed the external validity issue by the chance allocation of subjects.

The sociologist, similarly, has not met all the validity concerns by simply drawing a random sample. Conceding that he has taken a necessary step toward achieving external validity and generalization of his differences, the internal validity problem remains.

Random assignment is only one method of reaching toward internal validity. Experimental-design control, exclusive of randomization, is another. Consider the case of a pretest-posttest field experiment on the effect of a persuasive communication. Randomly choosing those who participate, the social scientist properly wards off some major threats to external validity. But we also know of other validity threats. The first interview in a two-stage study may set into motion attitude change and clarification processes which would otherwise not have occurred (e.g., Crespi, 1948). If such processes did occur, the comparison of a first and second measure on the same person is internally invalid, for the shift is a measurement-produced artifact.

Even when a measured control group is used, and a persuasive communication produces a greater change in an experimental group, the persuasive effect may be internally valid but externally invalid. There is the substantial risk that the effect occurs only with pretested populations and might be absent in populations lacking the pretest (cf. Hovland, Lumsdaine, & Sheffield, 1949; Schanck & Goodman, 1939; Solomon, 1949). For more extensive discussions of internal and external validity, see Campbell (1957) and Campbell and Stanley (1963).

The distinction between internal and external validity is often murky. In this work, we have considered the two classes of threat jointly, although occasionally detailing the risks separately. The reason for this is that the factors which are a risk for internal validity are often the same as those threatening external validity. While for one scientist the representative sampling of cities is a method to achieve generalization to the United States population, for another it may be an effort to give an internally valid comparison across cities.

SOURCES OF INVALIDITY OF MEASURES

In this section, we review frequent threats to the valid interpretation of a difference—common plausible rival hypotheses. They are broadly divided into three groups: error that may be traced to those being studied, error that comes from the investigator, and error associated with sampling imperfections. This section is the only one in which we draw illustrations mainly from the most popular methods of current social science. For that reason, particular attention is paid to those weaknesses which create the need for multiple and alternate methods.

In addition, some other criteria such as the efficiency of the research instrument are mentioned. These are independent of validity, but important for the practical research decisions which must be made.

Reactive Measurement Effect:
Error From the Respondent

The most understated risk to valid interpretation is the error produced by the respondent. Even when he is well mentioned and cooperative, the research subject's knowledge that he is participating in a scholarly search may confound the investigator's data. Four classes of this error are discussed here: awareness of being tested, role selection, measurement as a change agent, and response sets.

1. *The Guinea Pig Effect—Awareness of Being Tested.* Selltiz, Jahoda, Deutsch, and Cook (1959) make this observation:

> The measurement process used in the experiment may itself affect the outcome. If people feel that they are "guinea pigs" being experimented with, or if they feel that they are being "tested" and must make a good impression, or if the method of data collection suggests responses or stimulates an interest the subject did not previously feel, the measuring process may distort the experimental results. (p. 97)

These effects have been called "reactive effect of measurement" and "reactive arrangement" bias (Campbell, 1957; Campbell & Stanley, 1963). It is important to note early that the awareness of testing need not, by itself, contaminate responses. It is a question of probabilities, but the probability of bias is high in any study in which a respondent is aware of his subject status.

Although the methods to be reviewed here do not involve "respondents," comparable reactive effects on the population may often occur. Consider, for example, a potentially nonreactive instrument such as the movie camera. If it is conspicuously placed, its lack of ability to talk to the subjects doesn't help us much. The visible presence of the camera undoubtedly changes behavior, and does so differentially depending upon the labeling involved. The response is likely to vary if the camera has printed on its side "Los Angeles Police Department" or "NBC" or "Foundation Project on Crowd Behavior." Similarly, an Englishman's presence at a wedding in Africa exerts a much more reactive effect on the proceedings than it would on the Sussex Downs.

A specific illustration may be of value. In the summer of 1952, some graduate students in the social sciences at the University of Chicago were employed to observe the numbers of Negroes and whites in stores, restaurants, bars, theaters, and so on on a south side Chicago street intersecting the Negro-white boundary (East 63rd). This, presumably, should have been a nonreactive process, particularly at the predominantly white end of the street. No questions were asked, no persons stopped. Yet, in spite of this hopefully inconspicuous activity, two merchants were agitated and persistent enough to place calls to the university which somehow got through to the investigators; how many others tried and failed cannot be known. The two calls were from a store operator and the manager of a currency exchange, both of whom wanted assurance that this was some university nosiness and not a professional casing for subsequent robbery (Campbell & Mack, 1966). An intrusion conspicuous enough to arouse such an energetic reaction may also have been conspicuous enough to change behavior; for observations other than simple enumerations the bias would have been great. But even with the simple act of nose-counting, there is the risk that the area would be differentially avoided. The research mistake was in providing observers with clipboards and log sheets, but their appearance might have been still more sinister had they operated Veeder counters with hands jammed in pockets.

The present monograph argues strongly for the use of archival records. Thinking, perhaps, of musty files of bound annual reports of some prior century, one might regard such a method as totally immune to reactive effects. However, were one to make use of precinct police blotters, going around to copy off data once each month, the quality and nature of the records would almost certainly change. In actual fact, archives are kept indifferently, as a low-priority task, by understaffed bureaucracies. Conscientiousness is often low because of the lack of utilization of the records. The presence of a user can revitalize the process—as well as create anxieties over potentially damaging data (Campbell, 1963). When records are seen as sources of vulnerability, they may be altered systematically. Accounts thought likely to enter into tax audits are an obvious case (Schwartz, 1961), but administrative records (Blau, 1955) and criminal statistics (Kadish, 1964) are equally amenable to this source of distortion. The selective and wholesale rifling of records by ousted political administrations sets an example of potential reactive effects, self-consciousness, and dissembling on the part of archivists.

These reactive effects may threaten both internal and external validity, depending upon the conditions. If it seems plausible that the reactivity was equal in both measures of a comparison, then the threat is to external validity or generalizability, not to internal validity. If the reactive effect is plausibly differential, then it may generate a pseudo-difference. Thus, in a study (Campbell & McCormack, 1957) showing a reduction in authoritarian attitudes over the course of one year's military training, the initial testing was done in conjunction with an official testing program, while the subsequent testing was clearly under external university research auspices. As French (1955) pointed out in another connection, this difference provides a plausible reactive threat jeopardizing the conclusion that any reduction has taken place even for this one group, quite apart from the external validity problems of explanation and generalization. In many interview and questionnaire studies, increased or decreased rapport and increased awareness of the researcher's goals or decreased fear provide plausible alternative explanations of the apparent change recorded.

The common device of guaranteeing anonymity demonstrates concern for the reactive bias, but this concern may lead to validity threats. For example, some test constructors have collected normative data under conditions of anonymity, while the test is likely to be used with the respondent's name signed. Making a response public, or guaranteeing to hide one, will influence the nature of the response. This has been seen for persuasive communications, in the validity of reports of brands purchased, and for the level of antisocial responses. There is a clear link between awareness of being tested and the biases associated with a tendency to answer with socially desirable responses.

The considerations outlined above suggest that reactivity may be selectively troublesome within trials or tests of the experiment. Training trials may accommodate the subject to the task, but a practice effect may exist that either enhances or inhibits the reactive bias. Early responses may be contaminated, later ones not, or vice versa (Underwood, 1957).

Ultimately, the determination of reactive effect depends on validating studies—few examples of which are currently available. Behavior observed under nonreactive conditions must be compared with corresponding behavior in which various potentially reactivity conditions are introduced. Where no difference in direction of relationship occurs, the reactivity factor can be discounted.

In the absence of systematic data of this kind, we have little basis for determining what is and what is not reactive. Existing techniques consist of asking subjects in a posttest interview whether they were affected by the test, were aware of the deception in the experiment, and so forth. While these may sometimes demonstrate a method to be reactive, they may fail to detect many instances in which reactivity is a serious contaminant. Subjects who consciously dissemble during an experiment may do so afterward for the same reasons. And those who are unaware of the effects on them at the time of the research may hardly be counted on for valid reports afterward.

The types of measures surveyed in this monograph have a double importance in overcoming reactivity. In the absence of validation for verbal measures, nonreactive techniques of the kind surveyed here provide ways of avoiding the serious problems faced by more conventional techniques. Given the limiting properties of these "other measures," however, their greatest utility may inhere in their capacity to provide validation for the more conventional measures.

2. *Role Selection.* Another way in which the respondent's awareness of the research process produces differential reaction involves not so much inaccuracy, defense, or dishonesty, but rather a specialized selection from among the many "true" selves or "proper" behaviors available in any respondent.

By singling out an individual to be tested (assuming that being tested is not a normal condition), the experimenter forces upon the subject a role-defining decision—What kind of a person should I be as I answer these questions or do these tasks? In many of the "natural" situations to which the findings are generalized, the subject may not be forced to define his role relative to the behavior. For other situations, he may. Validity decreases as the role assumed in the research setting varies from the usual role present in comparable behavior beyond the research setting. Orne and his colleagues have provided compelling demonstrations of the magnitude of this variable's effect (Orne, 1959, 1962; Orne & Evans, 1965; Orne & Scheibe, 1964). Orne (1962) has noted:

> The experimental situation is one which takes place within context of an explicit agreement of the subject to participate in a special form of social interaction known as "taking part in an experiment." Within the context of our culture the roles of subject and experimenter are well understood and carry with them well-defined mutual role expectations. (p. 777)

Looking at all the cues available to the respondent attempting to puzzle out an appropriate set of roles or behavior, Orne labeled the total of all such cues the "demand characteristics of the experimental situation." The recent study by

Orne and Evans (1965) showed that the alleged antisocial effects induced by hypnosis can be accounted for by the demand characteristics of the research setting. Subjects who were not hypnotized engaged in "antisocial" activities as well as did those who were hypnotized. The behavior of those not hypnotized is traced to social cues that attend the experimental situation and are unrelated to the experimental variable.

The probability of this confounding role assumption varies from one research study to another, of course. The novelty of a test-taking role may be selectively biasing for subjects of different educational levels. Less familiar and comfortable with testing, those with little formal schooling are more likely to produce nonrepresentative behavior. The act of being tested is "more different." The same sort of distortion risk occurs when subject matter is unusual or novel. Subject matter with which the respondent is unfamiliar may produce uncertainty of which role to select. A role-playing choice is more likely with such new or unexpected material.

Lack of familiarity with tests or with testing materials can influence response in different ways. Responses may be depressed because of a lack of training with the materials. Or the response level may be distorted as the subject perceives himself in the rare role of expert.

Both unfamiliarity and "expertness" can influence the character as well as the level of response. It is common to find experimental procedures which augment the experting bias. The instruction which reads, "You have been selected as part of a scientifically selected sample . . . it is important that you answer the questions . . ." underlines in what a special situation and what a special person the respondent is. The empirical test of the experting hypothesis in field research is the extent of "don't know" replies. One should predict that a set of instructions stressing the importance of the respondent as a member of a "scientifically selected sample" will produce significantly fewer "don't knows" than an instruction set that does not stress the individual's importance.

Although the "special person" set of instructions may increase participation in the project, and thus reduce some concern on the sampling level, it concurrently increases the risk of reactive bias. In science as everywhere else, one seldom gets something for nothing. The critical question for the researcher must be whether or not the resultant sampling gain offsets the risk of deviation from "true" responses produced by the experting role.

Not only does interviewing result in role selection, but the problem or its analogues may exist for any measure. Thus, in a study utilizing conversation sampling with totally hidden microphones, each social setting elicits a different role selection. Conversation samples might thus differ between two cities, not because of any true differences, but rather because of subtle differences in role elicitation of the differing settings employed.

3. *Measurement as Change Agent.* With all the respondent candor possible, and with complete role representativeness, there can still be an important class of reactive effects—those in which the initial measurement activity introduces real changes in what is being measured. The change may be real enough in these instances, but be invalidly attributed to any of the intervening events, and be invalidly generalized to other settings not involving a pretest. This process has been deliberately demonstrated by Schanck and Goodman (1939) in a classic study involving information-test taking as a disguised persuasive process. Research by Roper (cited by Crespi, 1948) shows that the well-established "preamble effect" (Cantril, 1944) is not merely a technical flaw in determining the response to the question at hand, but that it also creates attitudes which persist and which are measurable on subsequent unbiased questions. Crespi (1948) reports additional research of his own confirming that even for those who initially say "don't know," processes leading to opinion development are initiated.

The effect has been long established in the social sciences. In psychology, early research in transfer of training encountered the threat to internal validity called "practice effects": the exercise provided by the pretest accounted for the gain shown on the posttest. Such research led to the introduction of control groups in studies that had earlier neglected to include them. Similarly, research in intelligence testing showed that dependable gains in test-passing ability could be traced to experience with previous tests even where no knowledge of results had been provided. (See Anastasi, 1958, pp. 190-191, and Cane & Heim, 1950, for reviews of this literature.) Similar gains have been shown in personal "adjustment" scores (Windle, 1954).

While such effects are obviously limited to intrusive measurement methods such as this review seeks to avoid, the possibility of analogous artifacts must be considered. Suppose one were interested in measuring the weight of women in a secretarial pool, and their weights were to be the dependent variable in a study on the effects of a change from an all-female staff to one including men. One might for this purpose put free weight scales in the women's restroom, with an automatic recording device inside. However, the recurrent availability of knowledge of one's own weight in a semisocial situation would probably act as a greater change agent for weight than would any experimental treatment that might be under investigation. A floor-panel treadle would be better, recording weights without providing feedback to the participant, possibly disguised as an automatic door-opener.

4. *Response Sets.* The critical literature on questionnaire methodology has demonstrated the presence of several irrelevant but lawful sources of variance. Most of these are probably applicable to interviews also, although this has been less elaborately demonstrated to date. Cronbach (1946) has summarized this literature, and evidence continues to show its importance (e.g., Chapman & Bock, 1958; Jackson & Messick, 1957).

Respondents will more frequently endorse a statement than disagree with its opposite (Sletto, 1937). This tendency differs widely and consistently among individuals, generating the reliable source of variance known as acquiescence response set. Rorer (1965) has recently entered a dissent from this point of view. He validly notes the evidence indicating that acquiescence or yea-saying is not a totally general personality trait elicitable by items of any content. He fails to note that, even so, the evidence clearly indicates the methodological problem that direction of wording lawfully enhances the correlation between two measures when shared, and depresses the correlation when running counter to the direction of the correlation of the content (Campbell, 1965b). Another idiosyncrasy, dependably demonstrated over varied multiple-choice content, is the preference for strong statements versus moderate or indecisive ones. Sequences of questions asked in very similar format produce stereotyped responses, such as a tendency to endorse the righthand or the lefthand response, or to alternate in some simple fashion. Furthermore, decreasing attention produces reliable biases from the order of item presentation.

Response biases can occur not only for questionnaires or public opinion polls, but also for archival records such as votes (Bain & Hecock, 1957). Still more esoteric observational or erosion measures face similar problems. Take the example of a traffic study.

Suppose one wanted to obtain a nonreactive measure of the relative attractiveness of paintings in an art museum. He might employ an erosion method such as the relative degree of carpet or floor-tile wear in front of each painting. Or, more elaborately, he might install invisible photoelectric timers and counters. Such an approach must also take into account irrelevant habits which affect traffic flow. There is, for example, a general right-turn bias upon entering a building or room. When this is combined with time deadlines and fatigue (Do people drag their feet more by the time they get to the paintings on the left side of the building?), there probably is a predictably biased response tendency. The design of museums tends to be systematic, and this, too, can bias the measures. The placement of an exit door will consistently bias the traffic flow and thus confound any erosion measure unless it is controlled. (For imaginative and provocative observational studies on museum behavior, see Melton, 1933a, 1933b, 1935, 1936; Melton, Feldman, & Mason, 1936; Robinson, 1928.)

Each of these four types of reactive error can be reduced by employing research measures which do not require the cooperation of the respondent and which are "blind" to him. Although we urge more methodological research to make known the degree of error that may be traced to reactivity, our inclination now is to urge the use of compensating measures which do not contain the reactive risk.

Error From the Investigator

To some degree, error from the investigator was implicit in the reactive error effects. After all, the investigator is an important source of cues to the respondent, and he helps to structure the demand characteristics of the interview. However, in these previous points, interviewer character was unspecified. Here we deal with effects that vary systematically with interviewer characteristics, and with instrument errors totally independent of respondents.

5. *Interviewer Effects*. It is old news that the characteristics of the interviewer can contribute a substantial amount of variance to a set of findings. Interviewees respond differentially to visible cues provided by the interviewer.

Within any single study, this variance can produce a spurious difference. The work of Katz (1942) and Cantril (1944) early demonstrated the differential effect of the race of the interviewer, and that bias has been more recently shown by Athey, Coleman, Reitman, and Tang (1960). Riesman and Ehrlich (1961) reported that the age of the interviewer produced a bias, with the number of "unacceptable" (to the experimenter) answers higher when questions were posed by younger interviewers. Religion of the interviewer is a possible contaminant (Hyman, Cobb, Feldman, Hart, & Stember, 1954; Robinson & Rohde, 1946), as is his social class (Lenski & Leggett, 1960; Riesman, 1956). Benney, Riesman, and Star (1956) showed that one should consider not only main effects, but also interactions. In their study of age and sex variables they report: "Male interviewers obtain fewer responses than female, and fewest of all from males, while female interviewers obtain their highest responses from men, except for young women talking to young men" (p. 143).

The evidence is overwhelming that a substantial number of biases are introduced by the interviewer (see Hyman et al., 1954; Kahn & Cannell, 1957). Some of the major biases, such as race, are easily controllable; other biases, such as the interaction of age and sex, are less easily handled. If we heeded all the known biases, without considering our ignorance of major interactions, there could no longer be a simple survey. The understandable action by most researchers has been to ignore these biases and to assume them away. The biases are lawful and consistent, and all research employing face-to-face interviewing or questionnaire administration is subject to them. Rather than flee by assumptions, the experimenter may use alternative methodologies that let him flee by circumvention.

6. *Change in the Research Instrument.* The measuring (data-gathering) instrument is frequently an interviewer, whose characteristics, we have just shown, may alter responses. In panel studies, or those using the same interviewer at two or more points in time, it is essential to ask: To what degree is the interviewer or experimenter the same research instrument at all points of the research?

Just as a spring scale becomes fatigued with use, reading "heavier" a second time, an interviewer may also measure differently at different times. His skill may increase. He may be better able to establish rapport. He may have learned necessary vocabulary. He may loaf or become bored. He may have increasingly strong expectations of what a respondent "means" and code differently with practice. Some errors relate to recording accuracy, while others are linked to the nature of the interviewer's interpretation of what transpired. Either way, there is always the risk that the interviewer will be a variable filter over time and experience.

Even when the interviewer becomes more competent, there is potential trouble. Although we usually think of difficulty only when the instrument weakens, a difference in competence between two waves of interviewing, *either increasing or decreasing,* can yield spurious effects. The source of error is not limited to interviewers, and every class of measurement is vulnerable to wavering calibration. Suicides in Prussia jumped 20% between 1882 and 1883. This clearly reflected a change in record-keeping, not a massive increase in depression. Until 1883, the records were kept by the police, but in that year the job was transferred to the civil service (Halbwachs, 1930, cited in Selltiz et al., 1959). Archivists undoubtedly drift in recording standards, with occasional administrative reforms in conscientiousness altering the output of the "instrument" (Kitsuse & Cicourel, 1963).

Where human observers are used, they have fluctuating adaptation levels and response thresholds (Campbell, 1961; Holmes, 1958). Rosenthal, in an impressive series of commentary and research, has focused on errors traceable to the experimenter himself. Of particular interest is his work on the influence of early data returns upon analysis of subsequent data (Rosenthal, Persinger, Vikan-Kline, & Fode, 1963; see also Kintz, Delprato, Mettee, Persons, & Schappe, 1965; Rosenthal, 1963, 1964; Rosenthal & Fode, 1963; Rosenthal & Lawson, 1963).

Varieties of Sampling Error

Historically, social science has examined sampling errors as a problem in the selection of respondents. The person or group has been the critical unit, and our thinking has been focused on a universe of people. Often a sample of time or space can provide a practical substitute for a sample of persons. Novel methods should be examined for their potential in this regard. For example, a study of the viewing of bus advertisements used a time-stratified, random triggering of an automatic camera pointed out a window over the bus ad (Politz Media Studies, 1959). One could similarly take a photographic sample of bus passengers modulated by door entries as counted by a photo cell. A photo could be taken one minute after the entry of every twentieth passenger. For some methods, such as the erosion methods, total population records are no more costly than partial ones. For some archives, temporal samples or agency samples are possible. For voting records, precincts may be sampled. But for any one method, the possibilities should be examined.

We look at sampling in this section from the point of view of restrictions on reaching people associated with various methods and the stability of populations over time and areas.

7. *Population Restrictions.* In the public-opinion-polling tradition, one conceptualizes a "universe" from which a representative sample is drawn. This model gives little or no formal attention to the fact that only certain universes are possible for any given method. A method-respondent interaction exists— one that gives each method a different set of defining boundaries for its universe. One reason so little attention is given to this fact is that, as methods go, public opinion polling is relatively unrestricted. Yet even here there is definite universe rigidity, with definite restrictions on the size and character of the population able to be sampled.

In the earliest days of polling, people were questioned in public places, probably excluding some 80% of the total population. Shifting to in-home interviewing with quota controls and no callbacks still excluded some 60%— perhaps 5% inaccessible in homes under any conditions, 25% not at home, 25% refusals, and 5% through interviewers' reluctance to approach homes of extreme wealth or poverty and a tendency to avoid fourth-floor walkups.

Under modern probability sampling with callbacks and household designation, perhaps only 15% of the population is excluded: 5% are totally inaccessible in private residences (e.g., those institutionalized, hospitalized, homeless, transient, in the military, mentally incompetent, and so forth); another 10% refuse to answer, are unavailable after three callbacks, or have moved to no known address. A 20% figure was found in the model Elmira study in its first wave (Williams, 1950), although other studies have reported much lower figures. Ross (1963) has written a general statement on the problem of inaccessibility, and Stephan and McCarthy (1958), in their literature survey, show from 3% to 14% of sample populations of residences inaccessible.

Also to be considered in population restriction is the degree to which the accessible universe deviates in important parameters from the excluded population. This bias is probably minimal in probability sampling with adequate callbacks, but great with catch-as-catch-can and quota samples. Much survey research has centered on household behavior, and the great mass of probability approaches employ a prelisted household as the terminal sampling unit. This frequently requires the enlistment of a household member as a reporter on the behavior of others. Since those who answer doorbells overrepresent the old, the young, and women, this can be a confounding error.

When we come to more demanding verbal techniques, the universe rigidity is much greater. What proportion of the population is available for self-administered questionnaires? Payment for filling out the questionnaire reduces the limitations a bit, but a money reward is selectively attractive—at least at the rates most researchers pay. A considerable proportion of the populace is functionally illiterate for personality and attitude tests developed on college populations.

Not only does task-demandingness create population restrictions, differential volunteering provides similar effects, interacting in a particularly biasing way when knowledge of the nature of the task is involved (Capra & Dittes, 1962). Baumrind (1964) writes of the motivation of volunteers and notes, "The dependent attitude of most subjects toward the experimenter is an artifact of the experimental situation as well as an expression of some subjects' personal need systems at the time they volunteer" (p. 421).

The curious, the exhibitionistic, and the succorant are likely to overpopulate any sample of volunteers. How secure a base can volunteers be with such groups overrepresented and the shy, suspicious, and inhibited underrepresented? The only defensible position is a probability sample of the units to which the findings will be generalized. Even conscripting sophomores may be better than relying on volunteers.

Returning to the rigidity of sampling, what proportion of the total population is available for the studio test audiences used in advertising and television program evaluation? Perhaps 2%. For mailed questionnaires, the population available for addressing might be 95% of the total in the United States, but low-cost, convenient mailing lists probably cover no more than 70% of the families through automobile registration and telephone directories. The exclusion is, again, highly selective. If, however, we consider the volunteering feature, where 10% returns are typical, the effective population is a biased 7% selection of the total. The nature of this selective-return bias, according to a recent study (Vincent, 1964), includes a skewing of the sample in favor of lower-middle-class individuals drawn from unusually stable, "happy" families.

There are more households with television in the United States than there are households with telephones (or baths). In any given city, one is likely to find more than 15% of the households excluded in a telephone subscription list— and most of these are at the bottom of the socioeconomic scale. Among subscribers, as many as 15% in some areas do not list their number, and an estimate of 5% over all is conservative. Cooper (1964) found an over-all level of 6% deliberately not listed and an additional 12% not in the directory because of recent installations. The unlisted problem can be defeated by a system of random-digit dialing, but this increases the cost at least tenfold and requires a prior study of the distribution of exchanges. Among a sample of known numbers, some 50% of dialings are met with busy signals and "not-at-homes." Thus, for a survey without callbacks, the accessible population of 80% (listed-phone households) reduces to 40%. If individuals are the unit of analysis, the effective sampling rate, without callbacks, may drop to 20%. Random-digit dialing will help; so, too, will at least three callbacks, but precision can be achieved only at a high price. The telephone is not so cheap a research instrument as it first looks.

Sampling problems of this sort are even more acute for the research methods considered in the present monograph. Although a few have the full population access of public opinion surveys, most have much more restricted populations. Consider, for example, the sampling of natural conversations. What are the proportions of men and women whose conversations are accessible in public places and on public transport? What is the representativeness of social class or role?

8. *Population Stability Over Time.* Just as internal validity is more important than external validity, so, too, is the stability of a population restriction more important than the magnitude of the restriction. Examine conversation

sampling on a bus or streetcar. The population represented differs on dry days and snowy days, in winter and spring, as well as by day of the week. These shifts would in many instances provide plausible rival explanations of shifts in topics of conversation. Sampling from a much narrower universe would be preferable if the population were more stable over time, as, say, conversation samples from an employees' restroom in an office building. Comparisons of interview survey results over time periods are more troubled by population instability than is generally realized, because of seasonal layoffs in many fields of employment, plus status-differentiated patterns of summer and winter vacations. An extended discussion of time sampling has been provided by Brookover and Back (1965).

9. *Population Stability Over Areas.* Similarly, research populations available to a given method may vary from region to region, providing a more serious problem than a population restriction common to both. Thus, for a comparison of attitudes between New York and Los Angeles, conversation sampling in buses and commuter trains would tap such different segments of the communities as to be scarcely worth doing. Again, a comparison of employees' washrooms in comparable office buildings would provide a more interpretable comparison. Through the advantage of background data to check on some dimensions of representativeness, public opinion surveys again have an advantage in this regard.

Any enumeration of sources of invalidity is bound to be incomplete. Some threats are too highly specific to a given setting and method to be generalized, as are some opportunities for ingenious measurement and control. This list contains a long series of general threats that apply to a broad body of research method and content. It does not say that additional problems cannot be found.

AN INTERLUDE: THE MEASUREMENT
OF OUTCROPPINGS

The population restrictions discussed here are apt to seem so severe as to traumatize the researcher and to lead to the abandonment of the method. This is particularly so for one approaching social science with the goal of complete description. Such trauma is, of course, far from our intention. While discussion of these restrictions is a necessary background to their intelligent use and correction, there is need here for a parenthesis forestalling excessive pessimism.

First, it can be noted that a theory predicting a change in civic opinion, due to an event and occurring between two time periods, might be such that this opinion shift could be predicted for many partially overlapping populations. One might predict changes on public opinion polls within that universe, changes in sampled conversation on commuter trains for a much smaller segment, changes in letters mailed to editors and the still more limited letters published by editors, changes in purchase rates of books on relevant subjects by that minute universe, and so on. In such an instance, the occurrence of the predicted shift on any one of these meters is confirmatory and its absence discouraging. If the effect is found on only one measure, it probably reflects more on the method than on the theory (e.g., Burwen & Campbell, 1957; Campbell & Fiske, 1959). A more complicated theory might well predict differential shifts for different meters, and, again, the evidence of each is relevant to the validity of the theory. The joint confirmation between pollings of high-income populations and commuter-train conversations is much more validating than either taken alone, just because of the difference between the methods in irrelevant components.

The "outcropping" model from geology may be used more generally. Any given theory has innumerable implications and makes innumerable predictions which are unaccessible to available measures at any given time. The testing of the theory can only be done at the available outcroppings, those points where theoretical predictions and available instrumentation meet. Any one such outcropping is equivocal, and all types available should be checked. The more remote or independent such checks, the more confirmatory their agreement.

Within this model, science opportunistically exploits the available points of observation. As long as nature abhorred a vacuum up to 33 feet of water, little research was feasible. When manufacturing skills made it possible to represent the same abhorrence by 76 centimeters of mercury in a glass tube, a whole new outcropping for the checking of theory was made available. The telescope in Galileo's hands, the microscope, the induction coil, the photographic emulsion of silver nitrate, and the cloud chamber all represent partial new outcroppings available for the verification of theory. Even where several of these are relevant to the same theory, their mode of relevance is quite different and short of a complete overlap. Analogously, social science methods with individually restricted and nonidentical universes can provide collectively valuable outcroppings for the testing of theory.

The goal of complete description in science is particularly misleading when it is assumed that raw data provide complete description. Theory is necessarily abstract, for any given event is so complex that its complete description may demand many more theories than are actually brought to bear on it—or than are even known at any given stage of development. But theories are more complete descriptions than obtained data, since they describe processes and entities in their unobserved as well as in their observed states. The scintillation counter notes but a small and nonrepresentative segment of a meson's course. The visual data of an ordinary object are literally superficial. Perceiving an object as solid or vaporous, persistent or transient, involves theory going far beyond the data given. The raw data, observations, field notes, tape recordings, and sound movies of a social event are but transient superficial outcroppings of events and objects much more continuously and completely (even if abstractly) described in the social scientist's theory. Tycho Brahe and Kepler's observations provided Kepler with only small fragments of the orbit of Mars, for a biased and narrow sampling of times of day, days, and years. From these he constructed a complete description through theory. The fragments provided outcroppings sufficiently stubborn to force Kepler to reject his preferred theory. The data were even sufficient to cause the rejection of Newton's later theory had Einstein's better-fitting theory then been available.

So if the restraints on validity sometimes seem demoralizing, they remain so only as long as one set of data, one type of method, is considered separately. Viewed in consort with other methods, matched against the available outcroppings for theory testing, there can be strength in converging weakness.

THE ACCESS TO CONTENT

Often a choice among methods is delimited by the relative ability of different classes of measurement to penetrate into content areas of research interest. In the simplest instance, this is not so much a question of validity as it is a limitation on the utility of the measure. Each class of research method, be it the questionnaire or hidden observation, has rigidities on the content it can cover. These rigidities can be divided, as were population restrictions, into those linked to an interaction between method and materials, those associated with time, and those with physical area.

10. *Restrictions on Content.* If we adopt the research strategy of combining different classes of measurement, it becomes important to understand what content is and is not feasible or practical for each overlapping approach.

Observational methods can be used to yield an index of Negro-white amicability by computing the degree of "aggregation" or nonrandom clustering among mixed groups of Negroes and whites. This method could also be used to study male-female relations, or army-navy relations in wartime when uniforms are worn on liberty. But these indices of aggregation would be largely unavailable for Catholic-Protestant relations or for Jewish-Christian relations. Door-to-door solicitation of funds for causes relevant to attitudes is obviously plausible, but available for only a limited range of topics. For public opinion surveys, there are perhaps tabooed topics (although research on birth control and venereal disease has shown these to be fewer than might have been expected). More importantly, there are topics on which people are unable to report but which a social scientist can reliably observe.

Examples of this can be seen in the literature on verbal reinforcers in speech and in interviews. (For a review of this literature, see Krasner, 1958, as well as Hildum & Brown, 1956; Matarazzo, 1962a.) A graphic display of opportunistic exploitation of an "outcropping" was displayed recently by Matarazzo, Wiens, Saslow, Dunham, and Voas (1964). They took tapes of the speech of astronauts and ground-communicators for two space flights and studied the duration of the ground-communicator's unit of speech to the astronauts. The data supported their expectations and confirmed findings from the laboratory. We are not sure if an orbital flight should be considered a "natural setting" or not, but certainly the astronaut and his colleagues were not overly sensitive to the duration of individual speech units. The observational method has consistently produced findings on the effect of verbal reinforcers unattainable by direct questioning.

It is obvious that secondary records and physical evidence are high in their content rigidity. The researcher cannot go out and generate a new set of

historical records. He may discover a new set, but he is always restrained by
what is available. We cite examples later which demonstrate that this weakness
is not so great as is frequently thought, but it would be naive to suggest that it
is not present.

11. *Stability of Content Over Time.* The restrictions on content just mentioned are often questions of convenience. The instability of content, however,
is a serious concern for validity. Consider conversation sampling again: if one
is attending to the amount of comment on race relations, for example, the
occurrence of extremely bad weather may so completely dominate all conversations as to cause a meaningless drop in racial comments. This is a typical
problem for index-making. In such an instance, one would probably prefer
some index such as the proportion of all race comments that were favorable.
In specific studies of content variability over time, personnel-evaluation studies have employed time sampling with considerable success. Observation during a random sample of a worker's laboring minutes efficiently does much
to describe both the job and the worker (Ghiselli & Brown, 1955; Thorndike,
1949; Whisler & Harper, 1962).

Public opinion surveys have obvious limitations in this regard which have
led to the utilization of telephone interviews and built-in-dialing recorders for
television and radio audience surveys (Lucas & Britt, 1950, 1963). By what
means other than a recorder could one get a reasonable estimate of the number
of people who watch *The Late Show?*

12. *Stability of Content Over Area.* Where regional comparisons are being
made, cross-sectional stability in the kinds of contents elicited by a given
method is desirable.

Take the measurement of interservice rivalry as a research question. As
suggested earlier, one could study the degree of mingling among men in
uniform, or study the number of barroom fights among men dressed in
different uniforms. To have a valid regional comparison, one must assume the
same incidence of men wearing uniforms in public places when at liberty.
Such an assumption is probably not justified, partly because of past experience
in a given area, partly because of proximity to urban centers. If a cluster of
military bases are close to a large city, only a selective group wear uniforms off

duty, and they are more likely to be the belligerent ones. Another comparison region may have the same level of behavior, but be less visible.

The effect of peace is to reduce the influence of the total level of the observed response, since mufti is more common. But if all the comparisons are made in peacetime, it is not an issue. The problem occurs only if one elected to study the problem by a time-series design which cut across war and peace. To the foot-on-rail researcher, the number of outcroppings may vary because of war, but this is no necessary threat to internal validity.

Sampling of locations, such as bus routes, waiting rooms, shop windows, and so forth, needs to be developed to expand access to both content and populations. Obviously, different methods present different opportunities and problems in this regard. Among the few studies which have seriously attempted this type of sampling, the problem of enumerating the universe of such locations has proved extremely difficult (James, 1951). Location sampling has, of course, been practiced more systematically with pre-established enumerated units such as blocks, census tracts, and incorporated areas.

OPERATING EASE AND VALIDITY CHECKS

There are differences among methods which have nothing to do with the interpretation of a single piece of research. These are familiar issues to working researchers, and are important ones for the selection of procedures. Choosing between two different methods which promise to yield equally valid data, the researcher is likely to reject the more time-consuming or costly method. Also, there is an inclination toward those methods which have sufficient flexibility to allow repetition if something unforeseen goes wrong, and which further hold potential for producing internal checks on validity or sampling errors.

13. *Dross Rate.* In any given interview, a part of the conversation is irrelevant to the topic at hand. This proportion is the dross rate. It is greater in open-ended, general, free-response interviewing than it is in structured interviews with fixed-answer categories; by the same token, the latter are potentially the more reactive. But in all such procedures, the great advantage is the interviewer's power to introduce and reintroduce certain topics. This ability allows a greater density of relevant data. At the other extreme is unobserved

conversation sampling, which is low-grade ore. If one elected to measure attitudes toward Russia by sampling conversations on public transportation, a major share of experimental effort could be spent in listening to comparisons of hairdressers or discussions of the Yankees' one-time dominance of the American League. For a specific problem, conversation sampling provides low-grade ore. The price one must pay for this ore, in order to get a naturally occurring response, may be too high for the experimenter's resources.

14. *Access to Descriptive Cues.* In evaluating methods, one should consider their potential for generating associated validity checks, as well as the differences in the universes they tap. Looking at alternative measures, what other data can they produce that give descriptive cues on the specific nature of the method's population? Internal evidence from early opinion polls showed their population biases when answers about prior voting and education did not match known election results and census data.

On this criterion, survey research methods have great advantages, for they permit the researcher to build in controls with ease. Observational procedures can check restrictions only for such gross and visible variables as sex, approximate age, and conspicuous ethnicity. Trace methods such as the relative wear of floor tiles offer no such intrinsic possibility. However, it is possible in many instances to introduce interview methods in conjunction with other methods for the purpose of ascertaining population characteristics. Thus, commuter-train passengers, window shoppers, and waiting-room conversationalists can, on a sample of times of day, days of the week, and so on, be interviewed on background data, probably without creating any serious reactive effects for measures taken on other occasions.

15. *Ability to Replicate.* The questionnaire and the interview are particularly good methods because they permit the investigator to replicate his own or someone else's research. There is a tolerance for error when one is producing new data that does not exist when working with old. If a confounding event occurs or materials are spoiled, one can start another survey repeating the procedure. Archives and physical evidence are more restricted, with only a fixed amount of data available. This may be a large amount—allowing split-sample replication—but it may also be a one-shot occurrence that permits only a single

analysis. In the latter case, there is no second chance, and the materials may be completely consumed methodologically.

The one-sample problem is not an issue if data are used in a clear-cut test of theory. If the physical evidence or secondary records are an outcropping where the theory can be probed, the inability to produce another equivalent body of information is secondary. The greater latitude of the questionnaire and interview, however, permit the same statement and provide in addition a margin for error.

————— •◆• —————

So long as we maintain, as social scientists, an approach to comparisons that considers compensating error and converging corroboration from individually contaminated outcroppings, there is no cause for concern. It is only when we naively place faith in a single measure that the massive problems of social research vitiate the validity of our comparisons. We have argued strongly in this chapter for a conceptualization of method that demands multiple measurement of the same phenomenon or comparison. Overreliance on questionnaires and interviews is dangerous because it does not give us enough points in conceptual space to triangulate. We are urging the employment of novel, sometimes "oddball" methods to give those points in space. The chapters that follow illustrate some of these methods, their strengths and weaknesses, and their promise for imaginative research.

⇢ TWO ⇠

PHYSICAL TRACES

Erosion and Accretion

————•◆•————

he fog had probably just cleared. The singular Sherlock Holmes had been reunited with his old friend, Dr. Watson (after one of Watson's marriages), and both walked to Watson's newly acquired office. The practice was located in a duplex of two physician's suites, both of which have been for sale. No doubt sucking on his calabash, Holmes summarily told Watson that he had made a wise choice in purchasing the practice that he did, rather than the one on the other side of the duplex. The data? The steps were more worn on Watson's side than on his competitor's.

In this chapter, we look at research methods geared to the study of physical traces surviving from past behavior. Physical evidence is probably the social scientist's least-used source of data, yet because of its ubiquity, it holds flexible and broad-gauged potential.

It is reasonable to start a chapter on physical evidence by talking of Sherlock Holmes. He and his paperbacked colleagues could teach us much. Consider that the detective, like the social scientist, faces the task of inferring the nature of past behavior (Who did the Lord of the Manor in?) by the careful generation and evaluation of current evidence. Some evidence he engineers (by questioning), some he observes (Does the witness develop a tic?), some he develops from extant physical evidence (Did the murderer leave his eyeglasses behind?). From the weighing of several different types of hopefully converging evidence, he makes a decision on the plausibility of several rival hypotheses. For example:

H_1: The butler did it.

H_2: It was the blacksheep brother.

H_3: He really committed suicide.

This chapter discusses only the physical evidence, those pieces of data not specifically produced for the purpose of comparison and inference, but available to be exploited opportunistically by the alert investigator. It should be emphasized that physical evidence has greatest utility in consort with other methodological approaches. Because there are easily visible population and content restrictions associated with physical evidence, such data have largely been ignored. It is difficult even to consider a patently weak source of data when research strategy is based on single measures and definitional operationism. The visibly stronger questionnaire or interview looks to be more valid, and it may be if only one measure is taken. In a multimethod strategy, however, one does not have to exclude data of any class or degree solely because it is weak. If the weaknesses are known and considered, the data are usable.

It may be helpful to discriminate between two broad classes of physical evidence, a discrimination similar to that between the intaglio and the cameo. On one hand, there are the *erosion measures,* where the degree of selective wear on some material yields the measure. Holmes's solution of the stairs on the duplex is an example. On the other hand, there are *accretion measures,* where the research evidence is some deposit of materials. Immediately one thinks of anthropologists working with refuse piles and pottery shards. The trace measures could be further subdivided according to the number and pattern of units of evidence. We might have two subclasses: remnants, where there is only one or a few indicators of the past behavior available, and series, where there is an accumulative body of evidence with more units, possibly deposited over a longer period of time. For purposes of simplicity, it is easier to consider just the two main divisions of erosion and accretion.

NATURAL EROSION MEASURES

Let us look first at some erosion measures. A committee was formed to set up a psychological exhibit at Chicago's Museum of Science and Industry. The committee learned that the vinyl tiles around the exhibit containing live, hatching chicks had to be replaced every six weeks or so; tiles in other areas of the museum went for years without replacement (C. P. Duncan, 1963, personal communication). A comparative study of the rate of tile replacement around the various museum exhibits could give a rough ordering of the popularity of the exhibits. Note that although erosion is the measure, the knowledge of the erosion rate comes from a check of the records of the museum's maintenance department.

In addition to this erosion measure, unobtrusive observation studies showed that people stand before the chick display longer than they stand before any of the other exhibits. With this additional piece of evidence, the question becomes whether or not the erosion is a simple result of people standing in one location and shuffling their feet, or whether it really does indicate a greater frequency of different people viewing the exhibit. Clearly an empirical question. The observation and the tile erosion are two partially overlapping measures, each of which can serve as a check on the other. The observation material is more textured for studies of current behavior, because it can provide information on both the number of viewers and how long each views the display. The erosion data cannot index the duration of individual viewing, but they permit an analysis of popularity over time, and do so with economy and efficiency.

Those readers who have attended American Psychological Association meetings have doubtless observed the popularity of conditioning exhibits displaying a live pigeon or monkey (a Skinner-boxed baby has also done well in recent years). This observation offers independent evidence for the general principle that dynamic exhibits draw more viewers than static ones. The hypothesis could be tested further by more careful comparison of tile wear about dynamic and static exhibits in the museum, making corrections for their positional distribution. At least part of the correction would be drawn from the previously mentioned research by Melton (1936) on response sets systematically present in museum traffic flow.

The wear on library books, particularly on the corners where the page is turned, offers an example of a possible approach that illustrates a useful overlap measure. One of the most direct and obvious ways to learn the popularity of books is to check how many times each of a series of titles has been removed from a library. This is an excellent measure and uses the records already maintained for other purposes. But it is only an indirect measure for the investigator who wants to know the relative amount of reading a series of books gets. They may be removed from the library, but not read. It is easy to establish whether or not there is a close relationship between degree of wear and degree of checkouts from the library. If this relationship is positive and high, the hypothesis that books are taken out but selectively not read is accounted for. Note that the erosion measure also allows one to study the relative use of titles which are outside the span of the library-withdrawal measure. Titles placed on reserve, for example, are typically not noted for individual use by library bookkeeping. An alternative accretion measure is to note the amount of dust that has accumulated on the books studied.

Mosteller (1955) conducted a shrewd and creative study on the degree to which different sections of the *International Encyclopedia of the Social Sciences* were read. He measured the wear and tear on separate sections by noting dirty edges of pages as markers, and observed the frequency of dirt smudges, finger markings, and underlining on pages. In some cases of very heavy use, "dirt had noticeably changed the color of the page so that [some articles] are immediately distinguishable from the rest of the volume" (p. 171). Mosteller studied volumes at both Harvard and the University of Chicago, and went to three libraries at each institution. He even used the *Encyclopaedia Britannica* as a control.

A variation of the erosion method had been suggested by Brown (1960) for studying the food intake of institutionalized patients—frequently a difficult task. If the question is one of overall food consumption of some administrative unit (say, a ward under special treatment conditions compared with a control ward), Brown makes the engagingly simple suggestion of weighing food trucks that enter and garbage trucks that leave. The unit could be varied to be an individual tray of food, the aggregate consignment to a floor or ward, or the total input and output of the hospital.

NATURAL ACCRETION MEASURES

There are large numbers of useful natural remnants of past behavior that can be exploited. We can examine now a few examples of behavior traces which were laid down "naturally," without the intervention of the social scientist.

The detective-story literature, again, is instructive. In a favorite example (Barzun, 1961), a case hinged on determining where a car came from. It was solved (naturally) by studying the frequencies to which the car's radio buttons were tuned. By triangulation of the frequencies, from a known population of commercial-station frequencies, the geographic source of the car was learned. Here was a remnant of past behavior (someone setting the buttons originally) that included several component elements collectively considered to reach a solution. Unimaginatively, most detective fiction considers much simpler and less elegant solutions—such as determining how fast a car was going by noting the degree to which insects are splattered on the windshield.

Modern police techniques include many trace methods, for example, making complex analyses of soil from shoes and clothing to establish a suspect's probable presence at the scene of a crime. One scientist (Forshufvud, 1961) uncovered the historic murder of Napoleon in 1821 on the basis of arsenic traces in remains of his hair.

Radio-dial settings are being used in a continuing audience-measurement study, with mechanics in an automotive service department the data-gatherers ("Z-Frank Stresses Radio," 1962). A Chicago automobile dealer, Z. Frank, estimates the popularity of different radio stations by having mechanics record the position of the dial in all cars brought in for service. More than 50,000 dials a year are checked, with less than 20% duplication of dials. These data are then used to select radio stations to carry the dealer's advertising. The generalization of these findings is sound if (a) the goal of the radio propaganda is to reach the same type of audience which now comes to the dealership and (b) a significant number of cars have radios. If many of the cars are without radios, then a partial and possibly biased estimate of the universe is obtained. It is reported, "We find a high degree of correlation between what the rating people report and our own dial setting research" (p. 83).

The same approach could be used to study the selective appeal of different radio stations. Knowing that various shopping centers draw customers from quite discrete economic populations, one could observe dial settings in cars parked in the shopping centers and compare them. As a validation check on the discrimination among the centers, one could (in metropolitan areas) note local tax stickers affixed to the automobiles and compare these with the economic data reported for tax areas by the U.S. Census.

Dial checking is difficult in public areas, because one cannot easily enter the car and make a close observation. And the locking of cars is a selective phenomenon, even if one would risk entering an unlocked car. Sechrest (1965b) has reported that a significantly larger proportion of college women lock their cars than do college men. He learned this by checking doors of automobiles parked adjacent to men's and women's dormitories.

DuBois (1963) reports on a 1934 study which estimated an advertisement's readership level by analyzing the number of different fingerprints on the page. The set of prints was a valid remnant, and the analysis revealed a resourceful researcher. Compare this with the anthropologist's device of estimating the prior population of an archeological site by noting the size of floor areas (Naroll, 1962). Among the consistently detectable elements in a site are good indicators of the floor areas of residences. When these can be keyed to knowledge of the residential and familial patterns of the group, these partial data, these remnants, serve as excellent population predictors.

Other remnants can provide evidence on the physical characteristics of populations no longer available for study. Suits of armor, for example, are indicators of the height of medieval knights.

The estimable study of McClelland (1961), *The Achieving Society,* displays a fertile use of historical evidence. Most of the data come from documentary materials such as records of births and deaths, coal imports, shipping levels, electric-power consumption, and remaining examples of literature, folk tales, and children's stories. We consider such materials in our discussion of archival records, but they are, in one sense, a special case of trace analysis. McClelland further reports on achievement-level estimates derived from ceramic designs on urns, and he indexes the geographic boundaries of Greek trade by archeological finds of vases. Sensitive to the potential error in such estimates, McClelland writes,

> So, rough though it is, the measure of the economic rise and fall of classical Greece was taken to be the area with which she traded, in millions of square miles, as determined by the location of vases unearthed in which her chief export commodities were transported. (p. 117)

This measure was related to the need-for-achievement level of classical Greece, estimated from a content analysis of Greek writings.

Following the anthropological tradition of refuse study, two recent reports demonstrate that refuse may be used for contemporary as well as historical research.

Hughes (1958) observes:

> It is by the garbage that the janitor judges, and, as it were, gets power over the tenants who high-hat him. Janitors know about hidden love-affairs by bits of torn-up letter paper; of impending financial disaster or of financial four-flushing by the presence of many unopened letters in the waste. Or they may stall off demands for immediate service by an unreasonable woman of whom they know from the garbage that she, as the janitors put it, "has the rag on." The garbage gives the janitor the makings of a kind of magical power over that pretentious villain, the tenant. I say a kind of magical power, for there appears to be no thought of betraying any individual and thus turning this knowledge into overt power. He protects the tenant, but, at least among Chicago janitors, it is not a loving protection. (p. 51)

Sawyer (1961) recounts the problem of estimating liquor sales in Wellesley, Massachusetts. In a city without package stores, the usual devices of observation of purchase or study of sales records are of no help. Sawyer solved the problem by studying the trash carted from Wellesley homes and counting the number of empty liquor bottles.

The duration of the sampling period is a consideration in studying traces of any product in which consumption of a visible unit takes a long time. The study must cover a large enough span to guarantee that a trace of the behavior will appear if, in fact, it did occur. With estimation of whisky consumption, there is the further demand that account be taken of such possibly confounding elements as holidays, birthdays, discount sales in nearby retail stores, and unusual weather. This is particularly true if estimates are being made of the relative consumption of specific types of liquor. A heat wave produces a substantial increase in the consumption of gin, vodka, and rum, while depressing consumption of scotch, brandy, and blended whiskies. Depending upon the area, an unusually high level of entertaining produces consumption of either more expensive or less expensive whisky than usual. The temporal stability of many common products that could be used to measure behavior is quite low.

Kinsey and his associates note the study of another trace measure—inscriptions in toilets. "With the collaboration of a number of other persons, we have accumulated some hundreds of wall inscriptions from public toilets" (Kinsey, Pomeroy, Martin, & Gebhard, 1953, p. 673). Their findings show a significant difference between men's and women's toilets in the incidence of erotic inscriptions, either writings or drawings. Sechrest (1965a), studying inscriptions in Philippine and United States toilets, also found a difference between frequencies of male and female inscriptions—although female inscriptions seemed relatively more frequent in the Philippines. A widely circulated United States joke runs, "When a girl can see the handwriting on the wall, she's in the wrong restroom." Sechrest also found indications of greater sexual and homosexual preoccupation in the U.S. sample.

Some accretion data are built up quickly, and the problem of deciding on the appropriate period of study is negligible. Take the debris accumulation of a ticker-tape parade. The New York Sanitary Commission regularly notes how many tons of paper float down onto the streets during a parade. One might use this as material in estimating the enthusiasm of response for some popular hero. Because the Sanitary Commission has been reporting on how hard it works for years, it is possible to employ a control level of tonnages showered down upon other heroes. Did John Glenn get a more or less enthusiastic response from the New Yorkers of his day than did Charles Lindbergh from the New Yorkers of his? At best, these data are suggestive, and the demise of the ticker-tape machine has meant a confounding of data for long-term historical analysis. While at one time, ticker-tape parades had a dominance of ticker tape in the air, today it is confetti. One can make corrections, of course, but they must be tenuous.

Litter can also serve as a measure of conformity to restrictions. One can measure with a direct criterion the effectiveness of antilitter posters which vary in severity or style.

Experimenter Intervention

The methods discussed so far have all been ones in which the social scientist has taken the data as they come and not intervened in any way to influence the frequency or character of the indicator material. There are conditions under which the social scientist can intervene in the data-production process without destroying the nonreactive gains characteristic of trace and erosion data. He might want to do this, for example, to speed up the incidence of critical responses—a sometimes nagging annoyance with slowly eroding or accreting materials. Or he might want to guarantee that the materials under study were in fact equivalent or equal before they were modified by the critical responses. The essential point is that his intervention should not impair the nonreactivity of the erosion and trace measures by permitting the subjects to become aware of his testing.

CONTROLLED EROSION MEASURES

John Wallace, our former colleague, once noted that it would be possible to estimate the activity level of children by measuring the rate at which they wear out shoes. It is theoretically possible to start at any point in time with the shoes that children are wearing, measure the degree of wear, and then later remeasure. The difference between the two scores might be a measure of the effect of some experimental variable. If the measurements were surreptitious, the experimenter would merely be noting a naturally occurring event and not involving himself with the materials.

Schulman and Reisman (1959) indexed the activity level of children by having them wear self-winding wristwatches which were adapted to record the child's amount of movement. Schulman, Kasper, and Throne (1965) have validated the "actometer" data against children's oxygen consumption.

Still another way to improve the data-gathering process is to manipulate the recording material. In some cases, one might treat the material to allow it to provide a more stable base. With floor tile, for example, surfaces are often coated to resist wear. Once the coating is worn through, erosion proceeds at a faster rate. For research purposes, it would be desirable to lay uncoated tiles and accelerate the speed with which information is produced.

In other cases, coating of materials may be desirable, either to provide a more permanent measure or to allow one where it otherwise would be impossible. The wear on public statues, reliefs, and so forth may provide an example. Throughout Europe, one may note with interest shiny bronze spots on religious figures and scenes. The rubbing which produced these traces is selective and becomes most visible in group scenes in which only one or two figures are shiny. The "Doors of Paradise" at the baptistry of San Giovanni in Florence demonstrate this particularly well.

A careful investigator might choose to work another improvement on the floor-erosion approach. An important bias is that each footfall is not necessarily an independent event. Once a groove on a stair becomes visible, for example, those who walk on that stair are more likely to conform to the position of the groove than are those who walked before it became visible. This is partly due to the physical condition of the stair, which tends to slide the person's foot into the groove, and also possibly due to a response tendency to follow in the footsteps of others. This may be partially controlled in newer settings by placing mats on the steps and noting their wear. The mats could also hide the already eroded grooves.

CONTROLLED ACCRETION MEASURES

Just as with erosion measures, it is sometimes desirable for the researcher to tamper with materials pertinent to an accretion comparison. Noted earlier was a fingerprint study of advertising exposure (DuBois, 1963). Another procedure to test advertising exposure is the "glue-seal record" (Politz Media Studies, 1958). Between each pair of pages in a magazine, a small glue spot was placed close to the binding and made inconspicuous enough so that it was difficult to detect visually or tactually. The glue was so composed that it would not readhere once the seal was broken. After the magazines had been read, exposure was determined by noting whether or not the seal was intact for each pair of pages, and a cumulative measure of advertising exposure was obtained by noting the total number of breaks in the sample issue. This method was developed because of a pervasive response-set tendency among questionnaire respondents to claim falsely the viewing or reading of advertisements. This particular measure was valuable in establishing the degree to which there was a spurious inflation of recall of advertisements. It was not used alone, but in consort with more standard interviewing practices to provide a validity check.

The content restrictions of this method are substantial. It does not provide data for a single page or advertisement, but instead only indicates whether or not a *pair* of pages were exposed to the person's eye. There is no direct evidence whether or not the person even looked at advertisements which appeared on this pair of pages. Nor is the method sensitive to how many people may have been exposed to a given pair of pages. One or more openings yield the same response.

The fingerprint method suffers from fewer restrictions, and it, too, could be improved by an unobtrusive move of the investigator. It is possible to select special paper which more faithfully receives fingerprints, thereby reducing the risk that the level of exposure will be underestimated. The greater fidelity of a selected paper would also improve the ability to discriminate among different fingerprints on the page. It is clearly impractical and unwise to base a complete study of advertising exposure on fingerprints; it is equally unwise not to consider coincidental methods which yield, as the glue seals do, independent validation data. Clearly, the greater the risk that awareness, response set, role evocation, and other variables present to valid comparisons, the greater the demand for independent, nonreactive, and coincidental measures.

From fingerprints to noseprints—and back to the museum for a final example. The relative popularity of exhibits with glass fronts could be compared by examining the number of noseprints deposited on the glass each day (or on some sample of time, day, month, and so forth). This requires that the glass be dusted for noseprints each night and then wiped clean for the next day's viewers to smudge. The noseprint measure has fewer content restrictions than most of the trace techniques, for the age of viewers can be estimated as well as the total number of prints on each exhibit. Age is determined by plotting a frequency distribution of the heights of the smudges from the floor, and relating these data to normative heights by age (minus, of course, the nose-to-top-of-head correction).[1]

TRANSFORMING THE DATA:
CORRECTIONS AND INDEX NUMBERS

The examples provided suggest that physical-evidence data are best suited for measures of incidence, frequency, attendance, and the like. There are exceptions. In a closely worked-out theory, for example, the presence or absence of a trace could provide a critical test or comparison. But such critical tests are rare compared to the times when the physical evidence—be it deposit or erosion—is one part of a series of tests.

When dealing with frequency data, particularly when they are in time-series form, it is essential to ask whether or not there are any corrections which may be applied to remove extraneous sources of variance and improve the validity of comparisons.

More so than most classes of data, the type of frequency data yielded by physical materials is subject to influences which can be known (and corrected for) without substantial marginal research effort.

The museum measures of noseprint deposits or tile erosion can serve as examples. We can use these data to answer questions about the popularity of a given exhibit over time. Are the hatching chicks as popular now as they once were? Is there a boom in viewing of giant panda exhibits? The answers to these questions might be of interest in themselves, or we might want them to evaluate the effect of some other variable. We could conceive of a study estimating the effect of newspaper stories on public behavior. Did a story on the birth of a baby leopard in the zoo increase the number of zoo visitors *and* the number of viewers of a leopard exhibit in the natural history museum? The effect may be too transitory for the erosion measure to pick up, but the noseprint deposits could index it. Or do accounts of trouble in a far-off spot increase the number of persons showing interest in museum collections from that area? The museum data might be one more outcropping of an effect that could be tested and used in consort with other measures to evaluate an effect.

In looking at the museum data, we could consider the newspaper-story question as a problem in the effect of an exogenous variable on a time series, and we are compelled to look for other sources of variation besides the story. We know something of the pool from which the critical responses come. Museum attendance varies seasonally (highest in summer, lowest in winter), varies cyclically (up on holidays, weekends, and school vacations), and has had a strong secular movement upward over time. All of these known influences on museum attendance are independent of the newspaper story. They may be partialled out of the total variance of the time series or, in descriptive statistics, be controlled in index numbers. Such corrections, however, are less critical for comparisons across areas. To the degree that these scores can be accounted for—in either inferential or descriptive terms—we achieve more sensitive research.

Auxiliary intelligence exists for most applications of physical-evidence data. It may be contained in records kept for other purposes, or come from prior knowledge. Consider the problem of estimating advertising exposure by the glue-seal method. In studying a single pair of pages, our only measure is the proportion of pages on which seals are broken. Of course, there are a number of variables known to influence the degree to which magazine pages are opened. The number of pages in the magazine, for example, or the magazine's policy of either clustering or dispersing advertisements throughout its pages will alter responses. Finally, readers of some magazines systematically and predictably read ads more than do readers of other magazines.

Each of these elements should be considered in evaluating the single medium under study. These factors might be combined into a baseline index which states the reasonable exposure expectation for an ad appearing in a very thin issue of Magazine A, with a dispersion strategy of ad placement. The observed score for the given pair of pages can thus be transformed into a number which is in some way related to the expected value.

This approach to "description" is the one argued in Chapter 1—description and all research inferences are comparisons. When the control is not developed within the data-gathering of the study (as it is not in most of the possible physical-evidence measures), it can be generated by analysis of other available intelligence.

With more elaborate comparisons than evaluating a single museum exhibit, the problems of extraneous variables and the need for their control in both inference and description become magnified. Keeping with the museum, take the problem of comparing two exhibits located in different sections of the museum. The same information used earlier—the known variation by season, holidays, and so on—is again core intelligence for comparison of the observed physical evidence. The concern becomes one of interactions. At those predictably high and low attendance times, we can expect a significant interaction between the accessibility of the exhibit and the over-all level of attendance. The interaction could bias measures of both the number of viewers and the duration of time spent viewing.

We should expect the more accessible exhibit to have a significantly higher marginal lead on noseprints during high-attendance periods than during low-attendance periods. Some of the interactive difference may come from the greater individual fatigue with large crowds, which might restrict the length of time each visitor spends in the museum. Or the size of the crowds may slow movements so that a number of people with fixed time periods to spend in the museum do not get around as much. Or there may be a population characteristic such that a larger share of peak-time visitors are indifferent viewers who lack a compelling interest in the over-all content of the museum. They may view either more casually or more erratically.

Corrections must be made for both the main effects and the interactions in such cases, and the easiest way to make them is to prepare corrections based on known population levels and response tendencies. We should speak of statue rubbings per thousand bypassers, or the rate of floor-tile replacement in a specific display area per thousand summer visitors. These figures are first-line transformations that are valuable. They can become more valuable if enough is known to consider them as the numerator of an index fraction. With the study of past behavior giving the denominator, indices can be produced which account for irrelevant variance and make for better comparisons.

Up to this point, we have been talking only of corrections applied to a single measure. Following in the index-number tradition, we can also consider a piece of physical evidence either as one component of an over-all index composed of several different classes of data or as an element in a set of physical evidence combined to make an aggregate index.

One might want an over-all measure, extending over time, of the completeness with which an institution is being used. This could supplement information on the extent to which it is being attended. In a library, for example, the various types of physical evidence available (dust collection, page wear, card-catalogue wear) could be gathered together and each individual component weighted and then combined to produce the over-all index. Similarly for museums.

Assume that one wanted to note the effect of an anxiety-producing set of messages on the alleged link between cigarettes and lung cancer. One could, in the traditional way, employ a before-after questionnaire study which measured attitudes toward cigarettes and obtained self-reports of smoking. Or, one could observe. If the anxiety-producing message were embedded in a lecture, at some point toward the middle, it would be possible to observe the frequency of cigarettes lit before, during, and after the mention of the deleterious effects of smoking. Or one could wire a sample of the chairs in the lecture hall and record the amount of squirming exhibited by the auditors at various points. Or, following Galton's (1885) suggestion, one could observe the amount of gross body movement in the audience. Or one could note the subsequent sale of books about smoking—ideally framing the setting so that equally attractive titles were available that argued the issue pro and con.

All of these alternatives are viable approaches to studying the effect of the message, with physical evidence an important element because of its ability to measure long-term effects and to extend the physical area of investigation beyond the immediate experimental setting. Depending on the degree of knowledge one had about the messages, the audience, and past effects, it would be possible to construct an index with differential weights for the various component measures of effect. Each of the single measures may be attacked for weakness, but taken cumulatively—as separate manifestations of an hypothesized effect—they offer greater hope for validity than any single measure, regardless of its popularity.

AN OVER-ALL EVALUATION OF
PHYSICAL EVIDENCE DATA

The outstanding advantage of physical evidence data is its inconspicuousness. The stuff of analysis is material which is generated without the producer's knowledge of its use by the investigators. Just as with secondary records, one circumvents the problems of awareness of measurement, role selection, interviewer effects, and the bias that comes from the measurement itself taking on the role of a change agent. Thus, physical evidence is, for the most part, free of reactive measurement effects. It is still necessary to worry over possible response sets which influence the laying down of the data. With erosion measures, this might be so obvious a bias as the tendency for people to apply more pressure to stairs when going up than when going down, or the less obvious tendency to turn right.

With accretion measures, there is the question of whether the materials have selectively survived or been selectively deposited. Do some objects have a higher probability of being discarded in public places than others? Or, equally an issue, do some materials survive the intervening events of time better? Archeological research has always faced the problem of the selective survival of materials. Some of this selection comes from the physical characteristics of the material: clay survives; wood usually does not. Other selection comes from the potential value of the material which might be discarded. In writing of the small decorated stamps (seals) used by the ancient Mexican cultures, Enciso (1953) noted, "If any gold or silver was used, the stamps have yet to be found or have been melted long ago. Wood and bone have not survived the ravages of time. This may explain the abundant survival of clay stamps" (p. iv). In Naroll's (1956) phrase, the clay stamps are "durable artifacts." We also discuss this bias in our comments on archival and available records, but it is significant here for the restrictions it places on the content of physical-evidence data and thereby the ability to generalize findings.

Any single class of physical evidence is likely to have a strong population restriction, and all physical-evidence data are troubled by population problems in general. It is not, for example, easy to get descriptive access to the characteristics of a possible population restriction. One has the remnant of past behavior—a groove or a pile—and it says nothing by itself of those who produced the evidence.

We also must be cautious of physical data because they may vary selectively over time or across different geographical areas. It is possible to get some checks on the character of these restrictions by employing supplementary methods such as the interview or the questionnaire. Some inferences about the character of population bias may come also from a time-series analysis of the data, possibly linking the physical-evidence data to time series of other data hypothesized to be selectively contributing to the variance. In a systematic investigation, a careful sampling of both times and locations is possible, and internal comparison of the findings may offer some clues. But the assumption must be that any set of physical evidence is strongly subject to population restrictions, and supplementary information is always required.

Other methods also have population restrictions, and it may be possible to turn the fact of a restriction into an asset. There are, for example, certain subsets of the population virtually impossible to interview. In such situations, an enterprising investigator should ask whether the subject is leaving traces of behavior or material which offer some help in inferring the subject's critical behavior. In this type of problem, the physical evidence is the supplementary data, and is used to fill in the population restrictions of other methods used concurrently.

As for the content available to the reach of physical-evidence methods, there are substantial limitations. It is not often that an investigator tests a theory so precise in its predictions that the appearance or absence of a single trace is a critical test of the theory. Most of the time, physical evidence is more appropriate for indexing the extent to which an activity has taken place— the number of footfalls, the number of empties tossed aside. Because these activities are influenced by many other variables, we seldom have an absolutely clean expression of some state of being—thus the necessity for corrections and transformations. Yet if enough information does exist, or can be produced, the content restrictions are controllable because they are knowable.

There is the positive gain that the amount of dross in physical evidence is low or negligible. Typically, what is measured is relatively uncontaminated by a body of other material which must be discarded as not pertinent to the research investigation. One can pinpoint the investigation closely enough to eliminate the dross—something not possible in the more amorphous method of conversation sampling, or of observation of "natural" behavior.

Compared with other classes of research methods, we have noted few examples of prior research using physical evidence. This is not through preference, but because we have been unable to find more. Physical-evidence data are off the main track for most psychological sociological research. This is understandable, but still regrettable. The more visible weaknesses of physical evidence should preclude its use no more than should the less visible, but equally real, weaknesses of other methods. If physical evidence is used in consort with more traditional approaches, the population and content restrictions can be controlled, providing a novel and fruitful avoidance of the errors that come from reactivity.

NOTE

1. The authors were told of such a research project, but have been unable to locate the source. If the study is not apocryphal, we should like to learn the source and give proper credit to so imaginative an investigator.

THREE

ARCHIVES I

The Running Record

————•◆•————

Possibly a wife was more likely to get an inscribed tablet if she died before her husband than if she outlived him.

he tablet cited here is a tombstone, and the quotation is from Durand's (1960) study of life expectancy in ancient Rome and its provinces. Tombstones are but one of a plethora of archives available for the adventurous researcher, and all social scientists should now and then give thanks to those literate, record-keeping societies which systematically provide so much material appropriate to novel analysis.

The purpose of this chapter is to examine and evaluate some uses of data periodically produced for other than scholarly purposes, but which can be exploited by social scientists. These are the ongoing, continuing records of a society, and the potential source of varied scientific data, particularly useful for longitudinal studies. The next chapter looks at more discontinuous archives, but here the data are the actuarial records, the votes, the city budgets, and the communications media which are periodically produced, and paid for, by someone other than the researcher.

Besides the low cost of acquiring a massive amount of pertinent data, one common advantage of archival material is its nonreactivity. Although there may be substantial errors in the material, it is not usual to find masking or sensitivity because the producer of the data knows he is being studied by some social scientist. This gain by itself makes the use of archives attractive if one wants to compensate for the reactivity which riddles the interview and the questionnaire. The risks of error implicit in archival sources are not trivial, but, to repeat our litany, if they are recognized and accounted for by multiple measurement techniques, the errors need not preclude use of the data.

More than other scholars, archeologists, anthropologists, and historians have wrestled with the problems of archival data. Obviously, they frequently have little choice but to use what is available and then to apply corrections. Unlike the social scientist working with a contemporaneous problem, there is little chance to generate new data which will be pertinent to the problem and which will circumvent the singular weakness of the records being employed.

Naroll (1962) recently reviewed the methodological issues of archives in his book *Data Quality Control.* His central argument focuses on representative sampling. Does the archeologist with his thousand-year-old pottery shards, or the historian with a set of two-hundred-year-old memoirs, really have a representative body of data from which to draw conclusions? This is one part of "Croce's Problem." Either one is uncertain of the data when only a limited body exists, or uncertain of the sample when so much exists that selection is necessary.

Modern sampling methods obviate the second part of the problem. We can know, with a specified degree of error, the confidence we can place in a set of findings. But the first part of Croce's problem is not always solvable. Sometimes the running record is spotty, and we do not know if the missing parts can be adequately estimated by a study of the rest of the series. That is one issue. But even if the record is serially complete, the collection of the secondary sources impeccable, and the analysis inspired, the validity of the conclusions must rest on assumptions of the adequacy of the original material.

There are at least two major sources of bias in archival records—selective deposit and selective survival. They are the same two concerns one meets in dealing with physical-evidence data. Durand's (1960) study of the ancient Roman tombstones illustrates the selective-deposit concern. Does a study of a properly selected sample of tombstones tell us about the longevity of the ancient Romans, or only of a subset of that civilization? Durand, as noted, suggests that the timing of a wife's death may determine the chance of her datum (CCCI-CCCL) being included in his sample. It is not only the wives who die after their husbands who may be underrepresented. There is, too, a possible economic or social-class contaminant. Middle- and upper-class Romans were more likely to have tombstones (and particularly those that survived until now) than those in the lower reaches of Roman society. This bias is a risk to validity to the degree that mortality rates varied across economic or social classes—which they probably did. The more affluent were more likely to have access to physicians and drugs, which, given the state of medicine, may have either shortened or lengthened their lives. It is to Durand's credit that he carefully suggests potential biases in his data and properly interprets his findings within the framework of possible sampling error.

This same type of sampling error is possible when studying documents, whether letters to the editor or suicide notes. We know that systematic biases exist among editors. Some try to present a "balanced" picture on controversial topics regardless of how unbalanced the mail. With the study of suicide notes, the question must be asked whether suicides who do not write notes would have expressed the same type of thoughts had they taken pen in hand. Any inferences from suicide notes must be hedged by the realization that less than a quarter of all suicides write notes. Are both the writers and nonwriters drawn from the same population?

The demographer cannot get new Romans to live and die; the psychologist cannot precipitate suicides. And therein is the central problem of historical data. New and overlapping data are difficult to obtain from the same or equivalent samples. The reduction of error must come from a close internal analysis which usually means fragmenting the data into subclasses and making cross-checks.

An alternative approach is feasible when reports on the same phenomenon by different observers are available. By a comparative evaluation of the sources, based on their different qualifications, inferences may be drawn on the data's accuracy (Naroll, 1960, 1961). In examining an extinct culture, for example, one can compare reports made by those who lived among the people for a long period of time with reports from casual visitors. Or there can be a comparison of the reports from those who learned the indigenous language and those who did not. For those items on which there is consensus, there is a higher probability that the item reported is indeed valid. This consensus test is one solution to discovery of selective deposit or editing of material. It does not eliminate the risk that all surviving records are biased in the same selective way; what it does do is reduce the plausibility of such an objection. The greater the number of observers with different qualifications, the less plausible the hypothesis that the same systematic error exists.

Sometimes selective editing creeps in through an administrative practice. Columbus kept two logs—one for himself and one for the crew. Record-keepers may not keep two logs, but they may choose among alternative methods of recording or presenting the data. Sometimes this is innocent, sometimes it is to mask elements they consider deleterious. In economic records, bookkeeping practices may vary so much that close attention must be paid to which alternative record system was selected. The depreciation of physical equipment is an example. Often deliberate errors or record-keeping policy can be detected by the sophisticate. At other times, the data are lost forever (Morgenstern, 1963).

One more example may serve. A rich source of continuing data is the *Congressional Record,* that weighty but sometimes humorous document which records the speeches and activities of the Congress. A congressman may deliver a vituperative speech which looks, upon reflection, to be unflattering. Since proofs are submitted to the congressman, he can easily alter the speech to eliminate his peccadillos. A naive reader of the *Record* might be misled in an analysis of material which he thinks is spontaneous, but which is in fact studied.

A demurrer is entered. Even if the data were originally produced without any systematic bias that could threaten validity, the risk of their selective survival remains. It is no accident that archeologists are pottery experts. Baked clay is a "durable artifact" that cannot be digested and decays negligibly. Naroll (1956) comments that artifacts survive because they are not consumed in use, are indifferent to decay, and are not incorporated into some other artifact so as to become unidentifiable. Discrete and durable, they remain as clues, but partial clues; other evidence was eaten, rotted, or re-employed. Short of complete destruction, decay by itself is no problem. It only becomes one when the rate and distribution of decay is unknown. If known, it may become a profitable piece of evidence—as Libby's (1963) work with radiocarbon dating shows.

For the student of the present, as well as of the past, the selective destruction of records is a question. Particularly in the political area, the holes that exist in data series are suspect. Are records missing because knowledge of their contents would reflect in an untoward way on the administration? Have the files been rifled? If records are destroyed casually, as they often are during an office move, was there some biasing principle for the research comparison which determined what would be retained and what destroyed?

When estimating missing values in a statistical series, one is usually delighted if all but one or two values are present. This gives confidence when filling in the missing cells. If the one or two holes existing in the series have potential political significance, the student is less sanguine and more suspicious of his ability to estimate the missing data.

ACTUARIAL RECORDS

Birth, marriage, death. For each of these, societies maintain continuing records as normal procedure. Governments at various levels provide massive amounts of statistical data, ranging from the federal census to the simple entry of a wedding in a town-hall ledger. Such formal records have frequently been used in descriptive studies, but they offer promise for hypothesis-testing research as well.

Take Winston's (1932) research. He wanted to examine the preference for male offspring in upper-class families. He could have interviewed prospective mothers in affluent homes, or fathers in waiting rooms. Indeed, one could pay obstetricians to ask, "What would you like me to order?" Other measures, nonreactive ones, might be studies of adoption records, the sales of different layette colors (cutting the data by the class level of the store), or the incidence of "other sex" names—such as Marion, Shirley, Jean, Jerry, Jo.

But Winston went to the enormous data bank of birth records and manipulated them adroitly. He simply noted the sex of each child in each birth order. A preference for males was indicated, he hypothesized, if the male-female ratio of the last child born in families estimated to be complete was greater than that ratio for all children in the same families. With the detail present in birth records, he was able to segregate his upper-class sample of parents by the peripheral data of occupation, and so forth. The same auxiliary data can be employed in any study to serve as a check on evident population restriction—a decided plus for detailed archives.

This study also illustrates the time-sampling problem. For the period studied, and because of the limitation to upper-class families, Winston's measure is probably not contaminated by economic limitations on the absolute number of children, a variable that may operate independently of any family sex preference. Had his study covered only the 1930s, or were he making a time-series comparison of economically marginal families, the time factor could offer a substantial obstacle to valid comparison. The argument for the existence of such an economic variable would be supported if a study of the 1930s showed no sex difference among terminal children, but did show significant differences for children born in the 1940s.

Economic conditions are only one of the factors important to errors due to timing. Wars, depressions, and acts of God are all events which can pervasively influence the comparisons of social science data. The subjective probability of their influence may be awkward to assign, yet the ability to control that influence through index numbers and other data transformations is a reasonable and proper practice.

There are many demographic studies of fertility levels in different societies, but Middleton (1960) showed a shrewd understanding of archival sources in his work. He developed two sets of data: fertility values expressed in magazine fiction, and actuarial fertility levels at three different time periods. For 1916, 1936, and 1956, he estimated fertility values by noting the size of fictional families in eight American magazines. A comparison with the population data showed that shifts in the size of fictional families closely paralleled shifts in the true U.S. fertility level.

Middleton had a troublesome sampling problem. Since only a small number of magazines continued publication over the period from 1916 to 1956, was the group of eight long-term survivors a proper sample? This durable group may not have been representative, but it was quite proper. The very fact that these eight survived the social changes of the 40 years argues that they probably reflected the society's values (or those of a sufficiently large segment of the society to keep the magazine economically alive) more adequately than those which failed. The issue was not one of getting a representative sample of all magazines, but, instead, of magazines which printed material that would have recorded more faithfully the pertinent research information.

Christensen (1960) made a cross-cultural study of marriage and birth records to estimate the incidence of premarital sex relations in different societies. He simply checked off the time interval between marriage and birth of the first child—a procedure which showed marked differences in premarital conception, if not in activity among cultures. His study illustrates some of the problems in cross-cultural study. The rate of premature births may vary across societies, and it is necessary to test whether this hypothesis can explain differences. Data on the incidence of premature births of later-born children in each society permit this correction. A population problem to be guarded against in these cross-cultural studies, however, is the differential recording of births, marriages, and the like. There are many societies in which a substantial share of marriages are not formally entered in a record-keeping system, although the parties initially regard the alliance to be as binding as do those in other societies where records are more complete. The incidence in Mexico of "free-union" marriages is both extensive and selective—more prevalent among working classes than other groups (Lewis, 1961).

Simple marriage records alone were used by Burchinal and Kenkel (1962) and Burchinal and Chancellor (1962). The records were used as a handy source by Burchinal and Kenkel to study the association between religious identification and occupational status. The records provided a great body of data from which to work, but also posed a sampling question. Are men about to be grooms a good base for estimating the link between religion and occupation? The small cadre of confirmed bachelors is excluded from the sample universe, and depending upon the dates of the records studied, there can be an interaction between history and groomdom.

A later study by Burchinal and Chancellor (1963) took the complete marriage and divorce records of the Iowa Division of Vital Statistics for the years 1953 and 1959. From these records, the authors compared marriages of same-religion and mixed-religion pairs for longevity. As might be expected, they found mixed marriages to be significantly shorter-lived than same-religion ones. Of the mixed marriages, those partners who described themselves as Protestants without naming a specific affiliation showed the highest divorce rate.

It might be well to note that such data may be contaminated by self-selection error. Persons entering mixed marriages may be more unstable or more quick to see divorce as a solution. Such people might not increase the chances of a durable marriage by choosing a mate of the same religion.

These same marriage records could be employed as tests of functional literacy. Taking a time series of marriage records, what is the proportion of people signing "X" at varying points in history?

Of all the marriage-record studies, probably none is more engaging than Galton's (1870) classic on hereditary genius. Galton used archival records to determine the eminence of subjects defined as "geniuses" and additional archives to note how their relatives fared on eminence. Few scientists have been so sensitive as Galton to possible error in drawing conclusions, and, in a section on occupations, he notes that many of the judges he studied postponed marriage until they were elevated to the bench. Even so, their issue of legitimate children was considerable. In Stein and Heinze's (1960) summary: "Galton points out that among English peers in general there is a preference for marrying heiresses, and these women have been peculiarly unprolific" (p. 87). And on the possible contaminant of the relative capacities of the male and female line to transmit ability:

> The decidedly smaller number of transmissions along the female line suggests either an "inherent incapacity in the female line for transmitting the peculiar forms of ability we are now discussing," or possibly "the aunts, sisters and daughters of eminent men do not marry, on the average, so frequently as other women." He believes there is some evidence for this latter explanation. (p. 89)

Galton (1872) even used longevity data to measure the efficacy of prayer. He argued that if prayer were efficacious, and if members of royal houses are the persons whose longevity is most widely and continuously prayed for, then they should live longer than others. Data showed the mean age at death of royalty to be 64.04 years, men of literature and science 67.55 years, and gentry 70.22 years.

Another pioneering study, Durkheim's *Suicide* (1951), shows an active exploration of archival source possibilities. He concluded that "the social suicide rate can be explained only sociologically" (p. 299) by relating suicide levels to religion, season of the year, time of day, race, sex, education, and marital status, doing all of this for different countries. All of these variables were obtained from available archives, and their systematic manipulation presaged the morass of cross-tabulations that were later to appear in socio-logical research.

Wechsler (1961) integrated three different classes of archival data in his correlational study of the relationships among suicide, depressive disorders, and community growth. He went to the census for data on population change, to mental-illness diagnoses in hospital records, and to the vital statistics of the state to get the suicide incidence.

Another study employing death records is Warner's (1959) work, *The Living and the Dead*. Death and its accoutrements in Yankee City were the subject of this multimethod research. Warner consulted official cemetery docu-ments to establish a history of the dead and added interviewing, observation, and trace analysis as aids to his description of graveyards. "Their ground and burial lots were plotted and inventory was taken of the ownership of the various burial lots, and listings were made of the individuals and families buried in them" (p. 287).

His findings are of interest for what they say of response tendencies in the laying down of physical evidence. Here the response tendencies, and the way in which they vary across social-class groups, become the major clues to the analysis. Warner found the social structure of Yankee City mirrored (if this be the proper verb) in the cemetery; he found evidence on family organization, sex and age differentiation, and social mobility. For example, the father was most often buried in the center of the family plot, and headstones of males were larger than those of females. In some cases, Warner found that a family which had raised its social status moved the graves of their relatives from less presti-gious cemeteries to more prestigious ones.

Tombstones would be an interesting source of data for comparative analy-sis of different cultures. In matriarchal societies, for example, is the matriarch's stone substantially larger than the husband's? Does the husband get a marker at all? What are the differences in societies with extended versus nuclear family structures?

Warner's findings tie in with Durand's (1960) study of ancient Rome. In both studies, the relative dominance of the male was demonstrated by the characteristics of the tombstones.

A more recent commentary on tombstones comes from Crowald (1964), who wandered through Moscow's Novo-Devich cemetery, noting the comparative treatment of old czarists and modern communists. After noting that over Chekhov's grave a cherry tree is appropriately blooming, he states:

> The cemetery also tells a quieter, more dramatic tale. Climbing out of some weedy grass is the washboard-sized marker of Maxim Litvinov, once a Stalin foreign minister and the wartime Soviet envoy to America. His mite of a marker reminds what happened to those who fell from Stalin's favor. (p. 12)

Just as in ancient Rome, the timing of a wife's death makes a difference in the nature of the tombstone. Here, this potential contaminant is used as a piece of evidence.

> Novo-Devich does show, too, that things have changed in Russia since Stalin. For example, there is the great marble monument to Rosa Kaganovich. She was the wife of Lazar Kaganovich, the Stalin lieutenant booted from power in 1957 by Premier Nikita S. Khrushchev. Kaganovich is in full disgrace, but he fell after Stalin died. So his wife, who died in 1961, still got her big place in the cemetery. Fresh flowers decorate her marble. (p. 12)

These objects are just big and small pieces of stone to the uninformed, but to the investigator who possesses intelligence on those buried and relates it to the stones, the humble and grandiose memorials are significant evidence.

In Rogow and Lasswell's (1963) discussion of "game politicians," they note:

> His relations with his immediate family were not close; indeed his wife and children saw less of him during his active life than certain key individuals in his political organization. As a result he is remembered less by his family than by the state which he dominated for so many years. His grave in the family plot is unattended, but his statue stands in front of the state capitol building. (p. 48)

And for a novelistic treatment of what remains behind, there is Richard Stern's (1960) commentary on Poppa Hondorp.

> The obituaries were Poppa Hondorp's measure of human worth. "There's little they can add or subtract from you then," was his view. Poppa's eye had sharpened over the years so that he could weigh a two-and-a-half-inch column of ex-alderman against three-and-a-quarter inches of inorganic chemist and know at a glance their comparative worth. When his son had one day suggested that the exigencies of the printer and make-up man might in part account for the amount of space accorded a deceased, Poppa Hondorp had shivered with a rage his son knew he should never excite again. "Don't mess with credos," knew young Hondorp, so the obituaries were sacrosanct; the *Times* issued mysteriously from an immaculate source. (p. 24)

Frequently, one has a choice among different archival sources, and a useful alternative are directories, whether of residents, association members, or locations. Ianni (1957–1958) elected to use city directories as the primary source of data in his study of residential mobility. An analysis of these directories over time allowed him to establish the rates of mobility, and then relate these mobility indices to the acculturation of ethnic groups.

It is obviously a tedious task to perform such an analysis, and the work includes a high amount of dross. If possible, such mobility levels might be more efficiently indexed by access to change-of-address forms in the post office. But the question here becomes one of population restriction. Is the gain in efficiency that comes from use of change-of-address forms worth the possible loss in completeness of sampling? The answer comes, of course, from a preliminary study evaluating the two sources of data for their selective characteristics.

For some studies, more selective directories are indicated, and the inclusion of a person in a directory serves as one element in the researcher's discriminations. *Who's Who in America* doesn't print everybody's name, nor does *American Men of Science*. W. H. Clark (1955) used both of these sources in his "A Study of Some of the Factors Leading to Achievement and Creativity with Special Reference to Religious Skepticism and Belief." Boring and Boring (1948) used *American Men of Science* to choose the psychologists studied in their useful article on the intellectual genealogy of American psychologists.

Fry (1933) had earlier used *Who's Who in America* in a study entitled "The Religious Affiliations of American Leaders" (see also Lehman & Witty, 1931).

Fry's work showed that if one depends on the editors of such directories for selective inclusion, one must also rely on the individuals listed for complete reporting. All of the problems associated with self-report are present, for the individual has a choice of whether or not he will included all data, and whether he will report accurately. The archive serves as an inexpensive substitute for interviewing a large sample of subjects stratified along some known or unknown set of variables. Fry found that a 1926 religious census showed 3.6% of the general population to be Jews, while only .75% of the entries in *Who's Who in America* were listed as Jews. Does this mean that Jews are less distinguished, are discriminated against in being invited to appear in the directory, or is there selective reporting by the Jews of their religion? Fry gave a partial answer to the question by a check of another directory—*Who's Who in American Jewry.* He found 432 persons in this directory who had reported no Jewish affiliation in *Who's Who in America,* thereby raising the Jewish percentage to 2.2. By raising the question of another plausible hypothesis for a comparison (3.6% of the population compared with .75% in the directory), he structured a question which was testable by recourse to a second archival source highly pertinent to the hypothesis.

Babchuk and Bates (1962) employed the membership list of the American Sociological Association in their work, "Professor or Producer: The Two Faces of Academic Man." After first procuring a list of all sociology Ph.D.s for a given period from the *American Journal of Sociology,* they referred to four different membership directories of the ASA for a measurement of the degree of identification with the profession. "A number of persons in the sample never became affiliated with the Association; this fact was interpreted as meaning that such persons lacked an 'orientation to [the] discipline' " (p. 342).

Kenneth Clark (1957) used the American Psychological Association's directory in his study of the psychological profession. For any study extending over a long time period, the APA directory can be frustrating. As the number of psychologist grew, the detail in the individual listings shrank. Thus, the number of items on which a complete time series could be produced were reduced as tighter and tighter editing took place. The measuring instrument was constant in its content for only a few pieces of information. The change in the number of available categories of information is a detectable shift in the quality of the measure. Other changes, such as increasingly difficult requirements for membership or individuals responding to the greater bulk of the directory by writing more truncated listings, may change the character of the instrument in a less visible way and produce significant differences which are, in fact, only recording artifacts.

Digging into the past, Marsh (1961) obtained the names of 1,047 Chinese government officials from the government directories of 1778 and 1831–1879. He then correlated the ranks of the officials with the time required to reach a particular rank and with other factors such as age and family background. If there was no differential recording, one may conclude with Marsh that the rich get there faster.

POLITICAL AND JUDICIAL RECORDS

An archival record—votes—is the dependent variable for office holders, the absolute criterion measure; but for the social scientist, it is only an indicator. Votes cast by the people determine the politician's most important piece of behavior (staying in office), and votes cast by the legislator are the definitive test of his position and alliances.

Dozens of studies are available that have evaluated voting statistics by party or by individual. The *ad hoc* rhetorical condemnations of an opponent's record are at one end of a scale that is anchored by sophisticated factor analysis on the other. In the interest of space, we have limited our examples to studies which have reported either unique or more convoluted manipulations of the essentially simple data.

The political slant of legislators has been a popular research topic. "Progressivism" in the United States Senate was assessed by Gage and Shimberg (1949). They wanted a sample of votes which would measure progressivism and picked ten bills for one congress and eight for another, getting coefficients of reproducibility of .88 and .91, respectively. With these data, they studied a series of questions: Are younger senators more progressive than older ones? (No); Do senators from the same state tend to vote the same? (No); Are regional differences significant? (Yes).

MacRae (1954b) also studied the same type of legislative tendency in his paper on the influence on voting of constituent pressure and congressional social grouping. He selected his sample of critical votes by consulting the roll calls published by the *New Republic* and the *CIO News*. His assumption was that these sources would only publish reports of votes on issues germane to their presumably liberal readers. From these, he obtained a "liberal index" depending upon the direction of the vote.

A finer breakdown was made by Dempsey (1962), who estimated conservative votes, but divided them along party and nonparty issues. His subject was party loyalty in the Senate, and he used the reports of roll-call votes on individual senators to provide a "Loyalty Shift Index."

Moving over to the House, and the employment of all roll-call votes, Riker and Niemi (1962) looked at the question of congressional coalitions. They took votes on 87 roll calls, noting whether a congressman (a) voted on the winning side, (b) voted on the losing side, (c) did not vote when eligible, (d) did not vote when ineligible. The rolls were classified into subsets, and finally an index of coalition was produced.

Farris (1958) also used roll-call votes to study coalitions within the Congress. His article is of strong interest, because it details the methodological issues the political scientist faces in isolating ideological groups. Farris elected to use Guttman scaling techniques on a sample of roll-call votes from the House in the seventy-ninth Congress. His sampling of votes was studied, and he excluded 94 of the 231 possible roll calls because either there was no quorum, the vote was nearly unanimous, or sharp partisanship was shown. His scales included bills on "foreign policy" and "labor." "It is possible to construct three-, four-, and five-position ideological groupings by cross-tabulating members' positions on the several analytic issues" (p. 328).

An elaborate set of analyses conducted by MacRae (1954a) illustrates a more complex analysis of multiple archival sources. MacRae asked how politicians with different seniority reduced the inherent insecurity of their elective jobs. The results are too extensive to report, but these are among the variables used:

- Seniority (number of consecutive terms of office)
- Number of representatives from each party elected in different years

- Rates of vote-getting performance (an index of the legislator's vote compared with a control of the gubernatorial vote by the candidate of the same party)

- Primary-election performance (ratio to nearest competitor)

- Guttman liberal-conservative scale of voting issues

- Voting behavior on key bills

Only two classes of data are used—general election statistics and legislative voting—but MacRae's analysis indicates the richness of these archives for the venturesome student.

The political scientist must work with roll-call votes; the desultory ayes and nays on voice are never traceable to their sources. An empirical question (one on which we can find no substantial research study) is the difference between bills voted on by roll call or by voice. It is reasonable to expect that a difference exists and that some systematic criterion is at work. It may be that only the more significant votes get a roll call, but it is also possible that some significant bills go through on a voice vote because leaders of both parties choose to avoid the record on some sensitive issues.

Taking the roll calls with proper hedging, though, there is the choice of which bills yield the best evidence for a particular research question, as well as directional decisions determining the liberal or conservative stand on particular bills. The population of congressmen voting sometimes varies substantially also, for some decide to evade a vote and a public stand on the bill. The "pairing" system, in which an absent congressman may announce what his vote would have been had he been present, eliminates some of his absentee error, but so long as congressmen avoid a vote, some population restriction is present.

The content analysis of political speeches is another workaday practice of politicians and diplomats. In a study of group tension, for example, Grace and Tandy (1957) studied thirteen speeches made by Soviet delegates before the League of Nations. Political tension may be indexed in many ways (see Bugental, 1948), but one method is to search for archival evidence of activities designed to reduce tension and uncertainty.

For congressmen, one device is to study the degree to which they make use of their franking (free mail) privilege. The rate of mail sent from congressional offices varies systematically, in a pattern closely linked to the proximity of the election year. We are not aware of any such study, but it should be possible to get an indirect measure of a congressman's perception of his job security by evaluating the use of this privilege. There are many speculations, for example, on what defines a "safe" seat for re-election to the Congress. A journalistic benchmark is a classification based on the extent of the congressman's victory. If he was elected by more than 55% of the vote, his seat is described as safe; if by less than 55%, it is described as dangerous. It would be of interest to study the extent of mail sent out (correcting for different-size constituencies) by the margin of victory in the last election. Such an analysis, combined with other intelligence, may provide a more empirical definition of how congressmen themselves designate "safe" and "dangerous" seats.

The behavior of the congressman can also be used to study those outside the Congress. It is a common practice for a congressman to insert into the *Congressional Record* newspaper columns which reflect his point of view. In a study of political columnists, Webb (1962a, 1963) employed these data for an estimate of liberalism-conservatism among twelve Washington columnists. Individual members of Congress were assigned a liberal-conservative score by evaluations of their voting record published by two opposing groups—the conservative Americans for Constitutional Action and the liberal Committee on Political Action of the AFL-CIO. The two evaluations correlated −.75 for Senators and −.86 for House members. Columnists were then ordered on the mean score of the Congressmen who placed their articles into the *Record*.

It would be valuable to supplement such an analysis with a comparative study of how various writers treat the same event. Cogley suggested this in his verse on the interpretation of the Papal encyclical, *Pacem in Terra:*

> David Lawrence read it right
> Lippmann saw a Liberal light,
> William Buckley sounded coolish,
> Pearson's line was mostly foolish . . .
> To play the game you choose your snippet
> Of Peace on Earth and boldly clip it
> (*cited in McCahill, 1963, p. 12*)

In off-year and primary elections, only a small share of eligible voters cast ballots. But this selective behavior is not damaging to validity, since the critical variables—election or no election, margin of victories—are posited directly on this selectivity. Lustig (1962) studied pro-integrationist voting by matching aggregate data on demographic characteristics and pro-integrationist votes. Precinct votes in a southern campaign between a segregationist and an integrationist were compared with census information. This is an admittedly gross approach, but the sanctity of the voting booth precludes, usually, a direct study of individual voting behavior. One can go back to survey questioning and relate these findings to the actual voting records, but the error in self-report of voting behavior is so great that such a potentially reactive approach is highly questionable. Digman and Tuttle (1961) have provided one of the few pieces of research in which investigators were able to sample individual ballots randomly. For most archival studies, however, this degree of precision is unobtainable.

The voting records of the people can also be used to measure the effect of experimenter intervention in pre-election settings. Among the memorable studies in social science is Gosnell's (1927) field experiment on getting out the votes. Selecting twelve electoral precincts, Gosnell divided them into experimental and control conditions. The experimental precincts were sent a series of nonpartisan messages encouraging registration and voting in a forthcoming election, while the control precincts received only the normal pre-election stimulation—generally of a politically partisan nature. The effect of the mail effort was determined by an analysis of registration lists, pollbooks, and census material. Here Gosnell intervened in a "natural" way, established controls, and employed inexpensive archival records as his tellingly appropriate dependent variable. Hartmann's (1936) study of "emotional" and "rational" political campaign pieces also used votes.

Bain and Hecock (1957) further demonstrated the ability to test persuasion principles in a natural laboratory free from the reactive biases of the university research suites. They were interested in the effect of physical position on alternative choices, and found data in the aggregate voting statistics from Michigan elections. Michigan was chosen because of (a) the absence of a law requiring ballots to be burned after the election (an obvious impediment to archival studies of voting behavior) and (b) the systematic rotation of candidates names on the Michigan ballot. This rotation is practiced in several states, and represents an assumption that position on the ballot does indeed have an effect. "Under [California] state law, the incumbent's name goes first on the ballot, and political handicappers give as much as a 20 per cent edge—greater than the margin of most senatorial victories—to this psychological primacy" ("Senator Salinger?" 1964, p. 28).

Because of the Michigan system of rotation, Bain and Hecock could work an orthogonal analysis, establishing the vote of each candidate and each position on the ballot. The findings supported the assumptions of veteran political hands and the ballot constructors: there was a significant position effect. It would be a provocative study to take this and other naturally occurring possibilities for a position effect (e.g., the sale of goods in a supermarket when placed in different shelf positions), and compare the results with those derived from the traditional experimental laboratory.

Schwartz and Skolnick (1962a) proposed a study of positive and negative incentives in tax compliance using changes in taxpaying in experimental and control groups as the dependent variable measure. This study would depend on the cooperation of the Internal Revenue Service, which cannot legally disclose information concerning the returns of any individual taxpayer (Schwartz, 1961). The problem can be avoided by group comparisons in which the individual's identity is not revealed to the researcher. Another device is to study tax compliance in a state such as Wisconsin where individual returns are legally available for research purposes.

The votes of a judicial body provide data for other than obvious research. Kort (1957, 1958), Schubert (1959, 1963), Nagel (1962), and Ulmer (1963) have employed mathematical analyses of past voting behavior by U.S. Supreme Court justices to predict future votes—a more systematic attempt at the common game played by working lawyers and constitutional law experts.

The same body of information, Supreme Court decisions, was used by Snyder (1959) in a study of the degree of uncertainty in the whole U.S. judicial system. In one measure, uncertainty was defined by the number of reversals of lower-court decisions by the high court. With the precedent principle of *stare decisis* at work in our court system, there should be few reversals if certainty is high. Moreover, to the degree that there is certainty (predictability) of outcome upon appeal, there will be cases fought up through the inferior courts.

Green (1961) demonstrated the large store of judicial data available to the social scientist. He gathered a sample of 1,437 cases from 1956–1957 police and court records of Philadelphia, in order to study uniformity in sentencing and the criteria by which sentences were decided. Three sets of variables were isolated as sentencing criteria: legal factors, legally irrelevant factors, and factors in the criminal prosecution. The relative severity of different types of sentences was measured by the extent of deprivation of civil liberty. A series of nonparametric tests "provide assurance that the deliberations of the sentencing judge are not at the mercy of his passions or prejudices but comply with the mandate of the law" (p. 102).

There is a very real population restriction in using such data—one that has been differential over time. It is a highly plausible hypothesis that appellate cases brought before the U.S. Supreme Court are not representative of the body of cases appearing before the inferior courts. Historically, a substantial share of high-court cases have involved affluent litigants, for the cost of steering a case through the courts is demanding of both money and time. Some of the change in representativeness over time has come from the increasing affluence of our society, but more has come from the growth of well-financed vested-interest groups who will assume the costs of litigation for a party. The spurting growth within civil-rights groups of both legal talent and money, documented by Vose (1959) and Krislov (1963), has meant an increasing number of cases before the appellate courts that might have never been appealed fifty years ago. Thus, any comparison over time of the behavior of the court system relative to some legal issue must take account of this variation.

There may be some bias from the selection of cases (a content restriction), for only a portion of the cases submitted to the Supreme Court are granted certiorari (i.e., accepted for ruling). In research on some issues, it may be that the Court has systematically excluded from consideration pertinent cases, or has excluded a critical subclass. As in all cases of archival analysis, it is necessary to determine whether or not confounding population restrictions exist. The advantage of legislative and judicial records is that one can learn something of the nature of these restrictions. It is a matter of record which legislators did not vote on roll calls, and which cases were rejected for consideration by the court.

OTHER GOVERNMENT RECORDS

Some government records are orthodox sources for the social scientist. The birth, death, and marriage archives, as we have already seen, can be used for straightforward descriptive work or for less direct applications. Other records have less visible, but equally fruitful, applications. In this section are examples of research which have used power failures, municipal water pressure, parking-meter collections, and the like as research data.

The weather is a reasonable start. Durkheim (1951), as noted above, used weather as one of the variables in his study of suicide. An early investigation by Lombroso (1891/1960) also used archival analysis to note the effect of weather and time of year on scientific creativity. He drew a sample of fifty-two physical, chemical, and mathematical discoveries and noted the time of their occurrence. His evidence, shaky as it is, showed that twenty-two of the major discoveries occurred in the spring, fifteen in the autumn, ten in the summer, and five in winter.

There are studies, too, on the relationship between phases of the moon and mental disorders. One made during World War II showed psychosomatic illnesses to increase in the South Pacific with the fullness of the moon. It was subsequently discovered that Japanese bombing attacks followed the same pattern.

Of all the studies using available records, few can measure up to E. L. Thorndike's (1939) work on the goodness of cities. Aware that "only the impartial study of many significant facts about cities enables us to know them" (p. 147), Thorndike gathered 37 core pieces of information about each of 310 United States communities. To develop his "goodness scale," he combined these to produce 297 characteristics for each city. And this in the era before computers! Examples of Thorndike's measures are infant death rate, percentage of sixteen- and seventeen-year-olds attending school, average salary of high school teachers, and per capita acreage of public parks.

Thorndike went further and gathered ratings of cities from various occupational groups. He noted that "thoughtful people realize that popular opinions about cities derived from brief visits and from what is heard and read about cities, are likely to err" (p. 142). How far they are likely to err (using his statistical data as criteria) is demonstrated by these findings: infrequency of extreme poverty correlates .69 with Thorndike's over-all goodness of cities, but −.18 for the judgments of clergymen and social workers; the infant death rate (reversed) correlates .82 with the aggregate statistical index, but .03 with businessmen's ratings of the cities. Few could read this report and not reap methodological profit.

Mindak, Neibergs, and Anderson (1963) took the ongoing records of parking-meter collections as one index of the effect of a Minneapolis newspaper strike. They hypothesized that one of the major effects of the strike would be a decrease in retail shopping. Since most of the parking meters were located in the downtown shopping area, revenue collection from them was a good piece of evidence on the strike's effect. The data showed marked decreases during the months of the strike, using a control of previous years.

City budgets were the stuff of Angell's (1951) study on the moral integration of American cities. He prepared a "welfare effort index" by computing local per capita expenditures for welfare and combined this with a "crime index" based on FBI data to get an "integration index."

Ross and Campbell (1965) showed that a close analysis of traffic fatalities discounted the claim that a crackdown on speeding in Connecticut had resulted in any significant decrease in the number of traffic fatalities.

A particularly interesting and novel use of data comes from the study of city water pressure as it relates to television viewing. For some time after the advent of television, there were anecdotal remarks about a new periodicity in water-pressure levels—a periodicity linked to the beginning and end of programs. As the television show ended, so the reports ran, a city's water pressure dropped, as drinks were obtained and toilets flushed. A graphic display of this hypothesis was provided by Mabley (1963), who published a chart showing the water pressure for the city of Chicago on January 1, 1963. This was the day of a particularly tense Rose Bowl football game, and the chart shows a vacillating plateau until the time the game ended, when the pressure level plummets downward.

Using this approach, one could study the relative popularity of different retirement times. Since a large amount of water is used by many people at bedtime, a comparison of the troughs at 9:00, 9:30, 10:00, and so on could be made. Similarly, a comparison could be made in the morning hours to estimate time of arising. Two problems arise. Do those who retire early use the same amount of water as those who retire late? It is, after all, possible that a smaller number of showers and baths would be taken by those who retire late— particularly in areas with a high number of apartment dwellers. Another difficulty of such a study is comparison across different time areas. Many people end the day by viewing television news. In the metropolitan Chicago area, for example, some three million people watch the 10:00 P.M. newscasts. But the last major television newscast in the Eastern areas is at 11:00 P.M. This one-hour variation might influence the times of people going to bed. The water-pressure index could help establish whether it did or not. Similarly, it could be used to study the relative amount of attention paid to entertainment and commercial content of television. The critical point of study in this research would be the water-pressure levels at the times of mid-show commercials. The prior decision of viewers to turn the set off at a specified hour would influence the water-pressure index for commercials at the beginning and end of shows, but should be a minor rival hypothesis for those embedded within the entertainment content of the program.

A similar measure, a more catastrophic one, has been manifest in the United Kingdom. This measure, electric-power failures, gives plausibility to the hypothesis that it is commercials (and not earlier decisions to turn the set off) which influence the drops in water pressure. At the time of the introduction of the United Kingdom's commercial television channel, a series of power failures hit the island. Whole areas were blacked out, and it was noticed that the timing of the power failures coincided with the time of commercials on the new television channel. The explanation provided was that viewers left their sets to turn on electric water heaters to make tea. The resulting power surge, from so many heaters plugged in simultaneously, overloaded the capacity of a national power system unequipped to handle such peaks. The commercials remain; new power stations have been built. This measure is a more discontinuous one than water pressure, but it would be of value to compare the water-pressure levels with power demands. If the hypothesis is correct that the English were plugging in water heaters, one should find a higher correlation between the two measures in the United Kingdom (with a small time lag as water precedes power) than in the United States.

Another imaginative link between two time series of archival data was provided by DeCharms and Moeller (1962). They gathered the number of patents issued by the U.S. Patent Office from 1800 to 1950. Relating these to population figures, they prepared a patent production index for 20-year periods over the 150-year span. These data were then matched to findings from a content analysis of children's readers for the same period, with a prime focus on achievement imagery. The matching showed a strong relationship between the amount of achievement imagery in their sample of books and the number of patents per million population.

THE MASS MEDIA

Among the most easily available and massive sources of continuing secondary data are the mass media. The variety, texture, and scope of this enormous data pool have been neglected for too long. In this section, we present a selected series of studies which show intelligent manipulation of the mass media. We have necessarily excluded most content analyses and focused on a few which illustrate particular points.[1]

It is proper to start this section by citing Zipf, who sought order in diverse social phenomena by his inventive use of data that few others would perceive as germane to scientific inquiry. In a model study, Zipf (1946) looked at the determinants of the circulation of information. His hypothesis was that the probability of message transfer between one person and another is inversely proportional to the distance between them (see also Miller, 1947; Stewart, 1947; Zipf, 1949). Without prejudice for content, he made use of the content of the mass media, as well as sales performance. How many and how long were out-of-town obituaries in the *New York Times?* How many out-of-town items appeared in the *Chicago Tribune?* Where did they originate? What was the sales level in cities besides New York and Chicago of the *Times* and *Tribune?* To this information from and about the mass media, Zipf added other archival sources. He asked the number of tons of goods moved by Railway Express between various points, and checked on the number of bus, railroad, and air passengers between pairs of cities. All of these were appropriate outcroppings for the test of his hypothesis on inverse proportionality, and in all cases the data conform, more or less closely, to his prediction.

Other investigators have used the continuing record of the newspaper for their data. Grusky (1963b) wanted to investigate the relationship between administrative succession and subsequent change in group performance. One could manipulate leaders in a small-group laboratory, but, in addition, one can go, as Grusky did, to the newspapers for more "natural" and less reactive intelligence. From the sports pages and associated records, Grusky learned the performance of various professional football and baseball teams, as well as the timing of changes in coaches and managers. Does changing a manager make a difference, or is it the meaningless machination of a front office looking for a scapegoat? It does make a difference, and this old sports-writer's question is a group-dynamics problem, phrased through the stating of two plausible rival hypotheses. In another study, Grusky (1963a) used baseball record books to study "The Effects of Formal Structures on Managerial Recruitment." He learned that former infielders and catchers (high-interaction personnel) were overrepresented among managers, while former pitchers and outfielders (low-interaction personnel) were underrepresented.

This public-record characteristic of the newspaper also allows linguistic analysis. If verbal behavior really is expressive, then one should be able to study a president's position on issues by studying the transcripts of his press conferences. Those answers on which a president stumbles in syntax, or which are prefaced by a string of evasive dependent clauses, may be symptomatic of trouble areas. Similarly, those questions which receive unusually long or short replies may reflect significant content areas.

Analysis of transcripts such as these can be very difficult, and often not enough substantive knowledge is available to rule out alternative hypotheses. A president is briefed on what are likely to be the topics of reporters' questions, and he has an opportunity to rehearse replies. The setting is not a nonreactive one, and the awareness of his visibility and the import of his answers may influence their content and form. One must also make each president his own control. The verbal styles of Eisenhower, Kennedy, and Johnson varied so greatly that any verbal index of syntax, glibness, or folksiness must be adjusted for the response tendencies of the individual president.

Less august reporting, that of the society news, served James (1958) as evidence of community structure. The reporting of social events is highly selective, of course, and most useful for studies of the upper class (cf. Coleman

& Neugarten, 1971). The court-tennis victory of a truckdriver is not reported, nor the visit of his wife to Dubuque for the weekend.

Comparison across different cities might be differentially affected by shifts in the selectivity of society editors. It is a good assumption that the size of the city in which the paper is printed is related to the selectivity of its social news: the larger the city, the greater the probability that a smaller segment of the city's population appears in the society pages.

Middleton (1960), mentioned earlier, conducted a longitudinal study of the fertility values in magazine fiction, linking them to the actuarial fertility figures. This research suggested that the media, if carefully selected, can serve as a mirror of the society's values—or at least of some selective elements within the society.

How are psychologists, psychiatrists, and other psychologically oriented personnel differentiated by the society? One can ask people of course, and one should. But of value, too, is a study of what the mass media contain on the question. Ehrle and Johnson (1961) plucked 4,760 cartoons, all of which pictured psychological personnel, from six different consumer magazines. Their evidence suggests no substantial differentiation among the groups. This finding could be further tested by observing psychologists at cocktail parties and noting how often they are asked, "Now how is a psychologist different from a psychiatrist?" Or one could ask the psychologists to relate their cocktail-party experience.

Ray (1965) has written of multiple confirmation through different sources of published material, noting as an example, "values of Hitler's Germany were compared with those of other countries by content analyses of plays (McGranahan and Wayne, 1948), songbooks (Sebald, 1962), handbooks for youth organizations (Lewin, 1947), speeches (White, 1949) and the press (Lasswell, 1941)."

Most of these have been examples of partial evidence contained in the mass media of attitudes or social structure. Even the most vitriolic critics of television commercials will admit that the media themselves are a force within the society for socialization of the young and attitude change of the old. Thus, they justify study. G. A. Steiner (1963), for example, demonstrated the salience of television for a national U.S. sample by showing the extreme alacrity with which sets are repaired. Before television, it had been said that a cigarette was the only object so compelling that deprivation would cause one to walk out in a snowstorm. This energy allocation is also inferred in the advertising slogan, "I'd walk a mile for a Camel."

Much work exists on the political bias of the media. A content analysis of press bias during presidential campaigns is as predictable as the campaigns themselves, but a fine, relatively unused, source is photographs. The element of editorial selectivity which is a contaminant in some other studies becomes the center of analysis. Editors have a large pool of photographs of a candidate from which to pick, and the one they eventually choose is a revealing piece of intelligence. One of the writers has noted this in American political campaigns, and Matthews (1957) has suggested that it is a phenomenon that might be studied across societies. Writing of the British press, he states:

> They [photographs] can be made to lie . . . as Lord Northcliffe was one of the first to discover. When he was using the *Daily Mail* to try to get Asquith out as Prime Minister and Lloyd George in, he once issued this order: "Get a smiling picture of Lloyd George, and underneath put the caption 'Do It Now,' and get the worst possible picture of Asquith and label it: 'Wait and See.'" (p. 165)

As in all these studies of the running record, there is the opportunity for time-series analysis. One could learn if a medium is changing in its posture to a candidate (or potential candidate), and observe when. This last information, on the time of modification, can help to validate other sources of data on the medium's attitude.

The selective practice has been so prevalent over time that it is likely to have little "instrument decay" to invalidate time-series analysis. It continues now, and offers some possibilities for interesting new research. A television interviewer told Malcolm X, the late Black Nationalist leader, that he was surprised at how much Malcolm smiled. The Negro leader said that newspapers refused to print smiling pictures of him. For less extreme, but still marginal, leaders, what is the pattern across time and regions? Of equal interest would be the photographic strategy toward Richard Nixon after his 1962 defeat for the California governorship. In a caustic and venomous statement immediately after the campaign, Nixon castigated the press for what he perceived as its anti-Nixon stance. To casual observers, there was an immediate decrease in the favorability of the Nixon photographs printed.

Tannenbaum and Noah (1959) studied press bias another way, analyzing the verbs that appeared in sports headlines. They asked how many runs in baseball equal a "romp" or how many points in football equal "X rolls over Y." In addition to providing descriptive information on the empirical limits of such verb usage, they demonstrated a home-town bias. The one-run margin might yield either "Sox Edged 8-7" or "Sox Bludgeon Yankees 8-7."

Winship and Allport (1943) were unconcerned with selling newspapers, but they did want to know something of the effect of positive and negative stimuli. Their study was conducted during the early years of World War II, and they were opportunistic enough to exploit the "victories" and "withdrawals" blazoned on headlines. Do potential readers buy more or fewer papers when positive headlines are used? For the measure of effect, they took the street-stand sales of newspapers from four major cities, ignoring the relatively invariant element of home-delivered newspapers. No significant sales difference could be traced to optimistic and pessimistic headlines.

Optimism is a central element in another study—Griffith's (1949) original and adroit research on horse-race betters. The newspapers supplied the odds, results, and payoffs for 1,386 horse races run in the spring and summer of 1947. His hypothesis is worth quoting:

> If the psychological odds equaled the a posteriori [odds] given by the reciprocal of the percentage [of] winners, the product of the number of winners and their odds would equal the number of entries at each odd group after correction of the odds had been made for loss due to breakage and take. If the product exceeds the number of entries, the psychological odds were too large; if the product is less than the number of entries, the odds were too small. (p. 292)

The results, which should receive some distribution beyond the archives of the *American Journal of Psychology,* suggest that long shots and favorites are overbet, while not enough money is put on horses with middle-range odds.

The DeCharms and Moeller (1962) study of patents and achievement imagery in children's readers was mentioned above. Others have worked with the content of books, attempting to puzzle out the popular mystery of why some books sell and others don't. Berreman (1940) gathered data on the sales of books as reported by the *New York Herald Tribune* book-review section and publicity outlays for individual titles, and performed a content analysis: sixty titles were grouped into twelve classes by setting, theme, and treatment of theme. He concluded, to oversimplify his complex Ph.D. dissertation, that content was more important than publicity. His findings suggest that content probably depressed the sale of the well-promoted poor sellers and "made" best sellers which had only feeble marketing efforts (cf. Harvey, 1953; Kappel, 1948).

Sales data permit the testing of hypotheses on the way in which items of popular culture rise and fall in favor. One hypothesis now being tested by Eugene Webb and Robert Armstrong is that sales of a book decline logarithmically once the sales peak has been reached. Data collected so far show only weak support for this hypothesis. Webb (1962b) demonstrated in a similar study that ratings of television westerns declined logarithmically once they started to slide in popularity.

Parker (1963) worked on the effect of the introduction of television by studying library records. His topic was the differential effect of television on the reading of books. A time series was prepared of withdrawals, by type of book, from libraries in a series of Illinois cities—both before and after television came to town. In one of the findings that looks like common sense (after the research is read), he learned that the withdrawals of nonfiction titles were unaffected, but that there was a significant drop in the withdrawal of fiction titles.

R. W. Jones (1960) used the extent of library facilities and personnel as the "index of progressivism" of a group of 154 Illinois towns. He corrected the raw figures by applying census data on community size, social class, race, occupation and income, population age, and rate of community growth.

Library withdrawals were also used by Parker (1964), who showed how a radio book-review program influenced the circulation of the books discussed.

Interest in library withdrawals was used by Vernon and Brown (1963), who measured the "dynamic information seeking process" among tuberculosis patients. They predicted (and found) that the patients of uninformative doctors would be significantly higher than patients of informative doctors in the degree to which they sought out information relevant to their disease. They indexed this by the proportion of patients in the two groups who took "tuber-culosis" and "nontuberculosis" books from a hospital library. In this study, the authors depended upon the reports of patients to define informative and uninformative doctors.

Rashkis and Wallace (1959) demonstrated that the researcher does not have to depend upon self-reports of the degree of attention paid by medical personnel. They observed the notes made by attending nurses on a patient's bedside record, notations that were both informal and required. The attention paid to the patient was measured by the frequency of these notes per patient. This helps to circumvent the possibility that perception of how much attention is being paid to one by medical personnel is heavily contaminated by the patient's degree of illness. The same amount of attention would probably be differentially perceived under preoperative, postoperative, and about-to-be-released states. The bedside chart may be more trustworthy.

Soviet writings on psychology could hardly be classed as mass media, but the findings of O'Connor's research are of substantive interest to any social scientist. O'Connor studied the amount of partisan philosophical (as opposed to empirical) content in Russian journal articles and notes "a tendency to move away from philosophical prolegomena in journal articles and towards a direct discussion of experimental material" (O'Connor, 1961, p. 14, cited in Brozek, 1964).

DATA TRANSFORMATIONS AND INDICES OF THE RUNNING RECORD

Of all the different classes of data treated in this monograph, none has so great a need for transformation as those cited in this chapter. Because the data are drawn from continuous records which typically extend over long periods of time, all the extraneous events of history are at work to threaten valid research comparisons.

Perhaps the most obvious of these is the change in the size of the popula-tion. The population increase has meant that the absolute values of actuarial and allied data are relatively useless for comparative purposes. In studies employing election records, for instance, the absolute number of votes cast provides an inadequate base for most research purposes. It gives Mr. Nixon little comfort, we are sure, to know that he garnered more votes in 1960, as a loser, than did any preceding winning candidate except Eisenhower. Similarly, the absolute number of entries associated with population level has changed over time. This secular trend in the data is often best removed. Thus, Ianni (1957–1958) had to construct a relative index of residential mobility over time, and DeCharms and Moeller (1962) transformed patent production to an index tied to population.

Time also works its effect by a change in the composition of a critical group. The number of congressmen in the House of Representatives may stay relatively stable over a long time period, but the characteristics of these congressmen change—and, in changing, produce a set of rival hypotheses for some investigator's explanation of a research comparison. A recent Supreme Court ruling on reapportionment of the House (to reflect population distribution more adequately) will mean substantial changes in the aggregate voting behavior of the House, influencing the decisional setting for all congressmen, both those there before the change and the new members.

With known changes in composition, it may be necessary to segregate research findings by time periods in which relatively homogeneous external conditions held. This is a grosser correction than the more continuous correction possible for data linked to population. Even with population, though, the only thoroughly reliable data—the census totals—are produced only once every ten years. The accuracy of intervening estimates, whether from the Census Bureau itself or the highly reliable *Sales Management* magazine, are high but still imperfect.

The frailty of individual sets of records, which is discussed below, has caused many investigators to employ indices which combine several different types or units of information. The adequacy of such combinations rests, of course, on the degree to which the component elements are adequate outcroppings of the research hypothesis, as well as the degree to which appropriate weights can be assigned to the elements. Setting these questions aside, however, it is apparent that combined indices must be employed when an investigator lacks a theory so precise and subtle as to predict a single critical test, or, when the theory's precision is adequate, no data exist for the critical test. For E. L. Thorndike's (1939) purpose in studying cities, there was no acceptable alternative to transforming such data as park area and property values into indices. And for MacRae (1954b) and Riker and Niemi (1962), the unstable nature of a single vote by a congressman forced the construction of indices of samples of votes, which were hopefully a less ephemeral source for comparisons. MacRae needed a "liberal index," Riker and Niemi, an "index of coalitions." Because the individual unit was highly suspect as a sampling of the critical behavior under study, the sampling had to be expanded. There occurs, too, the attendant questions of how the units are to be stated, weighted, and combined.

One of the major gains of the running record, then, is the capability to study a hypothesis as external conditions vary over time. Such analysis demands that the investigator consider all possible transformations before making comparisons, and also decide whether indices will provide a more stable and valid base for hypothesis testing. This requirement is not as pronounced in the discontinuous archival records cited in the chapter that follows nor among the observational and physical-evidence methods.

OVER-ALL EVALUATION OF
RUNNING RECORDS

It should be obvious that we prize the potential for historical analysis contained in running records.

> The best fact is one that is set in a context, that is known in relation to other facts, that is perceived in part in the context of its past, that comes into understanding as an event which acquires significance because it belongs in a continuous dynamic sequence. (Boring, 1963, p. 5)

If a research hypothesis, particularly for social behavior, can survive the assaults of changing times and conditions, its plausibility is far greater than if it were tested by a method which strips away alien threats and evaluates the hypothesis in an assumptive, one-time test. Validity can be inferred from a hypothesis' robustness. If the events of time are vacillating, as they usually are, then only the valid hypothesis has the intellectual robustness to be sustained, while rival hypotheses expire.

One pays a price in such time-series analysis, the necessary price of uncertainty. We again agree with that gentle stylist Boring (1963): "The seats on the train of progress all face backwards; you can see the past but only guess about the future" (p. 5). A hypothesis might not hold for anything but the past, but if the present is tested, and a new, possibly better, hypothesis produced, those same running records are available, as economical as ever, for restudy and new testing.

For all the gains, however, the gnawing reality remains that archives have been produced for someone else and by someone else. There must be a careful evaluation of the way in which the records were produced, for the risk is high that one is getting a cutrate version of another's errors. Udy (1964) wrote of ethnographic data:

> Researchers who use secondary sources are always open to the charge that they are cavalier and uncritical in their use of source materials, and cross cultural analysis—particularly when large numbers of societies are used with information taken out of context—is particularly vulnerable to such criticism. (p. 179)

At the beginning of this chapter, we detailed the operating questions of selective deposit and selective survival of archives. Both these contaminants can add significant restrictions to the content and contributing populations of the archival materials. In the discussion of individual research studies, we have noted how roll-call votes, marriage records, reports of congressional speeches, letters to the editor, crime reports, and other records are all subject to substantial population or content restrictions in their initial recording. To a lesser degree, the selective survival of records can be a serious contaminant, and in certain areas, such as politics, it is always a prime question.

Those contaminants which threaten the temporal and cross-sectional stability of the data are controllable through data transformation and indexing methods—if they can be known. Happily, one of the more engaging attributes of many of these records is that they contain a body of auxiliary data which allows the investigator good access to knowledge of the population restrictions. We have noted this for the absentee contaminant in congressional voting and the selective choice of cases in judicial proceedings. With the actuarial material on birth, marriage, and death, it is often possible to find within the records, or in associated data series such as the census, information which will provide checks on the extent to which the research population is representative of the universe to which the findings are to be generalized.

If the restrictions can be known, it is possible to consider the alternative of randomly sampling from the body of records, with a stratification control based on the knowledge of the population restriction. This is feasible for many of the records we have mentioned because of their massiveness. Indeed, even if no substantial population contaminants exist, it is often advisable to sample the data because of their unwieldy bulk. Since usually they can be divided into convenient sampling units, and also frequently classified in a form appropriate for stratification, the ability to sample archival materials, particularly those in a continuous series, is a decided advantage for this class of data. The sampling of observations, or of traces of physical evidence, is markedly more difficult.

The population restrictions are potentially controllable through auxiliary intelligence; the content restrictions are more awkward. For all the varied records available, there may still be no single set, or combination of sets, that provides an appropriate test of an hypothesis.

Something of this content rigidity is reflected in Walter Lippmann's (1955) discussion of the "decline of the west." Lippmann writes of the turn of the century when

> The public interest could be equated with that which was revealed in election returns, in sales reports, balance sheets, circulation figures, and statistics of expansion. As long as peace should be taken for granted, the public good could be thought of as being immanent in the aggregate of private trans-actions. (p. 16)

Yet many of the studies reported in this chapter have revealed the power of insightful minds to see appropriate data where associates only see "someone else's" records. There is little explicit in patent records, city water-pressure archives, parking-meter collection records, or children's readers to suggest their research utility. It required imagination to perceive the application, and a willingness to follow an unconventional line of data collection. Imagination cannot, of course, provide data if none are there. Our thesis is solely that the content limitations of archival records are not as great as the social scientist bound by orthodoxy thinks.

There is no easy way of knowing the degree to which reactive measurement errors exist among running archival records. These are secondhand measures, and many of them are contaminated by reactive biases, while others are not. The politician voting on a bill is well aware that his action will be noted by others; he may not be aware that an observer in the gallery made a note of the tic in his left eye when his name was called to vote. The records contributed by the person or group studied—the votes, the speeches, the entries written for directories—are produced with an awareness that they may be interpreted as expressive behavior. Thus, those errors that come from awareness of being tested, from role elicitation, from response sets, and from the act of measurement as a change agent are all potentially working to confound comparisons. With other data, such as the reports of presidential press conferences and census figures, the investigator has the additional bias of possible interviewer error passed along.

For data collected by a second party, by someone other than the producer (birth and death records, weather reports, power failures, patents, and the like), the risk of awareness, role, or interviewer contaminants is present but low. The main problem becomes one of instrument decay. Has the record-keeping process been constant or knowably variant over the period of study? As cited earlier, suicides in Prussia jumped 20% between 1882 and 1883. It may be that response sets on the part of the record keepers, or a change in administrative practice, threatens valid comparisons across time periods or geographic areas. To know of this variation is extremely difficult, and it represents one of the major drawbacks to archival records.

In summary, the running archival records offer a large mass of pertinent data for many substantive areas of research. They are cheap to obtain, easy to sample, and the population restrictions associated with them are often knowable and controllable through data transformations and the construction of indices. But all content is not amenable to study by archival records, and there is an ever present risk that reactive or other elements in the data-producing process will cause selective deposit or survival of the material. Against this must be balanced the opportunity for longitudinal studies over time, studies in which one may test a hypothesis by subjecting it to the rigor of evaluation in multiple settings and at multiple times.

NOTE

1. For general treatment of content analysis, see Berelson (1952); North, Holsti, Zaninovich, and Zinnes (1963); and Pool (1959).

FOUR

ARCHIVES II

The Episodic and Private Record

————•◆•————

*I*n the preceding chapter, we outlined the joys and sorrows of those archives on which there is typically a running time record. Here we continue our discussion of archives, but center on those which are more discontinuous and usually not a part of the public record. Such data are more difficult to come upon than the public records, unless the investigator is affiliated with some organization producing the material. The insurance sales of a casualty company, the nurse's record on a bedside clipboard, and last year's suicide notes from Los Angeles are more available to the "inside" investigator than they are to the curious outsider. But if these records are more difficult and costly to acquire than public records, they can often provide a gain in specificity of content. The amount of irrelevant dross commonly declines as an investigation is limited to a particular set of privately produced data.

We have already mentioned the risks of validity inherently present in archival records. The main analytic difference between the records mentioned in this and in the earlier chapter is the common inability to make longitudinal analyses of the private data. Sometimes security is the reason, sometimes the data are stored for shorter periods, sometimes financial and labor costs preclude an analysis over time. Whatever the cause, this is a major loss. The best defense against it is to find a related set and combine both—one continuous and the other discontinuous—for a more textured series of comparisons.

Some of the data in this chapter are episodic in character, but complete in reporting; many sources do maintain long and accurate record-keeping systems. The military is one such source, and Lodge (1963) has conducted a provocative correlational study with U.S. Navy records. All those who have learned his results on air crashes tend now, as passengers, to squint studiously at their pilots' height. Dipping back into the Navy records, Lodge collected reports of 680 jet plane accidents, and then searched other records for the height of the pilots. He learned that men exceeding the average height of seventy-two inches had significantly more accidents than their shorter contemporaries. This may be traced to the design of aircraft cockpits and the visual angle on instrument panels.

We have divided the sources into three gross classes; sales records, institutional records, and personal documents. All three are potential substitutes for direct observation of behavior. This is most obvious with personal documents, where the unavailability of a source may force the investigator to use whatever alternatives are available. But sales and institutional records may work in the same way, and can broaden the scope of an investigation which is primarily based on observation. They may fill in holes present in an observational series, or be used to produce a broader sampling of the behavior under study.

Chadwick Alger once suggested to us that it would be profitable for a political scientist to sit in the Delegates' Lounge of the United Nations and observe how much whisky was downed. By keying the consumption rate to action before the U.N., Alger felt that an index of tension might be developed. In such a setting, the sales records of the bar might be an even better measure, for they are less amenable to instrument-decay errors and permit a closer noting of type of drink ordered (Scotch, Canadian, Cuba libres, and so forth).

Brown (1960) suggested that records of soap consumption be substituted for ratings of the cleanliness of institutional patients—ratings which are, after all, observation one step removed. Brown points out two ways of measuring soap usage: a liquid soap could be measured by reading the level of liquid in the dispenser each day, or bar soap by a measure of the water displacement at the beginning and end of the period studied.

Two other examples, both employing records of whisky consumption, illustrate the substitution of sales records for observation. Hotel and restaurant records could be employed in a comparative study of occupations. One can observe members of an occupation and attribute traits to them, but valuable auxiliary information might come from the records on drink consumption and petty thievery in convention hotels. Do anthropologists take more soap and towels away with them than do mechanical engineers? Such an analysis is posited on the assumption that those who attend conventions (and who stay, steal, and drink in convention hotels) are a representative sample of the profession.

Hillebrandt (1962) sought data on the sale of alcoholic drinks at Chicago airports in his study of passenger anxiety produced by air crashes. He failed to use the proposed data because of the insensitivity of the instrument. At that time, the major Chicago airport had recently been completed, and the construction of bars had not caught up with demand. Thus, there was negligible variance from day to day in sales, and the small amount that existed seemed to be based upon the bartenders' speed, not on exterior factors.

SALES RECORDS

In a society as oriented to marketing and record keeping as ours, sales data abound for study of a varied body of content. As noted above, Hillebrandt (1962) did not get to use bar sales as a measure. He continued with his study, however, and used the volume of air passengers. With a complete set of data over time, he was able to transform the data, correcting for systematic sources of variance irrelevant to his hypothesis. He partialled out the seasonal variation in air traffic, for example, and accounted for the secular changes in traffic level at Chicago's two major airports. The residual material demonstrated that crashes were only a very short-term depressant on travel. Just as with the bar sales, there is some rigidity in his data which tends to blunt comparisons. A certain number of people have no alternative to flying, regardless of how dissettling was a major crash the day before. Webb and Campbell plan to continue this analysis with a complementary measure. With the same exogenous variable, they hope to plot the number and dollar value of trip insurance policies taken out by travelers at Chicago airports. Buying trip insurance is a low-cost and simple behavior which should index anxiety of air travelers. With the bar facilities now expanded to exceed demand, it will be possible to perform an analysis containing three sales components: bar sales, trip insurance sales, and ticket sales. Each of these must be corrected for the systematic biases present, but they should provide a more sensitive and nonreactive set of possible outcroppings of anxiety than any single variable study, particularly one based on the interviewing of travelers.

Insurance, a paid-for hedge against risk, is an admirable measure of the effect of disaster. Just as one can examine trip insurance sales and link them to crashes, one can examine the timing of casualty insurance sales and link them to the occurrence of hurricanes or tornadoes. Add to this sales of life insurance (compared to the time of death of close friends or relatives), and one has a three-way index of the general effect of disaster.

These same data could be used to test Zipf's (1946) hypothesis further. Is the amount of casualty insurance taken out inversely proportional to the distance from the disaster? How the mapping of insurance underwriting compares to a meteorological map of tornado probability would be a necessary control. It might be that the hypothesis holds only in areas which have had tornado experience. This would give support to Zipf's hypothesis, but even greater support would come if a significant amount of insurance were written in proximate areas with little or no tornado experience. What, in brief, is the nature of the generalization of effect?

How unlikely a source of research material is the sale of peanuts! Yet, continuing in the vein of study of anxiety or tension, peanut sales are a possibility that should be systematically explored. An anecdotal report appeared in the *Chicago Sun-Times* from the concessionaire in that city's baseball parks. He casually observed that peanut sales after the seventh inning of a game are significantly higher than earlier—but only during a tight game. If the game is one-sided, there is no late-inning increase in peanut purchasing. Is this a sound, nonreactive measure of involvement or tension? It may be, but it illustrates the problems associated with such archival measures—one must pay special heed to rival hypotheses. One hypothesis is that fans, during the increasingly tense moments of the late innings, absentmindedly lean over and compulsively crunch their way through more peanuts than earlier.

But one should look at population restrictions. It may be that the finding (if it may be legitimated as such) on the increase coming only in tight games is an artifact of selective attendance and not tension. There is a hyperbolic curve of attendance in a one-sided game. A substantial number of fans usually arrive late, and another substantial group leaves early if the game appears to be already decided. The population potential for peanut purchasing is thereby variable across innings, and the effect of a tight game should be to reduce the early departures and provide a larger base for sales in later innings. For a finer test, a simple corrective would be to transform the peanut sales into unit sales per X thousand fans per inning—a transformation possible by clocking turnstile movement in and out.

Another test of the hypothesis, using the same data, is possible, although we can report no findings. The tension hypothesis would get strong support if, in a population of one-sided games, fans left in substantial numbers early and sales stayed stable from the middle through the later innings. This would be reflected in an ascending consumption curve if correction were made for those in attendance.

But one other element of population restrictions remains to be considered. We have examined only the issue of the absolute number of fans available in the park to buy the peanuts. Is there any plausibility to the notion that those who leave early are more or less devoted to peanuts? One might determine this by interview at the exit gate, or by looking for traces of peanut shells in vacated seats.

Sales data can also be used to infer popularity and preference. The impact of Glenn's orbital flight was evidenced by record-breaking sales of the commemorative stamp issued to mark it. Similarly, the sale of commemorative Kennedy stamps and the great demand for Kennedy half-dollars after their issuance, as well as all the special books and the reappearance of *Profiles in Courage* on the best-seller list, provide persuasive evidence, if any were needed, of the man's influence on public thinking.

Another measure of the popularity of a man is the value of his autograph in the commercial market. The supply level must be controlled, of course, but it is of some interest that the following prices held at the end of 1964:

John Hancock	$250.00
Winston Churchill	225.00
Napoleon I	185.00
Charles Dickens	125.00
Ralph Waldo Emerson	110.00
César Franck	75.00
Daniel Webster	65.00
Calvin Coolidge	55.00
John Quincy Adams	37.50
Aldous Huxley	22.50

The sales and pictorial content of stamps are a useful but unused bit of expressive intelligence. An analysis of the illustrations on stamps may give indications of the state of political opinion in the nation. What does an analysis of illustrations printed during the early years of the Fascist regimes in Germany and Italy show? It has been suggested that stamp illustrations presage aggressive political action. Perhaps somewhere a philatelistic psychologist has prepared this study, using illustrated sets of stamp catalogs by year of issue.

A possible flaw in such analysis is a potential datum for another topic of study. Each nation does not print its own stamps. Many former colonial territories continue, as a cost-saving device, to use secondhand engravings and the printing facilities of the former governing power. The stamp illustration may thereby reflect an economic and not a political decision. But whether or not a former colonial territory still relies on the old power is itself a clue to relations between the two. One could, for example, compare former British and French colonies in Africa. Or compare new nations within what was a single colonial area. Guinea prints her own stamps; Mali buys hers from France.

The diffusion of information among physicians was the topic of Coleman, Katz, and Menzel's (1957) research. Instead of the more standard, and reactive, tactic of interviewing doctors, they elected to go to pharmacy records for information about which doctors prescribed what drugs when. Sampling at intervals over a fifteen-month period, they related the physician's adoption of new drugs to his social network. Such hardnosed data can be a useful check on interviewing data, provided the effect of collecting such records does not alter the behavior of the record-keepers. This is a very implausible risk with drug prescriptions, but a reasonable one when dealing with less legally controlled records. The danger is not so much in masking information as it is in improving it. The record-keeper may perform a more conscientious job because he knows that his work is being put to some use. If the investigator using such records stresses the greater glory to man that will come from the record-keeper offering his cooperation, he may actually be increasing the risk that the instrumentation process will change—thereby threatening the validity of comparisons over time.

The social-network variable employed by Coleman et al. can be measured by other methods than the standard interview or sociogram. To study the extent to which interaction among different departments of a university took place, one could use orthodox procedures. In addition, so humble a document as a desk calendar might be checked. This record can provide information on who lunched with whom, with what degree of frequency, and across what departments. Not everyone notes such engagements (a population restriction), and the desk calendar is not a likely source for learning of other engagements, such as social dinners or meetings so regular that they don't have to be noted (content restrictions). Staying just with the lunch dates, one route to learn the character of the restrictions would be to enlist the aid of waiters in faculty clubs. The reader can conjure up objections to this assistance.

Drug-sale records are in common use by pharmaceutical houses to evaluate the sales effort of their detail men. Both the houses and the detail men have learned that the verbal statement or the observed enthusiasm of a doctor for a new drug is a highly unstable predictor of what he will prescribe. If records are available for checks on self-reports, they should by all means be used. Such checks are particularly useful when the data are produced continuously by the same subjects, for then a correction can be applied to the self-reports. If the assumption can be made that the character of the error is constant over time, it may not be necessary to run both sets of data concurrently.

Something of an analogous correction can be seen with economic forecasters. Firms which employ more than one forecaster are said to compute the response-set characteristic of the forecaster (optimism or pessimism) and apply a secret correction to his periodic predictions. This is a rather interesting data transformation, since its existence shows the set rigidity of the forecasters. They, too, know whether they have been over- or underestimating, yet that knowledge does not produce potent enough feedback to overcome the response set. Morgenstern (1963) notes reports of the same type of corrections applied by Soviet planners in the 1930s.

Boring (1961) has detailed how a similar type of response error was an early *cause célèbre* in astronomy. Differences in reaction times among astronomical observers became known, and the phrase "personal equation" was coined to describe the bias. In an evolving history, the contaminant existed but was unknown, became known and the cause of study for the purpose of eliminating its biasing effect, and then became the substantive material of a large body of psychological research.

The sale of stocks was used by Ashley (1962) in a study interesting for what it says of positive and negative reward. Isolating firms which announced an unexpected dividend or earnings statement, either up or down, Ashley traced the stock prices following the announcement. An unexpectedly high dividend influenced the price of the stock for about fifteen days, while an unexpectedly low dividend or earnings statement had an effect for only about four days. There are other places to measure extinction than in a Skinner box. See, for instance, Winship and Allport's (1943) study on newspaper headlines, mentioned earlier, and Griffith's (1949) research on horse-race odds—both studies of optimism-pessimism. Hamilton (1942) has also conducted an interesting content analysis on the rise of pessimism in widely circulated Protestant sermons.

A more common use of sales records (but still surprisingly uncommon) is as a measure of propaganda effectiveness. Within advertising, particularly, there has been extensive writing on the inadequacy of survey methodology to predict the advertiser's major criterion, sales. An excellent annotated bibliography reviewing advertising's effect on sales has been prepared by Krueger and Ramond (1965).

Henry (1958) gives numerous examples of the discrepancies between respondents' report and sales figures, indicating that the reasons a consumer gives for buying a product cannot be relied upon. Reactive measures thus suspect, other methods of consumer preference measurement must be found.

Henry mentions an example of a controlled sales experiment on "shelf appeal." One brand of candy is sold in three types of wrappers, with variables such as shelf position and number of units displayed controlled. The dependent variable is the sales level of the different packages.

There is an ideal experiment medium for advertising research in direct-mail sales efforts. Lucas and Britt (1963) comment upon a number of studies which have varied such elements as the color of paper, inclusion of various incentives, and stamping a return envelope by hand or by meter. They also cite the example of a department store which might send out a monthly statement to customers containing one of ten variants of an advertisement selling a specific product. The average return per layout would then be determined by subsequent sales.

The large mail-order houses (Sears, Ward, Spiegel, and others) regularly conduct controlled experiments on different thematic appeals. This is easily performed by varying the content of the appeal and simply counting the returns attributable to the different sources. In a revealing finding, one of these houses discovered that an advertisement describing a self-riding lawnmower as something of an adult's toy dramatically outsold an appeal which argued its superior functional merits.

Using sales results of a promotional campaign, Blomgren and Scheuneman (1961) found a "scare" approach was less effective for selling seat belts than one that featured a professional racing driver and appealed to masculine control and relaxation.

Over thirty years ago, Jahoda-Lazarsfeld and Zeisel (1932) studied the impact of the depression by noting the level of grocery sales. The same measure is used now to evaluate the efficacy of different sales themes. A before-after design was used by the National Advertising Company (1963) to learn the effect of large outdoor signs placed in the parking lots of three shopping centers. They used store audits to determine the sales of products advertised on the signs and then compared these data to sales from a control sample of equivalent stores. Another method of "pretesting" advertising themes is to place treatments of the theme in prominent places within a supermarket and then observe sales. This has been done by comparing sales attributable to a single theme against a control of past sales, and also by employing multiple themes and comparing one against the other. In this latter approach, close attention has been paid to time-sampling problems, so as to protect the equivalence of the populations exposed to each version.

One could similarly experiment with vending machines, although we do not know of any such research. By random assignment of the display of experimental cigarette packages to machines, or by systematically varying exhortatory messages over machines, one could employ lever-pulling as the effectiveness measure.

Aside from the commercial applications of such research, direct-mail advertising, vending machines, and the like offer a fine natural laboratory for the study of persuasion. Mindak, Neibergs, and Anderson (1963) used the sales of tickets to parades and to a civic aquatennial as one of their several measures of the effect of a newspaper strike. Roens (1961) reported on the use of different combinations of media to carry the same propaganda theme (for Scott paper), and Berreman's (1940) study of factors affecting the sale of novels found that publicity elements had little effect.

DeFleur and Petranoff (1959) investigated subliminal persuasion by sales measures. Since the alleged subliminal effect was first reported (with no data) as the result of a filmed message, they flashed "Buy Product X" on a screen subliminally for several experimental weeks. The effect of this was measured by the deviation from normal of a food wholesaler's orders. No significant effect was observed.

The stuff of commercial persuasion, advertisements proper, has been employed in a number of ways for other purposes. The want-ad columns of newspapers have served as economic predictors (Fowler, 1962). Contrariwise, they may provide the data for historical analysis. The Security First National Bank of Los Angeles compiles a regional index of want-ad frequency and reports variance over time in this index coincidental with basic economic data. A management consulting firm prepares an index based only on advertisements for engineers and scientists. Although incomplete data are reported by Fowler, she writes that the firm "likes to consider its index as a leading indicator of how the economy fares, rather than a coincident indicator" (p. 12). That optimistic assessment illustrates the necessity for considering the time-linked nature of a measure. The statement was true for a long period of time—from the late 1940s possibly up to 1964. But since the employment of engineers and scientists is intimately tied to defense contracts, a major change in Defense

Department policy will throw off employment levels, thus the ads, thus the indicator. Just such a change occurred during Secretary Robert McNamara's administration, and the 1964 advertisement levels should be negatively correlated with the state of the economy.

Advertisements have also been used to test theories of social change. Assuming that ads reflect values, Dornbusch and Hickman (1959) sampled 816 issues of the *Ladies Home Journal* and analyzed the content of advertising to estimate the degree of "other-directedness" displayed. These data tested Riesman's hypotheses on the history of "other-directedness." Two classes of indices were employed: (a) endorsements by persons or groups and (b) claims that a product is related to satisfactions in interpersonal relations.

Singh and Huang (1962) made a cross-cultural study of advertising, comparing American and Indian advertising for similarity and relating the findings to socioeconomic and cultural factors. Since they used print advertising, it is important to take account of differential literacy rates in such comparisons. If the advertisers are addressing their messages to literate "prospects" and reflecting the values of those "prospects," the differential literacy rate may interact with magazine readership and prospect status to yield differences between societies that are spurious. This is less a concern with broadcast advertising, although there may be a population restriction in that those who either own or are more available to radio or television receivers vary systematically across countries.

INDUSTRIAL AND INSTITUTIONAL RECORDS

Among the finest work to be found on discussion of multiple methods and the criterion problem is that of the industrial psychologists. One rarely finds such attention to the relative merits of ratings versus observation versus performance versus interviewing versus questionnaires versus tests. Guion (1961) has offered an excellent short treatment of this subject, as have Ghiselli and Brown (1955) and Whisler and Harper (1962). But these have not supplanted the singular statements on "criteria of criteria" by R. L. Thorndike (1949).[1]

The number of private records marshalled by the industrial psychologists has been impressive. Amount and quality of output are probably the most

frequently used behavioral measures, and are usually expressed in some transformed score—the number of units produced by a worker or department per
unit of time, the amount of sales per unit of time, or the profitability of activity
by dollars invested by the firm. The known subjectivity of ratings by supervisors
or foremen increasingly moved many of the specialists in this area to pure
behavioral measures, but ratings remain because of the difficulty in making
behavioral measures comparable.

Private records have their difficulties, and Whisler and Harper (1962) are
helpful in illustrating problems in making comparisons across departments or
workers. The factors involved in any such comparison of records are numerous
and vary from one situation to another—the type of work, physical working
conditions, work group cohesion, and the like. Ghiselli and Brown (1955)
struggle with the problem of appropriate controls for work behavior and offer
a series of possible work standards: group average production, rates of selected
individuals known to be "good" workers (with some discounting then applied),
experimentally determined times for tasks, and "rational analysis" by people
familiar with the problem.

We review a body of studies with data drawn from the institutional records
of companies, schools, hospitals, and the military. A good share of these come
from industry, but the overlap with other institutions is marked.

Most of the current writers argue for multidimensional criteria. Ghiselli
and Brown (1955) give the humble example of a streetcar motorman, indicating a series of proficiency measures:

1. Number of collisions with pedestrians

2. Number of traffic violations

3. Number of commendations from public

4. Number of complaints from public

5. Number of times company rules broken

6. Number of sleepovers (tardiness)

7. Number of times schedules broken

8. Number of reprimands from inspectors

9. Rating by inspectors

10. Errors reported by dispatchers.

As always with multiple measures such as these, the question comes up of the advisability of combining the various measures into a single composite score. Consider in the list above the problem of weighting each of the ten variables. Ghiselli and Brown (1955) suggest multiple cutoffs—establishing a minimum performance level for *each* component element of the index. The way in which the variables are combined, and the final score reached, can be disastrously misleading if some minimum standard is not met on each of the tasks of the job. They offer the highly reasonable example that an airline pilot should be able to land a plane as well as take one off—perhaps not so gracefully, but still with an irreducible degree of proficiency (cf. Coombs, 1963).

Another multimeasure study, this one of ship effectiveness in the Navy, was conducted by Campbell (1956). Rather than rely solely on ratings by the captain or crew members, Campbell examined the ship records for reports of ship inspections, torpedo firings, re-enlistment rates of those aboard, requests for transfer, and disciplinary actions. Snyder and Sechrest (1959) combined behavioral violations and ratings in their work showing the positive effect of directive therapy in defective delinquents.

Re-enlistment rates are a measure of job turnover, and Evan (1963) explored this topic in research on student workers. Personnel records were examined to find a possible relationship between job turnover and departmental placement. He reasoned that a high level of interaction on the job with other student workers would have a stress-reducing effect and result in a lower rate of job turnover. He supported this hypothesis by showing that the larger the number of students with whom a worker could interact, the lower the rate of quitting.

Knox (1961) added absenteeism to job turnover and correlated both with age, seniority, and the distance of the worker's home from the factory. Melbin (1961) also used absenteeism and job turnover in research on psychiatric aids. He compared these data to archival reports on work assignments. The correlational methods limited his ability to establish cause-and-effect relationships, but he was able to trace a double-directioned effect between changes in work assignments and absences.

Job turnover is an ambiguous measure—sometimes it is an administrative action, sometimes an action dictated by the individual employee. R. L.
Thorndike (1949) holds that administrative actions should be considered as a
discrete class of criteria. Along with many others, Guilford (1956) used the
records of pay increases as his measure of the firm's appraisal of the individual.
Weitz (1958) suggests the imperfectly correlated measure of promotion within
the company, while Jay and Copes (1957) speak of job survival as a criterion.
Merely to stay on a job, without being fired, is indicative of an administrative
decision that the employee is not too bad.

Whisler and Harper (1962) also speak of seniority as a criterion and discuss
the implications of this in the union-management struggle over definition of
criteria. They state that seniority has appeal because of its qualities of objectivity and precision, and that it is not a simple case of the union wanting seniority
and the management fighting it. Promotion from within the management
group and the high value placed on experience is evidence of the use of
seniority within the management tier.

One could also observe other management actions which reflect the es-
teem with which an employee is held. The rug on the floor, the drapes on the
window, the white telephone, the second secretary, and the corner office are all
salient cues to an employee's success with the firm.

Other industrial research with absentee records has included Amthauer's
(1963) work on social psychological settings and Bernberg's (1952) study of
departmental morale. Amthauer took absenteeism as his dependent variable
and considered a string of independent variables: motivation, intelligence,
persistence, and stability, as well as the individual's relationship with appren-
tices and with instructors. Note that although absenteeism is not implicitly
reactive, the other measures of individual psychological characteristics were.
So, too, for Bernberg, who measured departmental morale by measures with
high reactive risk, but matched these against an elaborated set of absentee
measures. He took four variants of absenteeism as his variables: unexcused
absence of one day or longer, tardiness, absence of less than one day, and trips
to the medical unit not resulting from accident or disease. For a review of
studies focused on absenteeism in the industrial setting, see Brayfield and
Crockett (1955).

The unions keep books, too, and Stuart (1963) was canny enough to use grievance records in a study of racial conflict. He collected 364 verbatim records of the grievance board of a large union in the textile industry—data extending over a seven-year period. The complaints were analyzed to determine feelings, attitudes, and actions against Negro and Spanish-speaking workers who comprised a majority of the union. Their complaints are important evidence, but there is the risk of the bias one notes in studies of political speeches. Although the events occurred in the past, and the investigator did not intrude in the production of the data, the subjects were very much aware that their remarks were "on the record." This perforce limits the degree of generalization possible.

McGrath (1962) also used indirect data in his study of friendship and group behavior. The dependent variable was the competitive performance of rifle teams, plotted against whether the team had given favorable or unfavorable ratings to former teammates and how the team had been rated. I. D. Steiner (1964) comments on a possible restriction on generalization: "Additional research is needed to determine whether the individualistic orientation which was a boon to rifle teams would also promote productivity in situations calling for cooperative group action" (p. 434).

Hall and Willerman (1963) studied the effect of college roommates on grade performance. They set up experimental combinations of dormitory roommates with varying academic ability. Students rooming with high-ability students obtained better grades than those rooming with low-ability students; this condition held, however, only when the roommate was later born in his family. Hall and Willerman conclude that these results support Schachter's (1959) thesis that first-born students are more susceptible to influence and later-born ones are more influential.

Stouffer (Stouffer et al., 1949) was among those reporting on sick-call data, drawing statistics from the Office of the Air Surgeon on members of heavy bomber crews in the European theater during June, 1944. Sick-call rate was correlated with self-evaluations of physical condition. Stouffer suggests that the contrast between attitudes toward one's physical condition and behavior with respect to physical symptoms reflected the men's tendency to save up complaints until their tour of thirty missions was completed. He speculates that they might have been motivated by a fear of not completing a tour of combat duty and thus running the risk of postponing a return to the United States.

More military records were used by Fiedler and his associates (Fiedler, 1962; Fiedler, Dodge, Jones, & Hutchins, 1958). These studies examined "adjustment" in nonclinical populations—Army units and student populations. For the Army personnel, they obtained sick-call data, disciplinary-offense ratings, and court-martial records; for the students, course grades, number of visits to the student health center, and student counseling bureau visits. Little relationship was found among these measures of "adjustment," underlining the problem of combining pieces of evidence which *look* to be similar in reflecting some characteristics.

In a more circumscribed investigation, Mechanic and Volkart (1961) probed sick-call visits further, with a population of college students. They showed the frequency of visits to be positively related to the subject's degree of stress and his tendency to play the sick role. Medical visits are not a pure measure of a single trait, and few single archival measures are ever pure. The employment of multiple measures of the same hypothesized "trait" is always indicated (Campbell & Fiske, 1959). We stress this because many of the researchers who have been venturesome enough to employ nonreactive data have done so to define or classify subjects—often then administering questionnaires and interviews to the subjects. This is a highly appropriate device to combine research methods, but its validity is posited on the accuracy of the trait definition contributed by the initial record. A multiple-method approach is the best hedge against error (cf. R. L. Thorndike, 1949).

Schwartz and Stanton (1950) suggest a study of the social situation of the hospital combining observational and archival materials. The observation is of negative incidents in a ward, and the archive is a measure of incontinent behavior: the amount and type of laundry done for that ward. In their exploratory observational study, they kept complete records of the patients' daily activities, and were able to determine connections between certain types of negative incidents and incontinent behavior. They further suggest that the laundry record could be useful in establishing the effects of changes in therapeutic methods within a ward.

WRITTEN DOCUMENTS

The last major class of more or less private archives is personal documents. These have been more the bailiwick of the historiographer than the behavioral scientist, but a number of notable studies have been performed using personal documents. Cox (1926), in Volume 2 of Terman's *Genetic Studies of Genius,* used documentary evidence of all kinds, and, on the history of science side, we have Terman's early (1917) study estimating Galton's IQ. Centering on records of Galton's prowess between the ages of three and eight (he could read any English-language book by five and knew the *Iliad* and *Odyssey* by six), Terman compared them with the ages at which other children are able to accomplish the same or similar achievements and estimated Galton's IQ to be not far from 200.

There have been important methodological works, such as G. W. Allport's (1942) monograph, *The Use of Personal Documents in Psychological Science,* and facilitating methods papers, such as Dollard and Mowrer's (1947) system to determine the amount of tension in written documents by a "Discomfort Relief Quotient."

But for all this, written documents have been another of the underdeveloped data resources of social science. In the examples that follow, we cite some of the major studies using written documents and illustrate some of the rival hypotheses coincident with them.

One could not think of letters as a research source without bringing to mind Thomas and Znaniecki's (1918) classic study of the Polish peasant. Letters sent between Poland and the United States were one of the major elements in a data pool that included autobiographies, newspaper accounts, court proceedings, and the records of social agencies. Rather by happenstance, Thomas learned that there was an extensive correspondence between the two countries and that many of the letters were being thrown away. From this lead, advertisements were placed which offered to pay for each letter produced.

There are, to be sure, substantial questions about the population and content restrictions in the letters Thomas and Znaniecki gathered; there are in any body of voluntarily produced (even for pay) research materials. Typically, they only had one side of the exchange, a common and frustrating condition often bemoaned by biographers and historians. In a commentary on this study, Riley (1963) states:

> In all such instances, then, their data refer only to selected members of each group (family) and cover only part of the interaction. These gaps illustrate an important potential limitation in the use of available data generally: not having been assembled for the purpose of the investigation, the data may be fragmentary or incomplete, thus depriving the researcher of valuable information.
>
> Another limitation is that such privately owned and spontaneously produced materials may be rare or difficult to obtain. Owners of letters, diaries, or other personal documents may sometimes object to their use for research purposes. . . . Moreover, situations producing appropriate materials may be rare. The continuing exchange of letters, for example, seems to depend upon long-term or frequent separation of the members, as well as upon a custom of detailed letter writing. Nevertheless, there are no doubt many instances in which similar data are available for further research, as, for instance, when servicemen are separated from their families. (pp. 242–243)

Riley thus points out that the dross rate may be high ("situations producing appropriate materials may be rare"), and that population restrictions may be present ("exchange . . . seems to depend upon long-term or frequent separation . . . owners may sometimes object to their use"). Specifically for cross-cultural comparison purposes, there is the question of differential literacy rates. How many of the Polish peasants could write? If they could not, and had letters written for them by others, say, village scribes, did the presence of these intervening persons serve to alter the content of the letters? On the voluntary supplying of the letters, did the correspondent give up only a biased sample? A money incentive might have to be prohibitively high to pry loose some love letters, for example, or letters which detailed complaints about the correspondent's frugality in sending money back home.

In Sunday feature articles, one sometimes reads another group of one-way letters: those sent from children in summer camp to their parents. By themselves, they are instructive of a child's perception of the surrounding world. Salzinger (1958) got the other end of this candid correspondence as well, and analyzed the content of mail from children and parents, comparing the letters for similarity on "wants," "demands," and "requests."

Janowitz (1958) dealt with letters and diaries captured from German soldiers. His concern was the impact of propaganda on these troops, and "when these letters dealt with the German writer himself, or his small circle of friends, they contained testimony of considerable value. Many made valuable propaganda documents, especially captured undelivered mail" (p. 734). This last point is of interest, for the undelivered mail is a subset of mail which is most recent and most pertinent for evaluation of propaganda effect. Letters captured on the person of troops may also be particularly valuable, for they contain not only the most recent expressions of feeling, but may also include letters the writer may have been postponing mailing. Such uncertain writings may be prime indicators of attitudes and morale, for the easy stereotypes of "I'm fine Ma and the food's not bad" are more likely to be quickly dispatched.

Letters to political figures are another source of data. For some magnificent examples of these, as well as a general treatment of the topic, one can examine *Dear F. D. R.* (Sussman, 1963, an earlier report of which is in Sussman, 1959. See also Dexter, 1963).

A particularly fine discussion of possible sources of error in letters is presented in Dexter's (1964) chapter on letters to congressmen. He notes that congressmen do not necessarily see any cause for alarm in a barrage of negative mail.

> One "pro-labor" Senator, out of curiosity, had his staff check up the writers of 100 letters he received advocating support of a higher minimum wage. It was found that 75 writers were eligible to register, but of these only 33 actually were registered. Furthermore, the letters were advocating his support of a measure on which he had been particularly active, and the content of the mail showed no realization of the stand he had so publicly taken. The Senator could scarcely get excited about these letter writers as either a source of opposition or of support on the basis of that issue. (p. 399)

If the only goal of the senator is to stay in office, the mail from an ineligible voter is only so much dross. His greater concern is the lack of any intelligence from the great mass of eligible voters who don't write.

Dexter goes on to discuss why mail is important, but speaks of the congressman's description of "genuine," "junk," and "stimulated" mail. Of interest is the way in which they are discriminated.

> It [mail] is not believed if "junk," i.e., press releases or other broadcast mailings, nor if it be stimulated. Stimulated mail is not entirely easy to define.

In its pure form it consists of virtually identical postcard messages written under the instigation of a single company, union or interest group. (One company even mailed the postcards for its workers, fearing that they would not know who their congressman was.) Congressmen look for signs of stimulation—similarity of phrasing ("They all used the same argument.") or even stationery ("They handed out the paper.") and time of mailing ("You could tell the hour or minute someone pushed the button.") . . . it is hard to fool a congressman as to when mail is stimulated. Some organizations urge their members to write in their own words, on their own stationery, and as personally as possible. Congressional assistants tell us that perhaps one in fifty persons who write such a letter will enclose the original printed notice from the organization urging an individualized apparently spontaneous letter. (p. 403)

As for the extent of this false element in spontaneous mail,

Most of the mail sent on the Reciprocal Trade Act was in some sense stimulated . . . [for] Eastern and Southern congressmen . . . Westinghouse, Dow, Monsanto, and Pittsburgh Plate Glass may have stimulated 40 percent or more of all the mail received on the issue in 1954. . . . Mail in favor of reciprocal trade was equally stimulated and perhaps by even fewer prime movers. Our impression is that three-fourths of all antiprotectionist mail was stimulated directly or indirectly by the League of Women Voters. (pp. 403-404)

A check on the true level of protest mail was made by the Xerox Corporation. Flooded with negative letters after sponsorship of a television series on the United Nations, they hired a group of handwriting experts to examine the mail. "A total of 51,279 protests had been received. The handwriting experts determined that the letters were written by 12,785 persons. The latter figures practically equalled the number of favorable letters" (Kupcinet, 1965). No mention is made of an equivalent analysis of the "pro" letters.

This selective bias in the population mailing letters to congressmen or others results in an invalid generalization on the state of public opinion, but it can serve as evidence of how the major pressure groups are responding. The bias itself is not fatal; only not knowing of it is.

Earlier, we mentioned the problem of population-restriction bias in suicide notes, observing that less than 25% of all suicides leave final notes. Osgood and Walker (1959) took this into account in their study of motivation and language behavior. Reasoning from behavioral principles, they predicted that the content of suicide notes should differ significantly from control notes and simulated suicide notes. Persons about to take their life should be highly motivated (something of an understatement), and this motivation should increase the dominant responses in their hierarchies; a higher than normal level of stereotypy should be present. Content analysis by six different stereotypy indices supported their prediction. This study is a good example of relating "natural phenomena" that exist in the outside world to principles derived from laboratory experimentation. There are many tests for theoretical postulates available in settings other than the laboratory, and joint testing in the laboratory and outside may yield powerful validity checks.

Spiegel and Neuringer (1963) also tested a specific hypothesis by the employment of suicide notes. They examined the proposition that inhibition of the experience of dread ordinarily evoked by suicidal intention is a necessary condition for suicidal action. They drew on the Los Angeles County Coroner's office for their material, noting a control of "false" suicide notes. Other suicide-note studies have been conducted by Gottschalk and Gleser (1960) and by Schneidman and Farberow (1957).

Art work is another expressive personal document that may provide data—as is shown by all the clinical psychologists who look at Van Gogh's paintings and say, "That man was in trouble!" An equally post hoc analysis, but with more analytic elegance, has been contributed by Barry (1957). He studied the complexity of art form as related to severity of socialization. From Whiting and Child's seventy-six nonliterate societies on which socialization data are available, he found thirty with at least ten extant examples of graphic art—either displays in museums or illustrations in ethnographic reports. There was a low-level association between complexity of art form and degree of severity of socialization. The unknown question is whether a higher or lower level of association would have been detected had the data been available for more than 30 societies. Were those who were more gentle in socialization less likely to produce art work which has survived to the present? Note, too, that there is the selective screen of museum curators and ethnographers. Materials might have survived physically from the other 46 societies, but have been defined as of insufficient artistic or scientific worth to display behind glass or on paper.

What might be considered an equally primitive art form was studied by Solley and Haigh (1957) and by Craddick (1961). Both investigations showed that the size of children's drawings of Santa Claus was larger before Christmas than after. Sechrest and Wallace (1964) asked whether the size of the Santa Claus drawing might be traced to a generalized expansive euphoria associated with the excitement of the season, and whether children might be expected to draw almost any object larger during the Christmas season. Their experimentation showed this was not the case, and the Santa Claus was the only one of three objects drawn larger. Craddick (1962) also found that the mean size of drawings of witches decreased at Halloween time. Berger (1954), working from doodles in the notebooks of college students, found a correlation of .75 between graphic constriction in the doodles and neurotic tendency.

A CONCLUDING NOTE

In this review of archival studies, we have seen the versatility of the written record. Not only has the content of study varied, but also the functions these data have served.

For some research purposes, there were few alternatives to archives—not a particularly luminary recommendation, but certainly a compelling one. With suicides, for example, there is no choice but to wait until a population defines itself operationally. Once this happens, one can go to farewell notes, biographical material, and interviews with relatives; but one cannot go to the subject. So, too, for the general student of the past. For one like Terman (1917), who chose to study Galton, there was no easy alternative to consulting the written record.

In a limited content area, the archival record provides *the* dependent variable. Just as votes are the ultimate criterion for the politician, sales and work performance are the ultimate criteria for some applied social scientists. It has been of interest in the history of research in both advertising and personnel that relatively direct criterion variables have been ignored, while less pertinent ones were labored over. (Measuring "willingness to buy" by questionnaire methods is an example, although it does have some utility in prediction studies.)

There are also a few studies in which records were used as a medium through which theoretical principles could be tested. Such studies are too few, but these records offer superb opportunities to validate hypotheses generated in less natural and more reactivity-prone settings. There are restrictions, but it should be recognized that there are restrictions in any single class of information. Berlyne (1964), in commenting on some highly controlled experimental work, wrote:

> Skinner and his associates have concentrated on situations in which an animal can perform a particular kind of response repeatedly at a high rate. The findings yielded by this kind of experiment have been extrapolated without much hesitation, and not always with specific empirical warrant, to a diversity of human activities, including those on which the most important social problems hinge. (pp. 115-116)

Osgood and Walker (1959) used suicide notes to study the effect of heightened motivation on response hierarchies. Also using records as a testing medium, Mosteller and Wallace (1963) went to records of 1787–1788 for their comparative study of a Bayesian procedure with a classical statistical approach. They demonstrated that both procedures reached the same conclusion on the disputed authorship of some of *The Federalist Papers*.[2]

The great majority of these studies, however, have used the archives for indirect evidence. Stuart's (1963) study of union grievances and the state of race relations, Parker's (1963) study of library withdrawals to show the effect of television, and the measurement of the size of Santa Clauses (Craddick, 1961; Sechrest & Wallace, 1964; Solley & Haigh, 1957) all reveal the inventive unveiling of valuable evidence. But only partial evidence—for the reasons traced in the preceding chapter show the need for care in generalizing from such analyses. Here, as with the running public records, there is a heavy demand for consideration of possible data transformations and for the construction of multiple indices. If it is agreed that the archives typically provide only partial evidence, and if the desirable research strategy is to generate multiple displays of overlapping evidence, then the way in which these partial clues are pieced together is critical.

We should recognize that using the archival records frequently means substituting someone else's selective filter for your own. Although the investigator may not himself contaminate the material, he may learn that the producer or repository already has. A thoughtful consideration of the sources of invalidity may provide intelligence on these, either by suggesting astute hedges or new analyses to answer rival hypotheses. In any event, the Chinese proverb still holds:

The palest ink is clearer than the best memory.

NOTES

1. For other articles of methodological interest on criteria, see Bass (1952), Brogden and Taylor (1950), Fiske (1951), Gordon (1950), MacKinney (1960), Rush (1953), Severin (1952), and Turner (1960).

2. For an excellent general treatment of "identifying the unknown communicator," see Paisley (1964), where studies in painting, literature, and music are reviewed.

⚘ FIVE ⚘

SIMPLE OBSERVATION

———•◆•———

Who could he be? He was evidently reserved, and melancholy. Was he a clergyman?—he danced too well. A barrister?—He was not called. He used very fine words, and said a great deal. Could he be a distinguished foreigner come to England for the purpose of describing the country, its manners and customs; and frequenting city balls and public dinners with the view of becoming acquainted with high life, polished etiquette, and English refinement?—No, he had not a foreign accent. Was he a surgeon, a contributer to the magazines, a writer of fashionable novels or an artist?—No: to each and all of these surmises there existed some valid objection.—"Then," said everybody, "he must be somebody."—"I should think he must be," reasoned Mr. Malderton, with himself, "because he perceives our superiority, and pays us much attention."

—(Sketches from Boz)

Charles Dickens displayed a ready touch for observationally scouring the behavior of this mysterious gentleman for evidence with which to classify him—even going so far as to put out the hypothesis that the man was a participant observer. In this chapter, the first of two on observational methods, our interest is focused on situations in which the observer has no control over the behavior or sign in question, and plays an unobserved, passive, and nonintrusive role in the research situation. The next chapter details studies in which the observer has played an active role in structuring the

113

situation, but in which he is still unobserved by the actors. Since we have limited our discussion to measures with low risks of reactivity, the visible "research-observer" approach and the participant-observation method have been mini-mized here.[1]

Visible Observers

The patently visible observer can produce changes in behavior that dimin-ish the validity of comparisons. Arsenian (1943) noted that the simple presence of an adult sitting near a door seemed to lend assurance to a group of nursery-school children. The opposite change was noted by Polansky and associates (1949) in studying the effect of the presence of observers among young boys at a summer camp. There the observers were a threat and became objects of active aggression. Not only is change produced which reduces the generalizability of findings, but if one were comparing children in two settings varying in the visibility of observers or the reaction to observers, internal validity would take a blow.

The effect of the observer may erode over time, as Deutsch (1949) has shown, and thereby produce a selective contaminant in observational data series. The defense against this is to permit the effect of the observer contami-nant to wear off, and start analysis with data subsequent to the time when the effect is negligible. This is similar to experimental controls for practice effect in learning experiments, and presumes that the effect will wear off quickly enough not to waste too much data. And that in turn is based on the researcher's ability to measure the independent effect of observation in the series.

Bales (1950) tested whether different arrangements of observers would selectively bias group behavior. Observers sat with the group, or behind a one-way screen with the group aware they were there, or behind the screen with the group unsure if they were there. He found no difference in group behavior under these conditions. All conditions were applied in a laboratory, however, and all the groups knew they were being tested. These factors might overpower the possibly weaker effects of the physical position of the observer.

No matter how well integrated an observer becomes, we feel he is still an element with potential to bias the production of the critical data substantially. The bias may be a selective one to jeopardize internal validity, or, perhaps more plausibly, it may cripple the ability of the social scientist to generalize his findings very far beyond his sample. A number of writers (cf. Bain, 1960; Gullahorn & Strauss, 1960; Gusfield, 1960; Wax, 1960) have argued for the participant-observation method as a device to circumvent some of the contaminations of studies employing an "outside" observer. It may do that, but there is still a high risk of contaminants surviving to invalidate comparisons.

Participant Observation

Riley (1963) has suggested that the participant-observation studies are subject to two classes of error—"control effect" and "biased-viewpoint effect." The control effect is present when the measurement process itself becomes an agent working for change: "the difficulty with control effect in participant observation, and in many other research designs, is that it is unsystematic" (p. 71). The biased-viewpoint effect includes what we have discussed under the label of intra-instrument processes. The instrument (the human observer) may selectively expose himself to the data, or selectively perceive them, and, worse yet, shift over time the calibration of his observation measures.

This has been suggested by Naroll and Naroll (1963), who speak of the anthropologist's tendency to be disposed to "exotic data." The observer is more likely to report on phenomena which are different from those of his own society or subculture than he is to report on phenomena common to both. When the participant observer spends an extended period of time in a foreign culture (a year among the Fulani or six months with a city gang), those elements of the culture which first seemed notable because they were alien may later acquire a more homey quality. His increased familiarity with the culture alters him as an instrument.

Riley (1963) suggests that the control effect may be reduced by the observer assuming an incognito role, even though ethical questions are raised, but,

> on the other hand, the covert observer may find complete immersion in the system, and subsequent likelihood of a biased viewpoint, more difficult to avoid. Limited to his specified role, he may be cut off from valuable channels of information, unable to solicit information not normally accessible to his role without arousing suspicions. (p. 72)

Associated with this class of observation is the use of the informant, who is a participant observer one selective screen away from the investigator. Back (1960) writes of the traits of the good informant (knowledgeability, physical exposure, effective exposure, perceptual abilities, availability of information, motivation) and points out some of the difficulties of receiving valid and appropriate data from informants.

Dalton (1964) gives an excellent pro-and-con analysis of participant observation in his commentary on the methods used in *Men Who Manage*. Dalton's pro list is longer than the con one, and he employs the intriguing terminology of "established circulator" and "peripheral formalist."

As a final note on participant observation, we cite Lang and Lang's (1960) report, in which participant observers became participants. Two scientific observers of audience behavior at a Billy Graham Crusade in New York made *their* "Decision for Christ" and left the fold of observers to walk down the aisle. This is in itself an interesting measure. What a testimony to the Reverend Mr. Graham's persuasive skills, when sociological observers are so swayed that they leave their posts!

Stephen Leacock said, "Let me hear the jokes of a nation and I will tell you what the people are like, how they are getting along, and what is going to happen to them" (quoted in Manago, 1962). This may be too haughty a claim for conclusions possible from one set of observational data, but we note below studies which produce impressive findings from the opportunistic use of observation of events over which the investigator has no control.

These simple observation studies have been organized into the following categories: exterior physical signs, expressive movement, physical location, language behavior (conversation sampling), and time duration. The breadth of these measures is notable, and they are "simple" only in that the investigator does not intervene in the production of the material.

EXTERIOR PHYSICAL SIGNS

Most of the exterior physical signs discussed are durable ones that have been inferred to be expressive of current or past behavior. A smaller number are portable and shorter-lived. The bullfighter's beard is a case in point. Conrad

(1958) reports that the bullfighter's beard is longer on the day of the fight than on any other day. There are supporting comments among matadors about this phenomenon, yet can one measure the torero's anxiety by noting the length of his beard? The physical task is rather difficult, but not impossible in this day of sophisticated instrumentation. As in all these uncontrolled measures, one must draw inferences about the criterion behavior. Maybe it wasn't the anxiety at all. Perhaps the bullfighter stands further away from the razor on the morning of the fight, or he may not have shaved that morning at all (like baseball pitchers and boxers). And then there is the possible intersubject contaminant that the more affluent matadors are likely to be shaved, while the less prosperous shave themselves.

A less questionable measure is tattoos. Burma (1959) reports on the observation of tattoos among some nine hundred inmates of three different institutions. The research measure was the proportion of inmates with tattoos: "significantly more delinquents than nondelinquents tattoo themselves." Of course, one could hardly reverse the findings and hold that tattooing can be employed as a single measure of delinquency. Returning to the bull ring for a moment, "There are many ordinary bullfighters, but ordinary people do not fight bulls" (Lea, 1949, p. 40).

More formal classification cues are tribal markings and scars. Doob (1961) reports on a walk he and an African companion took through a Nigerian market.

> I casually pointed to a dozen men, one after the other, who had facial scars. My African friend in all instances named a society; then he and I politely verified the claim by speaking to the person and asking him to tell us the name of his tribe. In eleven instances out of twelve, he was correct. Certainly, however, he may have been responding simultaneously to other cues in the person's appearance, such as his clothing or his skin color. (p. 83)

In a report whose authors choose to remain anonymous (Anonymoi, 1953–1960), it was discovered that there is a strong association between the methodological disposition of psychologists and the length of their hair. The authors observed the hair length of psychologists attending professional meetings and coded the meetings by the probable appeal to those of different methodological inclinations. Thus, in one example, the length of hair was compared between those who attended an experimental set of papers and those who attended a series on ego-identity formation. The results are clear-cut. The "tough-minded" psychologists have shorter-cut hair than the long-haired psychologists. Symptomatic interpretations, psychoanalytic inquiries as to what is cut about the clean-cut young man, are not the only possibilities. The casual ambiguity of the correlation was clarified when the "dehydration hypothesis" (i.e., that lack of insulation caused the hard-headedness) was rejected by the "bald-head control," i.e., examining the distribution of baldheaded persons (who by the dehydration hypothesis should be most hardheaded of all).

Clothes are an obvious indicator, and A. M. Rosenthal (1962), wrote of "the wide variance between private manners and public behavior" of the Japanese:

> Professor Enright [British lecturer in Japan] and just about every other foreigner who ever visited Japan have noted with varying degrees of astonishment that there is a direct relationship between the politeness of a Japanese and whether or not he is wearing shoes. (p. 20)

It is quite likely that this relationship reflects the selective distribution of shoes in the Japanese society more than any causal element, an example of a population restriction. The economically marginal members of the Japanese population should, one would think, be more overt in expressing hostility to foreign visitors than those who are economically stable—and possession of shoes is more probably linked to affluence than it is to xenophobia.

Shoe styles, not their presence, have been used as the unit of discrimination in the United States society where almost everybody does wear shoes. Gearing (1952), in a study of subculture awareness in south Chicago, observed shoe styles, finding features of the shoe to correspond with certain patterns of living. In general, the flashier shoe more often belonged to the more culture-bound individual. Similar concern with feet was shown by the OSS Assessment Staff (1948) when, because standard uniforms reduced the number of indicators, they paid special attention to shoes and socks as a prime indication "of taste and status."

Despite the general consensus on clothing as an indicator of status, little controlled work has been done on the subject. Flugel (1930) wrote a discursive book on clothing in general, and Webb (1957) reported on class differences in attitudes toward clothes and clothing stores. Another investigation shows many differences between clothing worn by independent and fraternity-affiliated college males. Within the fraternity groups, better grades are made by the more neatly dressed (Sechrest, 1965b).

Kane (1958, 1959, 1962) observed the clothing worn by outpatients to their interviews. He has considered pattern, color, texture, and amount of clothing, relating these characteristics to various moods, traits, and personality changes. In a more reactive study, Green and Knapp (1959) associated preferences for different types of tartans with need achievement; it would be of interest to see if this preference pattern were supported in clothing purchased or worn.

A southern chief of detectives has discussed using clothing clues as predictor variables. In a series of suggestions to police officers, he noted the importance of dress details. When Negroes are planning a mass jail-in, "The women will wear dungarees as they enter the meeting places" ("Civil Rights," 1965).

Jewelry and other ornamental objects can also be clues. Freud gave his inner circle of six, after World War I, rings matching his own. On another intellectual plane, observers have noted that in some societies one can find illiterates who buy only the top of a pen and then clip it to clothing as a suggestion of their writing prowess. One could observe the frequency of such purchases in local stores, or less arduously, examine sales records over time from the manufacturer, considering the ratio of tops to bottoms for different countries or regions. The observation method would have an advantage in that one could make coincidental observations on the appearance of those purchasing the tops alone, or isolate a sample for interviewing. The archival record of top and bottom shipments is infinitely more efficient, but more circumscribed in the content available for study.

As part of their study of the social status of legislators and their voting, MacRae and MacRae (1961) observed the houses lived in by legislators and rated them along the lines suggested by Warner (Warner, Meeker, & Eells, 1949). This house rating was part of the over-all social-class index produced for each legislator.

Observation of any type of possession can be employed as an index if the investigator knows that there is a clear relationship between possession (ownership) of the object and a second variable. Calluses, for example, can serve as an observable indicator of certain classes of activity. Different sports make selective demands on tissue, for example, and the calluses that result are reliable indicators of whether one is a squash player or a golfer. Some occupations may also be determined by similar physical clues.

With these measures used alone, validity is often tenuous. Phillips (1962) is unusual in giving multiple indicators of the changes in Miami resulting from the influx of a hundred thousand Cubans. Two years following the Castro revolution, he observed:

Bilingual street signs (No Jaywalking; Cruce por la Zona para Peatones)

"A visitor hears almost as much Spanish as English."

Signs in windows saying "Se Habla Espanol"

Stores with names like "Mi Botanica" and "Carniceria Latina"

Latin-American foods on restaurant menus

Supermarkets selling yucca, malanga, and platanos

The manufacture of a Cuban type of cigarette

Radio broadcasts in Spanish

Spanish-language editorials in the English-language newspapers

Services held in Spanish by forty Miami churches.

Perhaps Phillips was overstating his case, but the marshalling of so much, and so diverse, observational evidence is persuasive. For a prime source in such studies of the unique character of cities, and their changes, there is that eminent guide, the classified telephone directory. It can yield a wide range of broad content information on the economy, interests, and characteristics of a city and its people. Isolating the major U.S. cities, which ones have the highest numbers of palmists per thousand population?

EXPRESSIVE MOVEMENT

The more plastic variables of body movement historically have interested many observers. Charles Darwin's (1872) work on the expression of emotions continues to be the landmark commentary. His exposition of the measurement of frowning, the uncovering of teeth, erection of the hair, and the like remains provocative reading. The more recent studies on expressive movement and personality measurement are reviewed by Wolff and Precker (1951). Of particular interest in their chapter is the emphasis on consistency among different types of expressive movement. They review the relation between personality and the following measures: facial expression, literary style, artistic style, style of speech, gait, painting and drawing, and handwriting. Not all of these studies are nonreactive, since the central criterion for this is that the subject is not aware of being measured.

Examples of using expressive movement as a response to a particular stimulus—that is, stimulus-linked rather than subject-linked—are provided in the work of Maurice Krout (1933, 1937, 1951, 1954a, 1954b). Although this work was done in a laboratory setting, it was under facade conditions. That is, subjects were unaware of the true purpose of the research, considering the experiment a purely verbal task. There is a good possibility for application of Krout's (1954a) approach in less reactive settings. He elicited autistic gestures through verbal-conflict situations, and his analysis deals primarily with digital-manual responses. An example of his findings is the correlation between an attitude of fear and the gesture of placing hand to nose. Darwin (1872) mentioned pupil dilation as a possible fear indicator.

Kinesics as a subject of study is relevant here, although as yet large amounts of data are not available. Birdwhistell (1960, 1963) has defined kinesics as being concerned with the communicational aspects of learned, patterned, body-motion behavior. This system of nonverbal communication is felt to be inextricably linked with the verbal, and the aim of such study is to achieve a quantification of the former which can be related to the latter. Some "motion qualifiers" have been identified, such as intensity, range, and velocity. Ruesch and Kees (1956) have presented a combination text-picture treatment in their book, *Nonverbal Communication*. An example of the impressionistic style of observation is provided by Murphy and Murphy (1962), who reported on the differences in facial expressions between young and old Russians: "While faces of old people often seemed resigned, tired and sad, generally the children seemed lively, friendly, confident and full of vitality" (p. 12).

Something of the detail possible in such studies is shown in Wolff's (1948, 1951) work on hands. In the first study, Wolff observed the gestures of mental patients at meals and at work, concluding, "I found sufficient evidence that correlations exist (1) between emotional make-up and gesture, (2) between the degree of integration and gesture" (1948, p. 166). The second study was anthropometric, and Wolff compared features of the handprints of schizophrenics, mental defectives, and normals. The hands were divided into three major types: (a) elementary, simple and regressive; (b) motor, fleshy and bony; and (c) small and large. On the basis of an individual's hand type, measurements, nails, crease lines, and type of skin, she delineates the main characteristics of their personality, intelligence, vitality, and temperament.

Without necessarily endorsing her conclusions, we report the finding of a confused crease-line pattern peculiar to the extreme of mental deficiency. Other structural characteristics such as concave primary nails, "appeared to a greater or lesser degree in the hands of mental defectives . . . but were completely absent in the hands of the control cases" (Wolff, 1951, p. 105).

A journalistic account of the expressive behavior of hands has been given by Gould (1951, cited in Doig, 1962). Here is his description of Frank Costello's appearance before the Kefauver crime hearings:

> As he [Costello] sparred with Rudolph Halley, the committee's counsel, the movement of his fingers told their own emotional story. When the questions got rough, Costello crumpled a handkerchief in his hands. Or he rubbed his palms together. Or he interlaced his fingers. Or he grasped a half-filled glass of water. Or he beat a silent tattoo on the table top. Or he rolled a little ball of paper between his thumb and index finger. Or he stroked the side piece of his glasses lying on the table. His was video's first ballet of the hands. (p. 1)

It is of interest that conversations of male students with females have been found to be more frequently punctuated by quick, jerky, "nervous" gestures than are conversations between two males (Sechrest, 1965b).

Schubert (1959) has suggested that overt personal behavior could be used in the study of judicial behavior. In presenting a psychometric model of the Supreme Court, he suggests that the speech, grimaces, and gestures of the judges when hearing oral arguments and when opinions are being delivered are rich sources of data for students of the Court.

On the other side of the legal fence, witnesses in Hindu courts are reported to give indications of the truth of their statements by the movement of their toes (Krout, 1951). The eminent American legal scholar J. H. Wigmore (1935, 1937), in works on judicial proof and evidence, speaks of the importance of peripheral expressive movements as clues to the validity of testimony.

That these cues can vary across societies is demonstrated by Sechrest and Flores (1971). They showed that "leg jiggling" is more frequent among Filipino than American males, and held that jiggling is a "nervous" behavior. As evidence of this, they found jiggling more frequent in coffee lounges than in cocktail lounges.

The superstitious behavior of baseball players is a possible area of study. Knocking dust off cleats, amount of preliminary bat swinging, tossing dust into the air, going to the resin bag, and wiping hands on shirts may be interpreted as expressive actions. One hypothesis is that the extent of such superstitious behavior is related to whether or not the player is in a slump or in the middle of a good streak. This study could be extended to other sports in which the central characters are relatively isolated and visible. It should be easier for golfers and basketball players, but more difficult for football players.

From a practical point of view, of course, coaches and scouts have long studied the overt behavior of opponents for clues to forthcoming actions. (It is known, for example, that most football teams are "right sided" and run a disproportionate number of plays to the right [Griffin, 1964].) Does the fullback indicate the direction of the play by which hand he puts on the ground? Does the linebacker rest on his heels if he is going to fall back on pass defense? Does the quarterback always look in the direction in which he is going to pass, or does he sometimes look the other way, knowing that the defense is focusing on his eyes?

A police officer reported eye movement as a "pickup" clue. A driver who repeatedly glances from side to side, then into the rearview mirror, then again from side to side may be abnormally cautious and perfectly blameless. But he may also be abnormally furtive and guilty of a crime. Another officer, in commenting on auto thefts, said, "We . . . look for clean cars with dirty license plates and dirty cars with clean plates," explaining that thieves frequently switch plates (Reddy, 1965).

In a validation study of self-reported levels of newspaper readership, eye movement was observed when people were reading newspapers in trains, buses, library reading rooms, and the street (Advertising Service Guild, 1949). A number of interesting eye movement and direction studies have been conducted in controlled laboratory settings. Discussion of them is contained in the following chapter on observational hardware.

PHYSICAL LOCATION

The physical position of animals has been a favored measure of laboratory scientists, as well as of those in the field. Imanishi (1960), for example, described the social structure of Japanese macaques by reporting on their physical grouping patterns. The dominant macaques sit in the center of a series of concentric rings.

For people, there are the familiar newspaper accounts of who stood next to whom in Red Square reviewing the May Day parade. The proximity of a politician to the leader is a direct clue of his status in the power hierarchy. His physical position is interpreted as symptomatic of other behavior which gave him the status position befitting someone four men away from the Premier, and descriptive of that current status position. In this more casual journalistic report of observations, one often finds time-series analysis: Mr. B. has been demoted to the end of the dais, and Mr. L. has moved up close to the middle.

The clustering of Negroes and whites was used by Campbell, Kruskal, and Wallace (1966) in their study of seating aggregation as an index of attitude. Where seating in a classroom is voluntary, the degree to which the Negroes and whites present sit by themselves versus mixing randomly may be taken as a presumptive index of the degree to which acquaintance, friendship, and preference are strongly colored by race, as opposed to being distributed without regard to racial considerations. Classes in four schools were studied, and significant aggregation by race was found, varying in degree between schools. Aggregation by age, sex, and race has also been reported for elevated trains and lunch counters (Sechrest, 1965b).

Feshbach and Feshbach (1963) report on another type of clustering. At a Halloween party, they induced fear in a group of boys, aged nine to twelve, by telling them ghost stories. The boys were then called out of the room and were administered questionnaires. The induction of the fear state was natural, but their dependent-variable measures were potentially reactive. What is of interest to us is a parenthetical statement made by the authors. After describing the ghost-story-telling situation, the Feshbachs offer evidence for the successful induction of fear: "Although the diameter of the circle was about eleven feet at the beginning of the story telling, by the time the last ghost story was completed, it had been spontaneously reduced to approximately three feet" (p. 499).

Gratiot-Alphandery (1951a, 1951b) and Herbinière-Lebert (1951) have both made observations of children's seating during informal film showings. How children from different age groups clustered was a measure used in work on developmental changes.

Sommer (1961) employed the position of chairs in a descriptive way, looking at "the distance for comfortable conversation." Normal subjects were used, but observations were made after the subjects had been on a tour of a large mental hospital. Distances among chairs in a lounge were systematically varied, and the people were brought into the lounge after the tour. They entered by pairs, and each pair was asked to go to a designated area and sit down. A simple record was made of the chairs selected.

The issue here is what one generalizes to. Just as the Feshbachs' subjects drew together during the narration of ghost stories, it would not be unrealistic to expect that normal adults coming from a tour of a mental hospital might also draw closer together than would be the case if they had not been on the tour. Their seating distance before the tour would be an interesting control. Do they huddle more, anticipating worse than will be seen, or less?

Sommer (1959, 1960, 1962) has conducted other studies of social distance and positioning, and in the 1959 study mentions a "waltz technique" to measure psychological distance. He learned that as he approached people, they would back away; when he moved backward during a conversation, the other person moved forward. The physical distance between two conversationalists also varies systematically by the nationality of the talkers, and there are substantial differences in distance between two Englishmen talking together and two Frenchmen in conversation. In a cross-cultural study, this would be a response-set characteristic to be accounted for.

Sommer's work inspired a study in Germany (Kaminski & Osterkamp, 1962), but unfortunately it is not a replication of Sommer's design. A paper-and-pencil test was substituted for the actual physical behavior, and 48 students were tested in three mock situations: classroom, U-shaped table, and park benches. Sechrest, Flores, and Arellano (1965) studied social distance in a Filipino sample and found considerably greater distance in opposite-sex pairs as compared with same-sex pairs. Other tests include measuring the distance subjects placed photographs away from themselves (Beloff & Beloff, 1961; Smith, 1958) and Werner and Wapner's (1953) research on measuring the amount of distance walked under conditions of danger.

Sommer (1960) noted how the physical location of group members influenced interactions. Most communication took place among neighbors, but the corner was the locus of most interaction. Whyte (1956) observed that air conditioners were dispersed in a nonrandom way in a Chicago suburban community, and Howells and Becker (1962) demonstrated that those who sat facing several others during a discussion received more leadership nominations than did those who sat side by side.

Leipold's (1963) dissertation carried the work further, paying special attention to the individual response-set variable of "personal space," the physical distance an organism customarily places between itself and other organisms. Leipold gathered personality-classification data on a group of 90 psychology students, divided them into two groups on the basis of introversion-extraversion, and administered stress, praise, or neutral conditions to a third of each group. He evaluated the effect of the conditions, and the tie to introversion-extraversion, by noting which of several available seats were taken by the subjects when they came in for a subsequent interview. The seats varied in the distance from the investigator. In one of his findings, he reports that introverted and high-anxious students, defined by questionnaire responses, kept a greater physical distance from the investigator (choosing a farther chair) then did extraverted and low-anxious students. Stress conditions also resulted in greater distance.

That random assignment doesn't always work is shown in Grusky's (1959) work on organizational goals and informal leaders—research conducted in an experimental prison camp. He learned that informal leaders, despite a policy of random bed assignments, were more likely to attain the bottom bunk. Grusky also considered such archival measures as number of escapes, general transfers, and transfers for poor adjustment. On all of these measures, leaders differed significantly from nonleaders. It must be remembered that this was an experimental prison camp, and the artificiality of the research situation presents the risk that a "Hawthorne effect" may be present. What would be valuable would be another study of regular prison behavior to see if these findings hold in a nonexperimental setting.

On still another plane, the august chambers of the United Nations in New York, Alger (1965) observed representatives at the General Assembly. Sitting with a press card in the gallery, he recorded 3,322 interactions among representatives at sessions of the Administrative and Budgetary Committee. Each interaction was coded for location, initiator, presence or exchange of documents, apparent humor, duration, and so on. His interest was in defining the clusters of nations who typically interacted in the committee.

Using the same approach, it might be possible to get partial evidence on which nations are perceived as critical and uncertain during debate on a proposed piece of U.N. action. Could one define the marginal, "swing" countries by noting which ones were visited by both Western and Bloc countries during the course of the debate? Weak evidence, to be sure, for there is the heavy problem of spatial restriction. One can only observe in public places, and even expanding the investigation to lobbies, lounges, and other public meeting areas may exclude the locus of the truly critical interactions. This bias might be selective, for if an issue suddenly appeared without warning, the public areas might be a more solid sampling base than they would be for issues which had long been anticipated and which could be lobbied in private. That the outside observer must have a broad understanding of the phenomenon and parties he is observing is indicated in Alger's study. He comments on the high level of interaction with the Irish delegate, which was not a reflection of the political power of Ireland, but instead the result of the easy affability of the man. This affability might truly influence the power position of his country, and hence be an important datum in that sense, but it is more likely to confound comparisons if it is used as evidence on a nation.

Barch, Trumbo, and Nangle (1957) used the behavior of automobiles in their observational study of conformity to legal requirements. We are not sure if this is more properly coded under "expressive movement," but the "physical position" category seems more appropriate. They were interested in the degree to which turn-signalling was related to the turn-signalling behavior of a preceding car. For four weeks, they recorded this information:

1. Presence or absence of a turn signal

2. Direction of turn

3. Presence of another motor vehicle 100 feet or less behind the turning motor vehicle when it begins to turn

4. Sex of drivers.

Observers stood near the side of the road and were not easily visible to the motorists. There was the interesting finding that conforming behavior, as defined by signalling or not, varied with the direction of the turn. Moreover, a sex difference was noted. There was a strong positive correlation if model and follower were females, and also a high correlation if left turns were signalled. But on right turns, the correlation was low and positive. Why there is a high correlation for left turns and low one for right turns is equivocal. The data, like so many simple observational data, don't offer the "why," but simply establish a relationship.

Several of the above findings have been verified and perturbingly elaborated by a finding that signalling is more erratic in bad weather and by drivers of expensive autos (Sechrest, 1965b). Blomgren, Scheuneman, and Wilkins (1963) also used turn signals as a dependent variable in a before-after study of the effect of a signalling safety poster. Exposure to the sign increased signalling about 6%.

OBSERVATION OF LANGUAGE BEHAVIOR: CONVERSATION SAMPLING

Language is a hoary subject for observation, with everything from phonemes to profanity legitimate game. Our interest here is more circumscribed and centers on language samples collected unobtrusively. This means excluding much useful research, Mahl's (1956) study of patients' speech in psychotherapy sessions, for example. The incidence of stuttering, slips of the tongue, and the like is important data, but because the data were collected in a therapist-patient setting, they do not apply here.

We would be curious to read the findings of a nonreactive study which investigated slips of the typewriter as a measure. The employment of these regularly appearing slips somehow evaded Freud (1920) in his major work on the topic. Sechrest (1965b) has demonstrated a higher number of gross errors (skipping lines, poor spacing, and repositioning of hands) when subjects are copying erotic passages than when copying passages from a mineralogy text. Winick (1962) studied some sixty thousand messages written by passers-by on a typewriter outside a New York store, but his analysis centered on coding of content. The data are also amenable to study of spelling errors, spacing, and the like.

We have taken one area of language research, conversational sampling, and traced it historically to illustrate the methodological issues.

Dittman and Wynne (1961) demonstrate a modern approach. They coded verbal behavior, with the source of language a radio program—the NBC show "Conversation." To study emotional expression, the authors examined "linguistic" phenomena (junctures, stress, pitch) and "paralinguistic" phenomena (voice set, voice quality, and vocalizations of three types). A problem comes from the possibility that a man's awareness of participation in a radio show—particularly the effects of nervousness on speech—could lead to conditions that bias the production of the critical responses.

Kramer (1963) has reviewed the literature on the nonverbal characteristics of speech, concentrating on personal characteristics and emotional correlates. In a later article (1964), he reports a methodological study of techniques to eliminate verbal cues. The three major methods are: a constant ambiguous set of words for various emotional expressions; filtering out the frequencies which permit word recognition; speech in a language unknown to the listener.

More satisfactory is language analysis which draws its samples from speech of subjects unaware of observation. One of the earliest mentions of conversation as a source of psychological data subject to quantification was made by Tarde (1901). Although he performed no studies on conversation himself, Tarde made several suggestions for potential areas of study, such as variation in speed of talking among cultures and categorization of topics by social-class differences.

For the first reported study of conversations, we can look at H. T. Moore's (1922) work on sex differences in conversation—a canny and delightful research that triggered a whole series of hidden-observer language studies.

Moore sought to prove that there was a definite mental differentiation between the sexes, regardless of what previous studies (to 1922) had shown. To test this, he argued for a content analysis of "easy conversation." Especially at the day's end, he held, conversation should provide significant clues to personal interest.

So Moore slowly walked up Broadway from 33rd Street to 55th Street about 7:30 every night for several weeks. He jotted down every bit of audible conversation and eventually collected 174 fragments. Each was coded by the sex of the speaker and by whether the company was mixed or of the same sex. It is not necessary to cite his findings at length, but one should not pass attention: in male to male conversations Moore found 8% in the category "persons of opposite sex"; for female to female conversations, this topic occupied 44% of the language specimens.

Some of the limitations of conversation sampling are obvious. Moore could record only intelligible audible conversation. Speech that is muttered, mumbled, or whispered may contain significantly different content than loud and clear speech. The representative character of the speech samples is further questioned by the representativeness of the speakers. Walkers on Broadway are probably not even a good sample of Manhattan. In short, there is a strong risk of sampling rigidity in both the talkers and the talk.

We can look, chronologically, at the conversation-sampling studies that followed Moore's and note the efforts of other investigators to reduce error due to data-collecting procedure.

Landis and Burtt (1924) published the first study stimulated by Moore's classic. They were sensitive to positional sampling biases and improved upon Moore's procedure by sampling a wider variety of places and situations. With an experimenter who "wore rubber heels and cultivated an unobtrusive manner," they gathered samples of conversation, adding an estimate of the social status of the speaker. The broadened locations included streetcars, campuses, railroad stations, athletic events, parties, department stores, theater and hotel lobbies, restaurants, barber shops, churches, and streets in both commercial and residential areas. After their analysis, Landis and Burtt concluded that the source of the collection was only a minor factor. Landis (1927) broadened the sampling base even further, reporting in an article entitled "National Differences in Conversation." He sampled conversations in Oxford and Regent streets in London and compared these results to the earlier Landis and Burtt (1924) findings from Columbus, Ohio.

The monitoring of telephone conversations was the device by which French, Carter, and Koenig (1930) measured the degree to which the most common words contributed to the total word usage of conversations. This study of the repetitiousness of language was later used as a control for the repetitiousness of speech of schizophrenics and college students (Fairbanks, 1944).

Stoke and West (1931) tried to limit the number of variables in their conversation-sampling study and restricted the sample to undergraduate college students, sampling from random bull sessions held at night in residence halls. The participant observers were 36 college students who worked with a checklist of probable topics and the data and number of people in the conversation. A limitation of this "observe—withdraw—record" approach is that the observer cannot hope to record adequately the duration of responses. The approach is also vulnerable to the criticism that the observers' reports are subject to bias, beyond the initial selective perception one, because of the gap between event and notation.

Moving away from the campus, and more to the Moore approach, Sleeper (cited in Murphy & Murphy, 1931) sampled conversations in the upper level of Grand Central Terminal in New York, during the rush hour from 5:00 P.M. to 6:30 P.M. Sleeper's procedure reflected the dross-rate problems of such data, as he added a recording variant by excluding all "environmentally stimulated" conversation.

Mabie (1931) and McCarthy (1929) employed free-play periods to sample the conversation of children. The visibility of the recorder is a great problem here, and the studies represent reactive methodology. It may be that, as Mabie claims, the children's awareness of her presence had no effect on their conversation. This is uncertain, and our inclination would be to consider that her presence, notebook in hand, would introduce a strong risk of biasing the character of the overheard statements. When asked by the children what she was doing, Mabie told them that she was writing down what the children liked to do during play periods. That response itself could predispose the children to verbalize evaluative comments more frequently.

Surreptitious observation is the only class which fits into what we would call nonreactive testing. Take the studied surreptitiousness of Henle and Hubble (1938). Students were again the subjects, and

> The investigators took special precautions to keep subjects ignorant of the fact that their remarks were being recorded. To this end, they concealed themselves under beds in students' rooms where tea parties were being held, eavesdropped in dormitory smoking rooms and washrooms, and listened to telephone conversations. (p. 230)

Without extending their explanation, Henle and Hubble report that "unwitting subjects were pursued in the streets, in department stores, and in the home."

Escaping from under the bed, Carlson, Cook, and Stromberg (1936) studied sex differences in conversation by monitoring lobby conversations at the intermissions of thirteen regular concerts of the Minneapolis Symphony and at six University of Minnesota concerts. The self-selection of subjects may be a serious risk to external validity (Who goes to Minneapolis Symphony concerts and who doesn't?), but the whispering problem is not so great in a research setting like a crowded theater, where a premium is placed on loudness.

The size of the group is a clear influence on the degree to which the experimenter must mask himself. For observing two-person communication, it may well be necessary to hide under a bed. In a large public gathering, the problem of visibility is solved; the individual providing the conversation sample expects to find unfamiliar people close to him, and the experimenter need not hide. Only the recording of the language need be hidden. But it is not as simple as that. Even though the presence of the observer may cause no surprise, the same situation which permits acceptance of the stranger may also have worked to inhibit a class or classes of verbal behavior. For some experiments, this may be unimportant—those in which the difference between public and private utterances is negligible. For other experiments, it may be substantial. This is an empirical question for each experimenter to solve. It must be accepted as one of the possible content limitations of conversational sampling.

Watson, Breed, and Posman (1948) displayed their concern about the representativeness of college students by deliberately excluding them from their sample of New York talkers. No campus locations were used, and an attempt was made to eliminate "anyone distinguishable as a college student." Working at all times of day and night, they sampled uptown, midtown, and downtown Manhattan, including the following locales: business, amusement, and residential streets and parks; subways, buses, ferries, taxis, and railroad stations; lobbies of movie houses and hotels; stores, restaurants, bars, night clubs. Each observer recorded verbatim what he had heard as soon as possible after hearing it. The sampling of respondents was resolved as well by Watson, Breed, and Posman as it has been by anyone.

Contrast this with the participant-observation type of approach suggested by Perrine and Wessman (1954). The investigator posed as a stranger to the state, initiated casual conversation with subjects, and then directed conversation to political issues by commenting on recent newspaper headlines and the like. The conversation was recorded as soon as possible after leaving the subject, along with sex, race, location, and estimated age and socioeconomic class. The enormous methodological issue in this type of conversation recording is the 60 to 70% rate of refusal. If nothing else, the eavesdropping approach reduces the problem of self-selection of the sample—at least that bias attributable to willingness to participate in a survey. Not everyone will chip into a conversation with some stranger who wants to talk about state politics. To use such data as the basis of inferring the state of public opinion is dubious.

Doob (1961) writes of a girl in an African market who "was carefully shadowed in the interest of scholarly research." In an approach described by Doob as "unsystematic eavesdropping," he notes:

> She began talking, and listening, before she entered the market's gate. Within a period of ten minutes—the duration of the research—she spoke with more than twenty people: some she greeted perfunctorily, others she talked to for a few moments concerning relatives and friends. No political or cosmic thoughts were aired. (p. 144)

Of interest is his point on a possible ethnocentric bias among foreign observers in Africa:

> Whereas people in the West . . . are likely to keep themselves occupied and to avoid long periods of complete solitude or, in contact with others, of silence, it may be that many Africans are perfectly content to be unoccupied except by their own feelings and thoughts and sense of well being. (p. 144)

All the studies of conversation reported here have relied on a content analysis of the conversational samples gathered. The essential problems have been the representativeness of the sample collected. The unobserved observer (secreted under a bed or among a crowd), must be sensitive to the limitations of self-selection of subjects, a problem of external validity, and the limitations of the probable partial character of public-conversation samples. Any public conversation may be constrained because of the "danger" of being overheard. Many of the inaudible comments in public are likely to be drawn from a different population of topics than those loudly registered. Moreover, as we noted earlier, the method requires a careful selection of both place- and time-sampling units to increase representativeness, and these controls will not be the same over different geographic locales. Sampling bus conversations in Los Angeles and in Chicago yields a population of very different subjects. Moreover, these data are typically loosely packed, and it takes a substantial investment in time and labor to produce a large enough residual pool of relevant data. For all these limitations, however, there are research problems for which private commentary is not a significant worry, for which the adroit selection of locales and times can circumvent selective population characteristics, and for which the issue is of sufficient currency in the public mind to reduce the dross rate. For these situations, conversational sampling is a sensitive and faithful source of information.

TIME DURATION

The amount of attention paid by a person to an object has long been the source of inferences on interest. For research on infrahuman species, notoriously incompetent at filling out interest questionnaires, visual fixation has been a popular research variable, as in the recent work of Berkson and Fitz-Gerald (1963) on the effect of introducing novel stimuli into the visual world of infant chimps. With humans who can fill out questionnaires, time-duration measures have been less popular, but are not uncommon. Frequently, a duration variable is imbedded in a body of other measures. H. T. Moore (1917) measured anger, fear, and sex interests by giving a subject multiplication tasks and then exposing him to distraction of different types. The time taken to complete the tasks was the measure of interest: the longer the time, the greater the interest in the distracting content.

In a study of museum visitors, Melton (1935) hypothesized a positive relationship between the degree of interest shown by a visitor in the exhibits and the number and quality of the permanent educational results of the museum visit. Melton was very careful to study response-set biases and situational cues which would contaminate his measure of the duration of observed time spent in viewing an exhibit. He demonstrated the "right-turn" bias, and experimented with changing the number of exits and installing directional arrows—all elements which significantly affected the length of a visit.

In one finding, for example, he reports that the closer an exhibit is to an exit, the less time will be spent at it. He posits an "exit gradient." Going further, he talks of the number of paintings in a gallery, the proportion of applied or fine arts in the room, and comes up with findings on "museum satiation." As the number of paintings in a gallery increases, the average total time in the gallery also increases, the total number of paintings visited increases, *and* the time per painting visited does not decrease but increases. Melton's attention to these cues provides a model seldom followed in observational research.

Washburne (1928) reported on an experiment conducted in the Russian school system which conceivably could have used time for a measure. Each child in the school was given his own garden plot, and at the same time had joint responsibility for a common garden tended by all the children. It is reported that records were kept to show the relative amount of interest that each child had in the two types of work. Although no mention is made of the measure used to determine amount of interest, time might be an appropriate one. Because it can be assumed that for equal care a greater amount of time would have to be spent on the individual garden, adjustments would have to be made in comparing the times for the two gardens.

A number of theoretical variables may be linked to time duration and time perception. Cortes (cited in McClelland, 1961, p. 327) has shown that a significantly larger number of high-need achievers have watches that are fast than do low-need achievers. Do the high achievers also perceive time duration differentially?

The lack of general emphasis on time-duration methods is partly due to difficulty of measurement. For accurate observation, the hurly-burly conditions of a natural setting are damaging; the laboratory control over instrumentation is almost necessary if precise observations of small time units are to be reached.

Sometimes this can be circumvented by a measure in which time is scaled in grosser units than microseconds. Jacques (1956) defined "responsibility" by measuring how long a worker is allowed to commit the resources of his task without direct supervision. Observation yields "a time span of responsibility" and a descriptive measure of the worker. For a duration measure like this, it would be foolish to calibrate the measurement in seconds. Many researchers demand ultrafine discrimination of time, and for them, natural observation is an awkward method. But where the unit is broader, observation in the natural setting becomes both feasible and desirable. Sometimes it is enough to say, "Professor X's interest in cutaneous sensation extended over a career of 38 years."

TIME SAMPLING AND OBSERVATION

For the permanent physical clues of observation—the scars, tattoos, and houses owned—the timing of when an observation is made may be relatively unimportant. It may be possible to conjure up conditions in which a tattoo may be so placed that it is differentially visible at various points in a day (with or without jacket, for example), but for the most part, the exterior signs are quite invulnerable to time-linked variance.

Many of the other simple observation materials—expressive movement, physical location, and language—are, however, subject to the objection that the critical behavior is variable over a day or some longer time period. The risk, or course, is that the timing of the data collection may be such that a selective population periodically appears before the observer, while another population, equally periodically, engages in the same behavior, but comes along only when the observer is absent. Similarly, the individual's behavior may shift as the hours or days of the week change. The best defense against this source of invalidity is to sample time units randomly.

Working in an industrial setting, Shepard and Blake (1962) observed employees and judged whether they were working or not. By a time-sampling design, they found a strong decline in percentage of workers working between 10:30 and 11:00—the time of a daily supervisors' meeting which drew them away from direct control over employees.

> Hence, the composition of supervisors' meetings was changed so as to ensure
> continuous supervision in the shop . . . thus the managers are correct in their
> . . . conclusion that more consistent control and direction are needed to
> correct for their tendency to be irresponsible. (pp. 88-89)

The technique has been extensively used in nursery settings, where there is a particular need for it because of the greater periodicity of behavior of infants and young children. Arrington (1943) has pointed out many of the factors which must be considered in assessing the results of time sampling recorded by the observer. The duration of the individual time sample must be chosen in accordance with behavior to be observed. Degree of sophistication, familiarity with the observer, previous experience in being observed, type of situation, and number of individuals in the situation are also thought to be factors contributing to "observation consciousness."

One of the important time-sampling studies of observation in a nursery setting was conducted by Thomas (1929). In recording the activities of the children, Thomas made use of a mapped floor plan and plotted movement against the plan. Olson (1929) used similar procedures, but concentrated on oral habits rather than movement patterns.

Barker and Wright (1951, 1954) have adopted an opposite strategy to time sampling. They sought to avoid the problem of selected behavior over time by a saturation method. Rather than sample behavior, they censused it. In their 1951 study, observations were made of one child for an entire day, with minute-by-minute notations. Eight observers were used in turn, each being wholly familiar with the child. For any child under ten, the authors feel the effects of observation are negligible. This may be subject to doubt, however, particularly in view of recorded statements detailing interaction between the observer and the child.

This strategy does solve a problem, but it provides other ones. It is practical for only relatively short periods of time (Imagine following a boy for a year!), and the method is predisposed to measurement of individuals, not groups. This latter point may be important for the probability of reactive effects creeping in, for, as we noted above, the size of the group may be an important factor in the degree of observation consciousness. A person tailing you about all day is quite different from one next to you in a theater lobby.

Yet these limitations are no more punishing than the limitations of other approaches, and the subtlety of links between behaviors can hardly be better described.[2] Either way, sampling or censusing, a measure of control is added over a usually uncontrolled variable.

OVER-ALL COMMENTS ON
SIMPLE OBSERVATION

The emphasis of this chapter has been on research in which the observer is unobserved, and in settings where the investigator has had no part in structuring the situation. The secretive nature of the observer, whether hidden in a crowd or miles away before a television screen, protects the research from some of the reactive validity threats. The subject is not aware of being tested, there is thereby no concomitant role-playing associated with awareness, the measurement does not work as an agent of change, and the interviewer (observer) effects are not an issue.

Moreover, there is the great gain that comes from getting the data at first hand. In studies of archival records and in the examination of trace and erosion evidence, there is always the uncertainty that others who came between the data and the investigator, processing or pawing it, left their own indistinguishable marks.

The first-hand collection of the data, usually of a contemporaneous event, also allows the gathering of other information to reduce alternative hypotheses. One may note characteristics of the subjects which permit a testing of rival hypotheses about the selective composition of the sample. To be sure, these are mostly limited to visual cues, but they can be extremely helpful. Similarly, the ability to observe the subjects in the act permits one to designate the individual actors, either for follow-up observation, or for study with other instruments like the questionnaire or interview. Such follow-up of individuals is difficult or impossible with archival and trace measures.

It would be difficult to overestimate the value of this potential for follow-up. One of the singular gains of simple observation is that it is a procedure which allows opportunistic sampling of important phenomena. Because it is often opportunistic, there is the attendant risk that the population under observation is an atypical group, one unworthy to produce generalizations. The follow-up studies may protect against this risk, as can adroit use of locational and time sampling.

Against this impressive list of gains must be balanced some possible sources of loss. Prime among these is the danger that the data-gathering instrument, the human observer, will be variable over the course of his observations. He may become less conscientious as boredom sets in, or he may become more attentive as he learns the task and becomes involved with it. If there are any ambiguities about how the behavior is to be coded, the effect of time may be to reduce the variation of coding (increase intra-observer reliability) as he works out operating definitions of which behaviors go with which codes. All of these can work to produce spurious differences in comparisons.

Errors of the observer, however, are not random, but show systematic biases that can be predicted, and hence corrected for, from the observer's expectations of the experimental or field situation. Campbell (1959) has inventoried twenty-one systematic sources of error that apply to the human observer.

That this may apply to the principal investigator, as well as his aides, has been demonstrated by Rosenthal's (1963) "On the Social Psychology of the Psychological Experiment." The implication of these studies is the demand for a greater emphasis on the necessity for saturated training of observers, hopefully under a "blind" condition in which they do not know what a "good" result or behavior will be.

The one other significant issue under the label of reactive threats comes from response sets on those observed. To a large measure, these are knowable— either through application of research conducted in other settings, or through direct observation of behavior under different conditions. Hopefully, there will be enough variation in the settings available for sampling to examine whether any systematic response sets are at work, and whether these can be isolated from other possible sources of variance. This is awkward when one is not actively manipulating the environment, and becomes one of the strong arguments for the unobserved observer to alter the research environment surreptitiously and systematically in an undetectable way.

The populations available for observation fluctuate according to both time and location. Thus, some caution should be employed in generalizing from research which gathered observations at one time in one place. If generalizations about the subject matter of conversations are to all people, and content varies by age, then the "place" should be considered as a sampling universe including varying locations which are likely to draw on different populations. When the concern is generalized to more limited settings, say, a study of the effect of different treatment conditions in prisons, then the place sample should be more than one prison for each condition hypothesized to have an effect.

It is not always possible to draw elaborate locational samples, but that should not deter observational research. If the setting is circumscribed by practical conditions, a proper defense is to employ time-sampling methods. Limited to a population of "tour" visitors to a mental hospital, one must bear the cross of a self-selected population unlikely to be representative of much. Imposing a time-sampling design, observing different groups who come on different days or in different months, for example, would markedly improve the solidity of a shaky base.

Both time and locational sampling should be employed if possible, for empirical research and introspection suggest that population variation is a substantial issue in observation. An added gain is that the investigator can also vary his observers over the sampling units and randomly assign them to different times and locations, thus adding a badly needed control. Not all research possibilities afford this chance, but it is a goal to be reached for.

McCarroll and Haddon (1961) took care to ensure that location and time factors would not affect their study of the differences between fatally injured drivers in automobile accidents and noninvolved drivers. At each accident site, a team consisting of the authors, medical students, and from one to eight police stopped noninvolved cars proceeding in the same direction as the accident car on the same day of the week and at the same time of the day.

The same time- and locational-sampling strategy will also help to counteract some of the risks in selective content. The population varies over place and time, and the content of their behavior similarly varies. If one can broaden the sampling base, he can expand the character of material available for study. It is not possible to know all about college students if observations are limited to afternoons in the fall; when these observations fall on Saturday, worse yet.

But all the finesse of the skillful investigator will not solve some content limitations. Much of behavior is precluded from public display and is available only through unethical action, elaborate instrumentation, or some titanic combination of both. This is potentially a variable problem across cultures, as one notes members of certain societies willing to display classes of behavior that are hidden or taboo in others. Cross-cultural observational studies are thereby threatened not only by the ethnocentric attribution of meaning, but also by the lack of equivalence in observable behavior across societies. As one increases the number of societies, of course, the probability is greater that an incomplete set of observations of public behavior will be available over all.

Finally, being on the scene often means a necessary exposure to a large body of irrelevant information. Because one cannot often predict when a critical event will be produced, it is necessary to wait around, observe, and complain about the high dross rate of such a procedure. The payoff is often high, as in the case of one patient observer who knew critical signs and was immortalized in the song, "My Lover Was a Logger." The waitress sings,

> I can tell that you're a logger,
> And not just a common bum,
> 'Cause nobody but a logger
> Stirs his coffee with his thumb.

NOTES

1. More standard treatments of research methods may be consulted for extensive discussion of observational techniques with the observer visible. See Festinger and Katz (1953), Goode and Hatt (1952), Good and Scates (1954), Kerlinger (1964), Madge

(1965), Riley (1963), and Selltiz, Jahoda, Deutsch, and Cook (1959). These same works also contain material on analysis of documentary and secondary source materials.

2. Edmond de Goncourt (1937) wrote of the goal of the *Goncourt Journal:* "What we have tried to do, then, is to bring our contemporaries to life for posterity in a speaking likeness, by means of the vivid stenography of a conversation, the physiological spontaneity of a gesture, those little signs of emotion that reveal a personality, those *imponderabilia* that render the intensity of existence, and, last of all, a touch of that fever which is the mark of the heady life of Paris" (p. xi).

SIX

CONTRIVED OBSERVATION

Hidden Hardware and Control

———•◆•———

his chapter discusses the investigator's intervention into the observational setting. In simple observational studies, research is often handicapped by the weaknesses of the human observer, by the unavailability of certain content, and by a cluster of variables over which the investigator has no control. To reduce these threats, a number of workers have elected to vary the setting actively or to substitute hardware devices for human record-keeping observers. We avoid here examples of the "speak clearly into the microphone, please" approach. The emphasis is on those investigations in which the scientist's intervention is not detectable by the subject and the naturalness of the situation is not violated.

HARDWARE: AVOIDING HUMAN
INSTRUMENT ERROR

When the human observer is the recording agent, all the fallibilities of the organism operate to introduce extraneous variance into the data. People are low-fidelity observational instruments. We have already noted how recording and interpretation may be erratic over time, as the observer learns and responds to the research phenomena he observes.

The fluctuations of this instrument can be brought under some degree of control by random assignment of observers to locations and time units. Random assignment will not, however, create a capacity in the organism which is not there, nor eliminate response sets characteristic of all members of the society or subcultures from which the observers are drawn.

Osgood (1953) illustrates the capacity weakness of the human observer in his comments on studies of language behavior in the first four or five months of a human's life: "From the total splurge of sounds made by an actively vocal infant, only the small sample that happens to strike the observer is recorded at all" (p. 684).

Not all observable behavior is so complex or so rapid, but there is enough to cause the consideration of a substitute mechanism for the observer. It might not be so bad if there were a random loss of material when the observer's perceptual system got overloaded. Unhappily, the nature of the material noted and not noted is likely to be a function of both the individual's idiosyncrasies and the systematic response sets learned in a given society. Again speaking of speech studies of early childhood, Osgood comments,

> The inadequate recording methods employed in most of the early studies make the data of dubious validity. The typical procedure was merely to listen to the spontaneous vocalizations of an infant and write down what was heard. The selective factor of auditory perception—listeners "hear" most readily those sounds that correspond to the phonemes of their own language—was not considered. (p. 684)

These same biases are at work with the recording of any language system that is unfamiliar to the observer—whether it be the occult language of a child, or the unfamiliar tones of a foreign language. Webb (1961) has noted this in his study of orthographies in African languages. His analysis was based on written records of the languages, many of which had been produced by missionaries, explorers, and other foreign nationals who came to Africa and learned the indigenous speech. In transcribing the sounds of these languages for others, there were selective approximations of the true sound, influenced by the tonal pattern of the characters in the observer's native language. Thus,

German observers heard umlauts that evaded the British. There is some possibility of control over this particular bias, since for some of the languages there are written transcriptions of the same words by nationals of various countries; these can be matched against the known tonal characteristics of the European languages to correct for the selective hearing. When multinational observations are missing, the task is much more difficult, and one must make inferences about the effect of perceptual biases based on the sound characteristics of the observer's native language.

A major gain from hardware recording, of course, is the permanence of this complete record. It is not subject to selective decay and can provide the stuff of reliability checks. Further, the same content can be the base for new hypothesis-testing not considered at the time the data were collected. Or material that was originally viewed as dross may become prime ore. For example, Bryan employs taped interviews in his study of call girls. Among other things, these are coded for the frequency of telephone calls received during the period of the interview. Such information serves as a partial check on the girl's self-report of business activity (J. Bryan, 1965, personal communication).

Hardware, of varying degrees of flexibility, has been used throughout the history of scientific observation. To reduce the risk of forgetting, if nothing else, permanent records were made of observed behavior. They may have noted less than the total behavior, but they did serve to reduce reliance on human memory. Boring (1961) writes of Galton, "an indefatigable measurer."

> He used to carry a paper cross and a little needle point, arranged so that he could punch holes in the paper to keep count of whatever he was at that time observing. A hole at the head of the cross meant *greater,* on the arm *equal,* and on the bottom, *less.* (p. 154)

Galton also contributed to that voluntary, self-descriptive reactive measure, the questionnaire, whose overuse William James (1890) anticipated: "Messrs. Darwin and Galton have set the example of circulars of questions sent out by the hundreds to those supposed able to reply. The custom has spread, and it will be well for us in the next generation if such circulars be not ranked among the common pests of life" (p. 194).

Evolving from such simple recording methods was the constriction of communication developed for work in small-group research in laboratory settings. Artificially, the participants were (or are) required to limit all communications to written notes, which are then saved by the investigator to provide a full record of all communication among participants. This is a very low-cost device, much cheaper than tape recording, but its stilted quality suggests a very high risk price for a very low dollar cost.

Other aids to the observer are pieces of apparatus which allow him to record his observations more quickly or more thoroughly. Sometimes the gain comes from forcing the observer into using a series of varied codes, sometimes it is just the gain of having a more permanent record of his perceptions of the behavior under study. Steiner and Field (1960), for example, timed vocal contributions to a group discussion by means of a polygraph, and a popular supplementary device has been the Interaction Chronograph, a recent use of which is reported in Chapple (1962).

A big boom exists, and properly, for audio tape recorders. With the development of superior omnidirectional and highly directional microphones, many of the former mechanical limitations have been resolved. The tape becomes the first source of data, and it is often considered the initial input into a hardware system. Thus, Andrew (1963) took tapes of sound patterns from primates (including man) and fed them into a spectograph for more detailed analyses.

Similarly, Heusler, Ulett, and their associates (Callahan, Morris, Seifried, Ulett, & Heusler, 1960; Heusler, Ulett, & Blasques, 1959; Heusler, Ulett, & Callahan, 1960; Ulett, Heusler, & Callahan, 1961; Ulett, Heusler, Ives-Word, Word, & Quick, 1961) developed what they termed a noise-level index for hospital wards. Their substantive concern was measuring the effects on drugs on hospital patients, and they planted tape recorders to pick up ward noises. These sounds are meshed in an integrator which provides a numerical total of the activity. Originally, this noise level had been rated by judges; in later work, however, the authors used a direct index of noise level, thus reducing biases, among them the possible confounding due to a judge's recognition of a patient's voice.

A highly opportunistic use of audiotapes was demonstrated by Matarazzo and his associates (Matarazzo, Wiens, Saslow, Dunham, & Voas, 1964) in their study of speech duration. The National Aeronautics and Space Administration

(NASA) made available to these investigators the audiotapes of conversations between astronauts and ground communicators for two orbital flights. From these tapes and the published transcripts of the communications (NASA Manned Spacecraft Center, 1962a, 1962b), they coded the duration of each unit of speech by means of an Interaction Chronograph. These data provided a test of propositions developed in the experimental laboratories and previously reported (Matarazzo, 1962b; Matarazzo, Weitman, Saslow, & Wiens, 1963). In space, as in the laboratory, the length of a response is positively correlated with the length of a question. It could hardly be claimed that the astronauts were thinking of Matarazzo's hypotheses at the time they were steering their craft, and the astronaut findings supported the work of the laboratory. This highly imaginative research dipped into archives that were available, archives known not to suffer from intermediary distortions.

The fidelity and breadth of content of the audiotapes give them an edge over written records for archival analysis. Not only are they uncontaminated by other hands, but they contain more pertinent material physically unavailable on the written record. Matarazzo, for example, could not have conducted so accurate a study had he been limited to transcripts alone. Interested in duration of speech, where the natural unit is a second of time, he would have had to make estimates of duration from word counts, which are pockmarked with substantial individual response-set errors in rate of speech, different levels of noncontent interjections (ummm's), and the like.

There is a weighty mass of research material almost untouched by social scientists, although known and used by historians. It is found in the oral archives of the national radio and television networks, which have kept disc, film, and tape recordings of radio and television shows over the years. The recent advent of video tape recordings has provided another dimension to these archives.

Videotapes are being used in some experimental research to validate the results of paper-and-pencil tests. A student of the effectiveness of television commercials has run some preliminary checks on an advertising exposure test. He called friends and asked them to send their secretaries to his office on the pretext of picking up a package. After arriving, the secretary was asked to wait in a reception room which contained newspapers, magazines, and a turned-on television set. A hidden television camera monitored her behavior as she turned to the printed material, watched television, or just sat. She left, unsuspecting, and was subsequently interviewed by standard questionnaire methods to determine her exposure to television commercials and magazines and newspapers. This is a more advanced variation of the obvious one-way mirror setting and provides a medium for a good check on observation and self-report data.

For some reason, still photography has never had much of a vogue as research hardware. Boring (1953/1963) mentions that "Voliva supported his theory of the flat earth by a photograph of twelve miles of the shore line of Lake Winnebago: you could see, he argued, that the shore is horizontal and bowed."[1] Both still and movie films have been used in the study of eye behavior—direction, duration of looking, pupil dilation, and the like.

The physical *location* of eyes was used by Politz (1959) in a study of commercial exposure of advertising posters placed on the outside of buses. Politz's equipment was movie cameras placed in buses and automatically activated in a series of short bursts spread throughout a day. The camera was faced outward, over the poster under study, and, in a switch on the Bunker Hill advice, a person whose two eyes could be seen in the developed film was classified as "in" the advertising audience. This design, which used a random sample of both locations and time, is exemplary for its control of a large number of extraneous variables that could jeopardize external validity. The visibility of the camera raises a question. It occupied a bus seat, and there is the probability that it attracted some attention. That is, the eyes counted as looking at the poster were looking at the camera instead. This should result in an overestimate of the size of the bus-poster advertising audience. If one could assume that the novelty of the camera would wear off over time, one could test the hypothesis by making a longitudinal analysis of the material. If the test materials were controlled for novelty and extinction themselves, the estimated audience level should decline over the time period if a significant number of people were viewing the camera and not the poster.

Walters, Bowen, and Parke (1963, cited in Bandura & Walters, 1963) recorded the eye movements of male undergraduates viewing a series of pictures of nude or almost nude males and females. The men were told that a moving spot of light on the film indicated the eye movements of a previous subject. For about half the subjects, the light roved over the bodies portrayed in the film, while with the other half, the light centered on the background of the pictures. The eye movement of the subjects was influenced, and

> Subjects who had been exposed to a supposedly sexually uninhibited model spent a significantly longer time looking at the nude and semi-nude bodies, and significantly less time looking at the background of the pictures. (Walters et al., 1963, cited in Bandura & Walters, 1963, p. 77)

Another investigation showed that the presence of a female inhibited the interest of male students in "sexy" magazines. The magazines were avoided with a woman present, but upon her leaving, they were quickly retrieved (Sechrest, 1965b).

Zamansky (1956, 1958) used "time looking" at different types of photos in his studies of homosexuality and paranoid delusions. Exline (1963, 1964) and Exline and Winters (1964) worked behind one-way mirrors to make controlled observations of mutual glances, time spent looking at someone while speaking to him, time spent looking when being spoken to, and the like.

Then, of course, there are the apparatus studies of pupil dilation. Gump (1962) reports that Chinese jade dealers were sensitive to this variable and determined a potential buyer's interest in various stones by observing the dilation of his pupils as pieces were shown (astute buyers countered this by wearing dark glasses).

Hess and Polt (1960) measured pupil dilation on 16-millimeter film and related it to stimulus materials. The stimulus objects were a series of pictures— a baby, a mother holding a child, a partially nude woman, a partially nude man, and a landscape. The six pictures elicited clear-cut differences in pupil size, and sex differences were present.

Commercial applications of this method have been based on work under the direction of Hess. See Foote (1962), "In the Eye of the Beholder" (1964), Krugman (1964), and West (1962).

The pupil-dilation studies have all been conducted in potentially reactive settings. Whether or not such a measure could be employed without the subject's awareness is questionable. There are technical difficulties with laboratory apparatus as is, and resolving field-use problems might be too much to expect.

But certainly the eye-direction and duration-of-looking measures are amendable to naturalistic use. If Politz (1959) was able to solve the technical problems of a jiggling bus, more stable situations should present little difficulty.

Many of our laboratory experiences could be replicated in natural settings. Landis and Hunt's (1939) method of studying movement responses could easily be applied in nonlaboratory settings. Shooting off a gun, the authors filmed the subject's gestural response pattern, which included such movements as drawing the shoulders forward, contracting the abdomen, and bending the knees. Facial patterns included closing the eyes and widening the mouth. It will be remembered that Krout found that a gesture of placing the hand to the nose was correlated with fear. With the stimulus of an unexpected gunshot, the immediate response may be independent of any contaminants due to the experimental setting.

HARDWARE: PHYSICAL SUPPLANTING OF THE OBSERVER

The hardware measures mentioned so far have been mainly concerned with reducing the risk associated with the human observer's fallibility as a measuring instrument—his selective perceptions and his lack of capacity to note all elements in a complex set of behaviors. Another use to which hardware has been put is to obtain research entrée into situations which are excluded by the usual simple observational method. Some of these content areas have been unattainable because of the privacy of the behavior, others because of the prohibitive costs of maintaining observational scrutiny over a substantial enough sample of time. Sitting in for the observer, hardware can help resolve both problems.[2]

"Blind bugging" via audiotapes is one such approach—a controversial one when applied in certain settings, and illegal in many. Jury deliberations are not observable because of standard legal restraints, but Strodtbeck and his colleagues (Strodtbeck & James, 1955; Strodtbeck, James, & Hawkins, 1957; Strodtbeck & Mann, 1956) received the approval of the court and counsel from both sides to place hidden microphones in the jury room. The use of concealed recording devices presents ethical questions that have been underlined by Amrine and Sanford (1956), Burchard (1957), and Shils (1959).

We may add as an aside that among the most astute devices for concealed recording is a microphone rigged in a mock hearing aid. It works extremely well in inducing the subject to lean over and shout directly into the recording apparatus. The presence of a dangling cord does not inhibit response.

The "cocktail-party effect" is an acoustical term for the process of listening to one among a multitude of talkers. First suggested by Pollack and Pickett (1957) and expanded by MacLean (1959), it was used by Legget and Northwood (1960) in conducting experiments at eight gatherings, relating recorded sound level to number of people attending and drawing on records for total consumption of food and drink. The experimenters found that the nature of the beverage served made no significant difference in the buildup of sound levels, that all-male gatherings were slightly quieter than mixed gatherings, and that the maximum sound levels were 80 to 85 decibels, "not quite high enough to cause permanent impairment of hearing" (Legget & Northwood, 1960, p. 18). See also Hardy (1959) and Carhart (1967).

Riesman and Watson (1964) met with failure in their attempts to record party conversations on tape:

> Losses of comments lasting over one minute occurred at the rate of about seven times per recorded hour . . . the critical objection lay . . . in the tape's sometimes useful lack of selectivity: the record was a long-drawn-out tissue of inanities in which the very diffuseness made analysis more difficult than when one was dealing with the more condensed material of recollection. (p. 299)

Which are the "better" data—the true conversation or the "condensed material of recollection"—is up to the investigator to decide. The loss of content, however, is a severe limiting condition, demonstrating the selective utility of some hardware. In this case, the recorder would be adequate for recording sound level, but inadequate for providing a complete record of conversations.

Many pieces of hardware have been developed for measuring the level of physical activity, a variable that has been viewed as symptomatic of many things. Perhaps the earliest mention of this type of measure was made by Galton (1884), who was at that time interested in the physical equivalents of metaphorical language. He took as his example the "inclination of one person toward another." This situation is clearly seen when two people are sitting next to each other at a dinner table, according to Galton. To demonstrate this empirically in quantitative terms (Galton, 1884; Watson, 1959), he suggested a pressure gauge with an index and dial to indicate changes in stress arranged on the legs of the chair on the side nearest the other person. Galton specified three necessary conditions for this type of experiment: the apparatus must be effective; it must not attract notice; and it must be capable of being applied to ordinary furniture. All of these criteria are appropriate for contemporary apparatus studies.

It is obvious that such a device may be a substitute for human observers when their presence might contaminate the situation, and where no convenient hidden observation site is available. Indeed, many of the studies discussed earlier as "simple observation" are amenable to mechanization, provided Galton's criteria can be met.

There is F. Scott Fitzgerald's fictional account in *The Last Tycoon,* of how the title character, a movie executive, evaluated the quality of rushes (preliminary, unedited film "takes") by observing how much they made him wiggle in his chair. The more the wiggles, the poorer the movie scenes. Simple observational measures could be made of twistings by a concealed observer, but they would clearly be inferior to a more mechanical device.

Galton (1885) suggested a fidget measure based on the amount of body sway among an audience. The greater the sway, the greater the boredom. "Let this suggest to observant philosophers, when the meeting they attend may prove dull, to occupy themselves in estimating the frequency, amplitude and duration of the fidgets of their fellow sufferers" (p. 175). The American playwright Robert Ardrey (1961) notes coughing as an audience response to boredom.

One cougher begins his horrid work in an audience, and the cough spreads until the house is in bedlam, the actors in rage, and the playwright in retreat to the nearest saloon. Yet let the action take a turn for the better, let the play tighten up, and that same audience will sit in a silence unpunctuated by a single tortured throat. (p. 85)

A mechanical device has been employed by Kretsinger (1952, 1959). He used what he terms an electromagnetic movement meter to study gross bodily movement in theater audiences—a very difficult observational setting because of inadequate illumination (see also Lyle, 1953). Kretsinger claims that this method was "objective, essentially linear, and completely removed from the subject's awareness." The technique

> was based upon a capacity operated electronic system often used in burglar alarm applications. As modified by the author, it consisted of an oscillator detector, a D.C. amplifier, and an Esterline-Angus ink writing recorder. A concealed copper screen was located near the head of the *S* watching the film. As the *S* moved, the effective capacity of the oscillator circuit varied, changing the frequency of its oscillation. This frequency shift was converted to a change in D.C. voltage amplified sufficiently to drive an ink pen on a moving paper chart . . . completely removed from the *S*'s awareness (Kretsinger, 1959, p. 74)

The importance of heeding population characteristics is borne out by his conclusion, "There was some evidence that the presence of girls had a disquieting effect upon the boys" (p. 77).

Cox and Marley (1959) devised another movement measure in their study of the restlessness of patients as a partial measure of the effect of various drugs. Their rather complex apparatus consists basically of a series of pulleys and springs, set under the springs of the bed, which record the displacement of the mattress. When the patient is perfectly motionless, the relay system does not operate, but the slightest movement will be recorded. A more simple device is possible with baby cribs: the activity level of the child is measured by shaving down one of the four crib legs and attaching a meter which records the frequency of jiggling. This is much less fine a measure than that of Cox and Marley, for the child could move without activating the meter. For studies which don't require such fine calibration, however, the simplicity of the device is appealing.

As beds, cribs, and chairs can be wired, so, too, can desks. Foshee (1958) worked on the hypothesis that a greater general drive state would manifest itself in greater activity. Here is a good theoretical proposition testable by a device appropriate for natural settings away from the laboratory. To measure activity, Foshee used a schoolroom desk which was supported at each corner by rubber stoppers. Attached to the platform which supported the desk was a mechanical level arrangement which amplified the longitudinal movements of the plat-form. Through an elaborate transmission system, the amplitude and frequency of the subject's movement could be measured. Foshee does not mention whether the subjects (in this case a group of mental defectives) were aware of the apparatus or not, but it would seem likely that the device could be con-structed to evade detection.

To reach into the difficult setting of a darkened movie house for the study of expressive movement, several investigators have employed infrared photog-raphy (Bloch, 1952; Field, 1954; Gabriele, 1956; Greenhill, 1955; Siersted & Hansen, 1951). This type of filming eliminates almost entirely the element of subject awareness of the observational apparatus. It is clearly superior to unaided observation because of the advantage of working in the dark; the brighter the light in which to see the subject, the brighter the light for him to see you. This is illustrated in Leroy-Boussion's (1954) visible-observer study of emotional expressions of children during a comedy film. Although Leroy-Boussion claimed to be only a projection aide during the film, she did have to eliminate certain subjects who "seemed to be aware" of her presence as an observer. It would thus seem likely that there were other subjects who did not make their awareness known to the investigator. Putting aside the question of reducing the sample size, the more important issue is whether those who were aware (and discarded as subjects) were a selective group (the more suspicious or paranoid, for example). Infrared photography drastically reduces such selective loss. Further, it is possible to match the infrared camera with the regular projection machine so that in subsequent analysis the photographs of audience reaction can be matched easily to the specific film sequence.

The danger of relying solely on interview or questionnaire self-reports is sharply illustrated in the Siersted and Hansen (1951) study. They supplemented their filming by interviewing the children who had seen the film. There were marked differences between these interview responses and both the filmed reactions and verbal comments made during the film (recorded with hidden tape recorders).

For some reason, the French have been leaders in research on movie hardware. Toulouse and Mourgue (1948) worked with respiratory reactions in order to index reactions to films, and it has even been suggested that the temperature of the room in which a film is viewed might be monitored as an indicator.

The estimation of attendance at an event or an institution can be carried out by planting observers who count heads. Another way is to mechanize and count circuit breaks. The "electric eye," particularly when supplemented by a time recorder, provides a useful record of frequency of attendance and its pacing. The photoelectric cells are typically set up on either side of a doorway so that any break of the current will register a mark on an attached recording device. As Trueswell (1963) shrewdly pointed out, however, this apparatus is not free from mechanical or reactivity contaminants. Particularly when the device is first installed, it is common for people to step back and forth through the light or to wave arms and legs, thus registering three or four marks for a single entry. Another difficulty is the placement of the cells. If they are set too low, it is possible for each leg to register a separate mark as the person walks through. If the doorway is wide enough to admit two people, a couple may walk together and register only one mark. It is important to note that these are not random errors which balance out, but are constant for the method. Because of this, it is equally important that human observers be there with the mechanical device, particularly in its early period of installation, to study whether any such errors are admitted to the data.

Ellis and Pryer (1959) have demonstrated the complexities possible with photoelectric cells in their study of the movements of children with severe neuropathology. Their apparatus consisted of a square plywood enclosure in which the children played. Electronic devices were located on the outside surface of the walls and arranged so that the beams crisscrossed the enclosure at two-foot intervals. Interruption of a beam would be recorded, with each beam recorded separately.

With the light beams visible, the behavior of subjects may be modified—either because they dart back and forth in a playful game with the beam, or because it inhibits their movement to know that they are under observation. Ellis and Pryer suggest modifications of their technique to avoid such risks, among them installing infrared exciter lamps, noiseless relays, and soundproofing.

As a final example of the use of hardware to get otherwise difficult content, there is Weir's (1963) report of her audiotape recordings of a two-and-a-half-year-old boy falling to sleep. The child practices language, working with noun substitution and articulation. In the evening of the day when he was first offered raspberries, he says, "berries, *not* bayreez, berries." Maccoby (1964), who summarized the study, states: "These observations provide insight into language learning processes which are ordinarily covert and not accessible to observation" (p. 211).

THE INTERVENING OBSERVER

Most of the observation studies reported so far have been ones in which the observer is passive. He may take the behavior as it comes, or he may introduce mechanization to improve the accuracy and span of his observations, but he has not typically altered the cues in the environment to which the person or group is responding. This passivity has two costs. It is possible that the behavior under study occurs so infrequently that an inordinate amount of effort is expended on gathering large masses of data, only a small segment of which is useful. Or, paying the second cost, the naturally occurring behavior is not stimulated by events of sufficient discriminability. The investigator may want four or five levels of intensity of a condition, say, when the convenient simple observation approach can produce only two.

Rather than pay these costs, many investigators have actively stepped into the research environment and "forced" the data in a way that did not attract attention to the method. In some cases, this has meant grading experimental conditions over equivalent groups, with each group getting a different "natural" treatment. In a smaller number of studies, the conditions have been varied over the individual. Both classes are illustrated in this section.

Allen Funt of the television show *Candid Camera,* perhaps the most visible of the hidden observers, gave up simple observation because of the high dross rate (Flagler, 1960). In the early years of the program, Funt's episodes consisted largely of studies of gestures and conversation (Hamburger, 1950; Martin, 1961). Particularly with conversation, Funt found that a large amount of time was required to obtain a small amount of material, and he turned to introducing confederates who would behave in such a way to direct attention to the topic of study.

In one magnificent sequence of film, Funt prepared a cross-cultural comparison of how men from different countries respond to the request of a female confederate to carry a suitcase to the corner. Filmed abroad, the episodes centered on the girl indicating she had carried the suitcase for a long time and would like a hand. The critical material is the facial expression and bodily gestures of the men as they attempted to lift the suitcase and sagged under the weight. It was filled with metal. The Frenchman shrugged; the Englishman kept at it. Funt has offered to open his extensive film library to social scientists. For students of response to frustration or unexpected stimuli, this is rich ground.

Obviously, experimental manipulation is not a contaminant. It is only when the manipulation is seen as such that reactivity enters to threaten validity. P. F. Carroll (1962, personal communication) showed that active initiation of stimuli can have its comic side. In an exploratory venture, he sent out wires to twelve distant friends, congratulating each on his "recent achievement." Back came eleven acknowledgments of humble thanks. This approach lacks control, for we cannot know how many acknowledged in puzzled courtesy and how many felt Carroll had given them their due. If the study is replicated, it might be well to send a control sample a wire saying, "It doesn't matter. We're with you anyway." The wire was an efficient way to stimulate a response. An analogue may be an attempt to teach automobile driving by operant conditioning procedures. It is possible, but may take a hazardously long time contrasted to active control by the teacher (Bandura, 1962).

Simple observation, mechanized or not, is appropriate to a broad range of imaginative and useful research comparisons. Some of these we have mentioned. The advantage of contrived observation is to extend the base of simple observation and permit more subtle comparisons of the intensity of effect.

The early work of Hartshorne and May yields good examples of the manipulating observer. In *Studies in Service and Self Control* (Hartshorne, May, & Maller, 1929), they report on a long series of experiments—the first behavioral studies of "service." Employing "production methods of measurement," they indexed service or helpfulness by the subject's willingness to produce something—a toy in a shop, or the posting of a picture. Similarly, they employed "self-sacrifice" techniques, measures on which the subject had to give up something.

The subjects were school children, and the active involvement of the experimenter (teacher) in defining alternatives of behavior was both expected and normal. The threat of subjects' awareness of being tested is less an issue in educational research, and the long line of studies on lecture versus discussion methods, as well as the current research on educational television, are a fine source of learning research because the risk of the contaminant is so reduced.

In the same way, it is not a patently false condition for a teacher to present students with the chance to help some other children in hospitals. Hartshorne and May (1928) graded the opportunities to help in an "envelope test." The student could put pictures, jokes, or stories in envelopes to give to hospitalized children, could promise to do so, or not do so. In another behavioral measure of sacrifice, one with more artificiality, however, the students were told they would be given some money. They were provided opportunities to bank it, give it to a charity, or keep it themselves. In another phase, one that presaged many small-group experiments, the children were given a choice of whether they would work for themselves or for the class in a spelling contest.

In Hartshorne and May's *Studies in Deceit* (1928), children were offered the opportunity not to return all of the coins distributed for arithmetic practice, to cheat by changing original answers in grading their own exam papers (which had previously been collected and then handed back with some excuse), to peek during "eyes-closed" tests and thus perform with unbelievable skill, to exaggerate the number of chin-ups when allowed to make their own records "unobserved." Forty separate opportunities were administered in whole or in part to about eight thousand pupils.

In one of their reports (May & Hartshorne, 1927) is found the first presentation of what is now known as Guttman scale analysis. The experimenters found high unidimensionality for a series of paper-regrading opportunities: those students who cheated when an ink eraser was required cheated on *every* easier opportunity.

These studies of Hartshorne and May in the Character Education Inquiry are the classics of contrived observation, and nothing so thorough and ingenious has been done since. It is unfortunate for subsequent measurement efforts that interpretation of the cheating results was viewed as specific to the situation. To be sure, honesty was found to be relative to situation; for example, in one study (May & Hartshorne, 1927), only 2% cheated when corrections required an ink eraser, while 80% cheated when all that was needed was either erasing or adding a penciled digit. But this is not inconsistent with the six cheating opportunities forming a single-factored test or unidimensional scale. The data show a Guttman reproducibility coefficient of .96. Even though the measure was only six items long, there was a Kuder-Richardson reliability of .72 which becomes .84 when corrected for item-marginal ceiling effects as suggested by Horst (1953). Pooling all their disguised performance tests for a given trait, the experimenters checked the character tests against reputational scores from the so-called Guess-Who tests. The validities ranged from .315 to .374. Although very low values in terms of the standards of their day, they are now recognized to be reasonable values typical of those found for personality tests. Of course, the reputational measures contributed their full share of the error in validity.

Contrived observation, then, is observation in which the stimuli or the available responses are varied in an inconspicuous way. For Hartshorne and May, the variation was primarily of the response alternatives.

The recent series of studies by Fantz and associates (Fantz, 1961a, 1961b, 1963, 1964; Fantz, Ordy, & Udelf, 1962) shows the more usual variation of the stimuli. They too worked with subjects where the reactivity risk is low—newborn infants. The simple response measure was visual fix on a target, with the stimulus varied along such dimensions as novelty, color, and patter. As far as a 48-hour-old infant is concerned, a series of concentric rings in his visual field is as natural as anything else.

Stechler (1964) also studied newborns, observing the effect of medication administered to the mother during labor on the baby's attentiveness. Each child received three stimuli, "held near the baby's face for a total of nine minutes.... An observer hidden from the babies recorded the total time they looked at and away from the stimuli" (p. 315).

A much more hardheaded group of subjects, automobile salesmen, were studied by Jung (1959, 1960, 1961, 1962) in his evaluations of the effect of various bargaining postures. The response measure was simple, the quoted price of an automobile with specified features, and three different bargaining postures were struck. In this well-designed series of experiments, confederates posed as customers and adopted one of these three poses: an eager, naive "I just got my license. Where do I sign?" approach, an engineering, price-sophisticated approach, and one in between. The differences among test conditions are smaller in absolute quotations than might have been expected—only $33 between the extremes in one study. Because the research was conducted in the heavily price-competitive Chicago area, the dollar differences may well be less than in areas in which competition is along other lines. The Chicago buyer, real or feigned, gets an automatic discount without any haggling. Jung has used the same feigned-shopper approach in studies of mortgage financing and the sale of mobile homes (Jung, 1963, 1964).

Brock (1965) turned the conditions around. His experimenter in a study of decision change was a paint salesman. After customers chose paint at a certain price, the salesman suggested either a more or less expensive paint. The salesman was more successful when he described himself as having recently bought the same amount of paint at a different price.

Franzen (1950) conducted a sales experiment with pharmacists. The confederate was again a "customer," who related various symptoms of illness to the pharmacist. The symptoms were graded by their severity as told by the "customer," and it was noted whether or not a visit to a physician was suggested. Examples of the symptoms, all of which could be related to early cancer, were loss of voice, sore on lip, heartburn and stomach trouble, and constipation.

Franzen also administered opinion questionnaires to an equivalent, randomly selected group of pharmacists. The results from the questionnaire are different from those of the field study. The contrived observation results, we suspect, have a higher predictive value than those from the questionnaires.

These findings recall the classic study comparing verbal attitudes and overt acts: LaPiere's (1934) research on prejudice. He and a Chinese couple visited 250 hotels and restaurants and were refused service just once. Yet when questionnaires were sent to those same places, asking if Chinese customers were welcome, some 92% answered negatively. As a control, LaPiere sent identical questionnaires to 100 similar establishments which his party had not visited, and the response was similar.

J. S. Adams (1963a, 1963b) has demonstrated in his important work on wages what fine research can be undertaken with simple productivity data. He conducted three experiments "to test how people behave when they are working on a relatively highly paid job for which they feel underqualified (that is, when they feel their pay, or outcome, exceeds their qualifications or input)" (1963b, p. 10).

The subjects were students who were hired for part-time temporary interviewing, not knowing they were part of an experiment. In the first experiment, they were paid $3.50 an hour and divided into two groups. The experimental group was led to believe that they were not qualified for the job as interviewers; they "were treated quite harshly." The control group was told they had met all qualifications for the job. With productivity the dependent variable, the experimental subjects produced significantly more than the control subjects.

In the second experiment, interest was focused on the relationship between method of pay and dissonance. Thirty-six students were hired for the same interviewing job and randomly assigned to the four conditions:

1. Experimental dissonance condition—students were paid $3.50 an hour and made to feel overpaid.

2. Control condition—students were paid $3.50 an hour and made to feel it was an equitable wage.

3. Experimental dissonance condition—students were paid 30 cents an interview and made to feel overpaid on a piece rate.

4. Control condition—students were paid 30 cents an interview and made to feel payment was fair.

Adams' (1963b) hypothesis was supported: "hourly workers in the dissonance condition had a higher mean productivity than their controls, whereas piece-workers in the dissonance condition had a lower mean productivity than their controls" (p. 13).

In the final experiment, Adams showed that pieceworkers who perceive that they are inequitably overpaid will perform better quality work at a lower productivity level than pieceworkers paid the same rate who believe that the wage is fair. The experimental subjects increased their "inputs" on each unit of work, thereby increasing the quality, but decreasing the quantity.

We have detailed this study because of the example that Adams provides of the shrewd hypothesis-testing potential of some of the rudimentary, but natural, measures available for experimental study.

The violation of prohibitions has offered the subject matter for several field studies of contrived observation. In these, the physical world of the observed was actively manipulated, and the dependent variables were simple motor acts.

Freed and his colleagues (Freed, Chandler, Mouton, & Blake, 1955) experimented with sign violation. To what extent will students violate a sign urging the use of an inconvenient side door rather than the customary main door of a university building? The degree of prohibition was varied on the sign (high, medium, or low) with the interesting fillip of a confederate who conformed to the sign or violated it. In a control condition, no confederate was present. Ninety subjects were assigned to nine different experimental groups, combinations of prohibition strength of the sign and a confederate's presence or behavior. They showed main effects for the two variables with no interaction between them. In an extension of these findings, another investigator (Sechrest, 1965b) found that a politely worded sign, "Please Do Not Use This Door," elicited fewer violations than the more abrupt "Use Other Door."

Violation of traffic signals was the dependent variable in a study by Lefkowitz, Blake, and Mouton (1955). An experimenter was again an active element in the setting—a male who dressed in either high- or low-status clothing. The confederate either conformed to or violated a traffic signal that ordered him to "wait" on a street corner. An observer a hundred feet from the corner noted the number of people on the corner who went along with the confederate. Would the difference in dress elicit differences in the number of pedestrians violating the light? Austin, Texas, was the locale, and pedestrians violated the sign more often in the presence of a model—significantly more often when the nonconforming model was in his higher-status dress.

Cratty (1962) attempted a replication of this study in Evanston, Illinois. He added observation of the race of violators and conformers, and his analysis suggests a significant difference between Negroes and whites on violations under *both* conditions. The racial composition of the sample could thus confound comparisons.[3] Cratty's findings also illustrate the problem of the cross-sectional stability of a research measure. To have good intersectional comparisons, the degree of usual conformity to the signs should be equivalent. Comparison of the Texas and Illinois data is muddied by a law-abiding difference. Only 1% of the Texas sample violated the sign when the confederate was absent; over 60% of the Illinois sample did.

Moore and Callahan (1943) conducted research in New Haven, concentrating on traffic and parking behavior. Three sets of studies are reported, all of them nonreactive, all examples of contrived observation. In the first set, the "parking" studies, observations were made over a four-year period. Moore and Callahan first observed the number and length of time parked of cars in areas where there was no formal ordinance against parking. Then a formal ordinance prohibiting parking was introduced, and the observation continued. Thus, there is a time-series analysis in which the baseline is the period preceding the introduction of signs.

In a second set of "administrative" studies, the militancy of enforcement of traffic violations was the independent variable. Parking was limited by ordinance (sign) to thirty minutes. In one condition, violations were tagged after eighty minutes and in a second condition, after forty-five minutes. The frequency and duration of parking under these two conditions were compared to a control condition in which no tickets were given at all.

The third set centered on rotary traffic. All studies in this group used a large circular tract of pavement from which five streets radiated. Observation consisted of noting the path in which the area was crossed.

Five observation periods were employed. The first was before there was any ordinance regulating the direction of traffic. The second was before a formal ordinance was enacted, but in the presence of signs to "keep right." The third followed enactment of the ordinance. The fourth was while the ordinance was visibly in effect—barriers would not allow cars through the center of the circle. Finally, the barrier and signs were removed when the ordinance was still in effect. The observed directions of flow under the five conditions were compared.

Another driving study, reported by Sechrest (1965b), was concerned with willingness of drivers to accept a challenge to "drag" at stop signals. The investigators challenged by pulling alongside a car, gunning the engine of their car, and looking once at their "opponent." They used different stimulus cars and recorded several attributes of the responding cars. Results showed a strong decline in acceptance of the challenge with increasing age and with presence of passengers other than the driver in the respondent's car. As for the stimulus cars? Very few drivers wanted to drag with a Volkswagen.

Traffic behavior offers a splendid opportunity for naturalistic experimentation. A large body of control data is already available, produced for engineering studies or by market-research firms to document the exposure of outdoor advertising. It should be possible, for example, to study the effect of different degrees of threat in a persuasive message by studying the degree to which drivers slow down, if they do, after passing different classes of signs—say, those threatening legal enforcement or the danger to personal safety. Radar devices or filming from an overhead helicopter could provide the measure of speed. What might be of particular interest in such a study would be the extinction rate under the different conditions. Does an enforcement warning have a faster rate of decay than a personal safety message? What happens if both classes are equated for initial effect on speed?

Another study relating to legal processes is that of Schwartz and Skolnick (1962b). They investigated the effect of criminal records on the employment opportunities of unskilled workers. Four employment folders were prepared for an applicant; all folders were identical save for description of the criminal-court record of the applicant. Each of 100 employers was assigned one of four treatment folders, and the employer was asked whether he could "use" the man described in the folder. The employers were never given any indication that they were participating in an experiment. Even when the applicant was described as having been acquitted with an excusing letter from a judge or acquitted without a letter, the incidence of employers who thought they might use the applicant dropped.

ENTRAPMENT

Jones (1946) has provided an excellent summary of early behavioral studies of character development, many of which follow the entrapment strategy of Hartshorne and May (1928). A recent example is the work of Freeman and

Ataov (1960). They contrived a situation in which the subjects had a chance to cheat by grading their own examinations by a scoring sheet. Using three classes of questions—fill-in blanks, multiple-choice, and true-false—they found the number of changed answers for each class. The three formed a Guttman scale with a reproducibility coefficient of .94.

One of the more interesting studies on honesty has been reported by Merritt and Fowler (1948), who "lost" two kinds of stamped and addressed envelopes, one containing a trivial message, the other a lead slug of the dimensions of a fifty-cent piece. They dropped the letters "on many different days and in many different cities to insure a representative sample of the public at large" (p. 91). While 85% of the control letters were returned, only 54% of the test (containing slug) were, and some 13% of the test letters that were returned had been opened. After the letters were dropped, there was a chance to work with auxiliary information on the unsuspecting subjects.

> Watching the pickup of the letters proved to be a most entertaining pastime. Some were picked up and immediately posted at the nearest mailbox. Others were examined minutely, evidently precipitating quite a struggle between the finder and his conscience, before being pocketed or mailed. Some were carried a number of blocks before being posted, one person carrying a letter openly for nine blocks before mailing it. A lady in Ann Arbor, Michigan, found a letter and carried it six miles in her car to deliver it personally, although she was not acquainted with the addressee. One letter, picked up in Harrisburg, Pennsylvania was mailed from York, Pennsylvania. Another picked up in Toledo, Ohio, was mailed in Cleveland. Still another from the Toledo streets was mailed from Monroe, Michigan. Two missives left on the steps of the cradle of liberty in Philadelphia failed to find their way into a mailbox. Two of five letters left on church steps during Sunday services failed to return. (p. 93)

Grinder (1961, 1962) and Grinder and McMichael (1963) have reported studies using a "ray gun" type of apparatus. Like Hartshorne and May (1928), their interest was in studying character, or "conscience development." Children operated a "ray gun" individually in a realistic game situation.

> Seated seven feet from a target box, subjects were asked to shoot the ray gun pistol 20 times at a rotating rocket. With each pull of the ray gun trigger, prearranged scores from zero to five were registered by score lights also housed in the target box. High scores were rewarded with a marksman,

sharpshooter, or expert badge . . . subjects cumulated their scores on a paper score sheet. Subjects were judged to have resisted temptation if the scores recorded on their score sheets indicated that they had not earned a badge (they could not honestly). They were judged to have yielded to temptation if their score sheet showed that they had falsified their scores in order to earn one of the badges. (Grinder & McMichael, 1963, p. 504)

Similar in its assumption of dishonesty by subjects is a study by Brock and Guidice (1963). The subjects were students ranging from the second to the sixth grade, and these children were individually asked if they would leave the class, go to another room, and participate in an experiment. Upon entering the room, the subject found the experimenter in a flustered state with her purse spilled and money lying on the floor. At this point, the experimenter left, saying she would be back shortly, and asking the subject to pick up the contents of her purse while she was gone. The measure used was the amount of money stolen by the subjects. There is a good risk that some of the children, having been told to go to another room for an "experiment," became suspicious. The effect of this is to make uncertain how many of those who took no money were honest and how many were acute. This bias could possibly interact with a practice effect on the part of the experimenter. Did she play her role differently over time, as she became more practiced or more bored? If professional actresses have problems "keeping fresh," it is reasonable to ask about amateurs.

The more complex the action of the confederate, the greater the risk of an experimenter effect, *and* the greater the possibility for more gradations in the experimental variable.

PETITIONS AND VOLUNTEERING

Petition-signing has been the dependent variable in observational studies by Blake, Mouton, and Hain (1956) and Helson, Blake, and Mouton (1958). In the first study, the strength of the plea to sign was varied, and frequency of signing was closely associated with this variable. A confederate was then introduced into this situation to provide varying reactions of another person. In some situations, he signed readily, in others refused, and in still others his response was unknown to the person approached. The behavior of the confederate influenced signing, and an interesting finding was that both variables operated independently—the strength of the plea and endorsement by another.

The Helson et al. (1958) study used petition-signing as a response behavior within a larger experimental setting. Students who had volunteered to participate in an experiment were taken by a guide to an experimental room. On the way, the pair was stopped, and a confederate asked the guide to sign a petition. After the guide (also a confederate) signed or did not sign, the subject was asked to sign. Four conditions were employed, with each student receiving one:

1. A petition on a proposal that had previously elicited 96% positive response and confederate signed

2. The same 96% positive proposal, but confederate refused to sign

3. A proposal that had received only a 15% positive response and confederate signed

4. The same 15% proposal; confederate did not sign.

Solicitation to sign a petition is a common enough event in academic settings, and may be becoming more common outside the cloistered world. Certainly it offers a broad freedom of movement in experimentation and structuring of contrived conditions. Searching for volunteers does, too, and several studies have used observation of the simple "volunteer-not volunteer" alternatives as the behavioral variable.

Schachter and Hall (1952) experimented with college students, employing different situational elements in eliciting volunteers for an experiment and then noting whether or not the volunteers did in fact show up for the experiment. Classes were divided into four groups and given different restraints. In one group, after a requesting speech, the listeners were asked to fill out a questionnaire, whether or not they wished to participate in the experiment. Those who did wish to participate were merely asked to check an appropriate place on the form. In a second group, the forms were passed around the room, and anyone who wanted to participate in the experiment could take one. A third group was asked to raise hands if interested; a fourth group also raised hands, but half of the class had been enlisted as confederates and "volunteered." Schachter and Hall's conclusion was that neither the high- nor low-constraint condition was particularly desirable in soliciting volunteers. If the experimenters made it easy to refuse, they got a high refusal rate, but high attendance among those who did volunteer. Contrariwise, placing high pressure on volunteering yielded a higher level of volunteers, but a smaller number who held to their promise.

Rosenbaum and Blake (1955) wanted to test the hypothesis that the act of volunteering is "a special case of conformance with social norms or standards, rather than . . . an individualistic act conditioned by an essentially unidentifiable complex of inner tensions, needs, etc." (p. 193). Subjects were plucked from students studying in the university library, and conditions were varied so that the subject saw either an acceptance or rejection of the request from a confederate. In a third group, the student accepted or rejected the volunteering request in the absence of a model. As predicted, acceptances were high with a conforming confederate, low with a nonconforming confederate, and in between on the control condition.

The University of Texas library was also the site of another study by Rosenbaum (1956). Volunteering was the dependent variable, and stimulus conditions included three request strengths (determined by a pilot study) and three background conditions employing confederates. The confederate entered the library, sat next to an unsuspecting student, and then the volunteer-seeker entered and started with the confederate.

Blake and his associates (Blake, Berkowitz, Bellamy, & Mouton, 1956) determined the effect on the level of volunteering of varying the attractiveness of alternatives to volunteering. The public or private character of the volunteering was also varied, with conditions altered so that a class might substitute volunteering time for time otherwise devoted to (a) a pop quiz, (b) released time from class, (c) a control, with no time gained. It might be observed that under the pop-quiz alternative, 98.8% of the subjects volunteered under the private-commitment situation and 100.0% under public commitment. The 1.2% above is accounted for by the single aberrant student who preferred a pop quiz to participation in an experiment.

Volunteering for social action was the subject of a study by Gore and Rotter (1963). The action in this case was the willingness of students in a southern

Negro college to engage in different types of segregation-protest activity. This criterion measure was correlated with previously obtained scores on control of reinforcement and social desirability scales, these scales not specifically dealing with the segregation issue. A generalized attitude toward internal or external control was shown to predict the type and degree of behavior subjects were willing to perform in attempts at social change.

AN OVER-ALL APPRAISAL OF HIDDEN HARDWARE AND CONTROL

As the discussion and example of observational research have progressed over these past two chapters, the reader may have been sensitive to a movement along a passivity-activity dimension. In the studies reported in the chapter on simple observation methods, the observer was a nonintervening passive onlooker of behavior that came before his eyes or ears. He may have scrambled about in different locations to reduce some population restrictions, but his role was a quiet, receptive one. In many ways, this is appropriate for the covert character of the studies we have outlined.

With the hardware employed in the studies cited in this chapter, the investigator engaged his data more—actively expanding the possible scope of the content of research and achieving a more faithful record of what behaviors did go on. Yet the hardware varied, too. Some of the hardware devices are static, while others are mobile. To the degree that the hardware is mobile (say, a microphone in a mock hearing aid versus one secreted in a table), the experimenter has flexibility to make more economical forays into locational sampling. He could sample in a number of locations by installing more permanent recording devices, but commonly a more feasible method is to sample occasions and time with mobile equipment. As electronic technology develops, more opportunities arise. It isn't so long ago that television cameras had to be anchored in one spot.

When, through deliberate choice or no realistic alternative, the investigator was limited to a fixed instrument, he was forced to depend on the character of the population which flowed past that spot and the content appropriate to it. The waiting game can give accurate and complete measurement of a limited population and limited content, and the decision to use such an approach is posited on two criteria, one "theoretical," one "practical." Are the limitations likely to be selective enough to inhibit the generalizability of the findings? Can the investigator absorb the time and money costs of developing material with a low saturation of pertinent data for his comparisons?

In the contrived-observation studies, the experimenters took the next step and intervened actively in the production of the data, striding away from passive and critically placed observations. The effect was to produce very dense data, of which a high proportion was pertinent to the research comparisons. Further, a finer gradation of stimuli was then possible, and more subtle shadings of difference could be noted. By active intervention, as the petition and volunteering studies of conformity show, it was also possible to make estimates of the interaction of variables, an extremely difficult matter with passive observation.

As the experimenter's activity increases, and he achieves the gains of finer measurement and control, the price paid is the increased risk of being caught— that the subjects of the observation will detect the recording device, or will suspect that the confederate is really a "plant." This is a high price, for if he is detected, the experimenter's research is flooded with the reactive measurement errors which the hidden-observation approach, regardless of its simplicity or complexity, is designed to avoid. At the extreme end of contrivance, when a confederate is a visible actor in the subject's world, it requires the greatest finesse to protect against detection and against changes in the behavior of the confederate damaging to comparison. The best defense, as always, is knowledge, and almost all of the observational approaches have built into them the capacity to examine whether or not population or instrument contaminants are working to confound the data.

NOTES

1. In the same article, Professor Boring comments on changes in the human observer as an instrument. "I remember how a professor of genetics many years ago showed me published drawings of cell nuclei dated both before and after the discovery

and description of chromosomes. Chromosomes kept showing up in the later drawings, not in the earlier" (p. 176).

2. Galton, writing from Africa, sent the following letter to his brother:

> I have seen figures that would drive the females of our native land desperate—figures that could afford to scoff at crinoline, nay more, as a scientific man and as a lover of the beautiful I have dexterously even without the knowledge of the parties concerned, resorted to actual measurement. Had I been a proficient in the language, I should have advanced, and bowed and smiled like Goldney, I should have explained the dress of the ladies of our country, I should have said that the earth was ransacked for iron to afford steel springs, that the seas were fished with consummate daring to obtain whalebone, that far distant lands were overrun to possess ourselves of caoutchou—that these three products were ingeniously wrought by competing artists, to the utmost perfection, that their handiwork was displayed in every street corner and advertised in every periodical but that on the other hand, that great as is European skill, yet it was nothing before the handiwork of a bounteous nature. Here I should have blushed bowed and smiled again, handed the tape and requested them to make themselves the necessary measurement as I stood by and registered the inches or rather yards. This however I could not do—there were none but Missionaries near to interpret for me, they would never have entered into my feelings and therefore to them I did not apply—but I sat at a distance with my sextant, and as the ladies turned themselves about, as women always do, to be admired, I surveyed them in every way and subsequently measured the distance of the spot where they stood—worked out and tabulated the results at my leisure (Pearson, 1914, p. 232).

3. It might be interesting to draw a sample of U.S. cities with varying degrees of reported racial tension and compare, by race, the extent to which minor violations such as walking on a red signal are committed.

SEVEN

A FINAL NOTE

————•◆•————

In the dialectic between impulsivity and restraint, the scientific superego became too harsh—a development that was particularly effective in intimidating adventurous research, because the young were learning more about methodological pitfalls than had their elders.

—(Riesman, 1959, p. 11)

avid Riesman's remarks on the evolution of communications research apply equally well to the broader panoply of the study of social behavior. As social scientists, we have learned much of the labyrinth that is research on human behavior, and in so doing discovered an abundance of cul-de-sacs. Learning the complexities of the maze shortened our stride through it, and often led to a pattern of timid steps, frequently retraced. No more can the knowledgeable person enjoy the casual bravura that marked the sweeping and easy generalizations of an earlier day.

The facile promulgation of "truth," backed by a few observations massaged by introspection, properly met its end—flattened by a more questioning and sophisticated rigor. The blackballing of verification by introspection was a positive advance, but an advance by subtraction. Partly as a reaction to the grandiosities of the past, partly as a result of a growing sophistication about the opportunities for error, the scope of individual research studies shrank, both in the range of content considered and in the diversity of procedures.

The shrinkage was understandable and desirable, for certainly no science can develop until a base is reached from which reliable and consistent empirical findings can be produced.[1] But if reliability is the initial step of a science, validity is its necessary stride. The primary effect of improved methodological practices has been to further what we earlier called the internal validity of a comparison—the confidence that a true difference is being observed. Unfortunately, practices have not advanced so far in improving external validity—the confidence with which the findings can be generalized to populations and measures beyond those immediately studied.

Slowing this advance in ability to generalize was the laissez-faire intellectualism of the operational definition. Operational definitionalism (to use a ponderously cumbersome term) provided a methodological justification for the scientist not to stray beyond a highly narrow, if reliable, base. One could follow a single method in developing data and be "pure," even if this purity were more associated with sterility than virtue.

The corkscrew convolutions of the maze of behavior were ironed, by definitional fiat, into a two-dimensional T maze. To define a social attitude, for example, solely by the character of responses to a list of questionnaire items is eminently legitimate—so much so that almost everything we know about attitudes comes from such research. Almost everything we know about attitudes is also suspect because the findings are saturated with the inherent risks of self-report information. One swallow does not make a summer; nor do two "strongly agrees," one "disagree," and an "I don't know" make an attitude or social value.

Questionnaires and interviews are probably the most flexible and generally useful devices we have for gathering information. Our criticism is not against them, but against the tradition which allowed them to become the methodological sanctuary to which the myopia of operational definitionalism permitted a retreat. If one were going to be limited to a single method, then certainly the verbal report from a respondent would be the choice. With no other device can an investigator swing his attention into so many different areas of substantive content, often simultaneously, and also gather intelligence on the extent to which his findings are hampered by population restrictions.

The power of the questionnaire and interview has been enormously enhanced, as have all methods, by the development of sensitive sampling procedures. With the early impetus provided by the Census Bureau to locational sampling, particularly to the theory and practice of stratification, concern about the population restrictions of a research sample has been radically diminished. Less well developed is the random sampling of time units—either over long periods such as months, or within a shorter period such as a day. There is no theoretical reason why time sampling is scarce, for it is a simple question of substituting time for location in a sampling design. Time sampling is of interest not only for its control over population fluctuations which might confound comparisons, but also because it permits control over the possibility of variable content at different times of the day or different months of the year.

The cost is high. And for that reason, government and commercial research organizations have led in the area, while academic research continues to limp along with conscripted sophomores. The controlled laboratory setting makes for excellent internal validity, as one has tight control over the conditions of administration and the internal structure of the questionnaire, but the specter of low generalizability is ever present.

That same specter is present, however, even if one has a national probability sample and the most carefully prepared questionnaire form or interview schedule. So long as one has only a single class of data collection, and that class is the questionnaire or interview, one has inadequate knowledge of the rival hypotheses grouped under the term "reactive measurement effects." These potential sources of error, some stemming from an individual's awareness of being tested, others from the nature of the investigator, must be accounted for by some other class of measurement than the verbal self-report.

It is too much to ask of any single class that it eliminate all the rival hypotheses subsumed under the population-, content-, and reactive-effects groupings. As long as research strategy is based on a single measurement class, some flanks will be exposed, and even if fewer are exposed with the choice of the questionnaire method, there is still insufficient justification for its use as the only approach.

If no single measurement class is perfect, neither is any scientifically useless. Many studies and many novel sources of data have been mentioned in these pages. The reader may indeed have wondered which turn of the page would provide a commentary on some Ouija-board investigation. It would have been there had we known of one, and had it met some reasonable criteria of scientific worth. These "oddball" studies have been discussed because they demonstrate ways in which the investigator may shore up reactive infirmities of the interview and questionnaire. As a group, these classes of measurement are themselves infirm, and individually contain more risk (more rival plausible hypotheses) than does a well-constructed interview.

This does not trouble us, nor does it argue against their use, for the most fertile search for validity comes from a combined series of different measures, each with its idiosyncratic weaknesses, each pointed to a single hypothesis. When a hypothesis can survive the confrontation of a series of complementary methods of testing, it contains a degree of validity unattainable by one tested within the more constricted framework of a single method (Campbell & Fiske, 1959). Findings from this latter approach must always be subject to the suspicion that they are method-bound: Will the comparison totter when exposed to an equally prudent but different testing method? There must be a multiple operationalism. E. G. Boring (1953/1963) put it this way:

> As long as a new construct has only the single operational definition that it received at birth, it is just a construct. When it gets two alternative operational definitions, it is beginning to be validated. When the defining operations, because of proven correlations, are many, then it becomes reified. (p. 222)

This means, obviously, that the notion of a single "critical experiment" is erroneous. *There must be a series of linked critical experiments, each testing a different outcropping of the hypothesis.* It is through triangulation of data procured from different measurement classes that the investigator can most effectively strip of plausibility rival explanations for his comparison. The usual procedural question asked is, Which of the several available data-collection methods will be best for my research problem? We suggest the alternative question: Which set of methods will be best?—with "best" defined as a series which provides data to test the most significant threats to a comparison with a reasonable expenditure of resources.

There are a number of research conditions in which the sole use of the interview or questionnaire leaves unanswerable rival explanations. The purpose of those less popular measurement classes emphasized here is to bolster these weak spots and provide intelligence to evaluate threats to validity. The payout for using these measures is high, but the approach is more demanding of the investigator. In their discussion of statistical records, Selltiz and her associates (Selltiz, Jahoda, Deutsch, & Cook, 1959) note:

> The use of such data demands a capacity to ask many different questions related to the research problem. . . . The guiding principle for the use of available statistics consists in keeping oneself flexible with respect to the form in which research questions are asked. (p. 318)

This flexibility of thought is required to handle the reactive measurement effects which are the most systematic weakness of all interview and questionnaire studies. These error threats are also systematically present in all observation studies in which the presence of an observer is known to those under study. To varying degrees, measurements conducted in natural settings, without the individual's knowledge, control this type of error possibility. In all of them—hidden observation, contrived observation, trace analysis, and secondary records—the individual is not aware of being tested, and there is little danger that the act of measurement will itself serve as a force for change in behavior or elicit role-playing that confounds the data. There is also minimal risk that biases coming from the physical appearance or other cues provided by the investigator will contaminate the results.

In the observational studies, however, hiding the observer does not eliminate the risk that he will change as a data-collecting instrument over time. Any change, for the better or worse, will introduce shifts that might be erroneously interpreted as stemming from the causal variable. This source of error must be guarded against in the same way that it is in other measurement classes—by careful training of the observer (interviewer), by permitting practice effects to take place before the critical data are collected, and by "blinding" the observer to the hypothesis. There is no way of knowing, of course, whether all reasonable precautions have worked. For this, the only solution is an internal longitudinal analysis of data from a single observer and cross-analysis of data from different observers at various times during the data collection.

Finally, none of the methods emphasized here, by themselves, can eliminate response sets which might strongly influence the character of the data. These must be brought under experimental control by manipulation of the setting itself (as in contrived field experimentation) or by statistical operations with the data if the character of the response sets is known well enough to permit adjustments. With archival records, it may be extremely difficult to know if response sets were operating at the time the data were produced.

These methods also may counter a necessary weakness of the interview and questionnaire—dependence upon language. When one is working within a single society, there is always the question whether the differential verbal skills of various subcultures will mislead the investigator. It is possible, if groups vary in articulateness, to overgeneralize the behavior or attitudes of the group or individuals with the greater verbal fluency. This risk is particularly marked for the interpretation of research reports which employ quotations liberally. The natural tendency of the writer is to choose illustrative quotations which are fluent, dramatic, or engaging. If the pool of good quotations is variable across the subcultures, the reader may mistakenly overvalue the ideas in the quotations, even though the writer himself does not. This is a question of presentation, but an important one because of the disproportionate weight that may be placed on population segments.

The differential capacity to use the language artfully is one source of error, while the absolute capacity of the language to convey ideas is another.[2] This is an issue strongly present in cross-cultural comparisons, where different languages may vary radically as a medium of information transfer. The effect of this is to limit the content possible for study with questionnaires or interviews. If one worked in New Guinea, for example, and had to depend upon the *lingua franca* pidgin widely spoken there, he would find it adequate to indicate an answer to "Where do you keep your fishing nets?" but too gross a filter to study the ethnocentrism of a tribe. Pidgin simply does not possess the subtle gradients required to yield textured responses to questions on attitudes toward neighboring tribes or one's own tribe. Although it is theoretically possible to learn all the regional dialects well enough to be competent in a language, in practice this does not occur. A more pragmatic approach is to search for observational or trace evidence which will document aspects of ethnocentrism (e.g., reactions to outsiders, disposition and use of weapons) and then relate it to the verbal responses in the inadequate pidgin.

One more weakness of the dependence on language is that sometimes there is silence. So long as a respondent talks, glibly or not, in a rich language or not, checks and controls can be worked on the reported content.[3] There are, however, situations in which refusals to cooperate preclude any chance of correcting distorted information. This usually results in a biased research population and not a rejection of all findings, because it is almost always possible to find some people who will discuss any topic. But it can also result in a complete stalemate if only the verbal report is considered as the research instrument.

An amusing example of this inability to get data by verbal report, and a nonreactive circumvention, is provided by Shadegg (1964). In his book on political campaign methods, Shadegg writes of a campaign manager who used every available means to learn the plans of his opponent, who, reasonably enough, was unwilling to grant a revealing interview. One method arranged for procuring the contents of his opponent's wastebasket: "He came into possession of carbon copies of letters . . . memos in the handwriting of his opponent's manager." Admittedly a less efficient method than the interview, it admirably met the criterion of being workable: "It took a lot of digging through the trash to come up with the nuggets. But . . . daily panning produced some very fine gold." The "investigator" did not limit himself to inferences drawn from observations of his opponent's public acts, but was able to develop ingeniously (although perhaps not ethically) a trace measure to complement the observation. Each aided the other, for the observations give a validity check on the nuggets among the trash (Was misleading material being planted?), and the nuggets gave a more accurate means of interpreting the meaning of the public acts.

Evidence of how others are sensitive to wastebaskets is seen in the practice in diplomatic embassies of burning refuse under guard, the discussion of refuse purchase by industrial spies ("Litter Bugged," 1964), and the development of a new electric waste-basket that shreds discarded paper into unreadable bits.

Generally speaking, then, observational and trace methods are indicated as supplementary or primary when language may serve as a poor medium of information—either because of its differential use, its absolute capacity for transfer, or when significant elements of the research population are silent.

The verbal methods are necessarily weak along another dimension, the study of past behavior or of change. For historical studies, there is no alternative but to rely mainly on records of the past time. Behavioral research on the distant past is rare, however; more common are studies which center on experiences within the lifetime of respondents. For example, there is a large literature on child-rearing practices, in which mothers recollect their behavior of years past.

A sole dependence on this type of data-gathering is highly suspect. It may be enough to note that Thomas Jefferson, in his later years, observed that winters weren't as cold as they used to be. Available records could be used to check both Mr. Jefferson and other observers of secular changes in winter's fierceness.

For more current evidence on the fallibility of such recall data, see McGraw and Molloy (1941); Pyles, Stolz, and Macfarlane (1935); Smith (1958); and Weiss and Dawis (1960)—all of whom comment on, or test, the validity of mothers' recall of child-rearing practices. Weiss and Dawis wrote, "It is indefensible to assume the validity of purportedly factual data obtained by interview" (p. 384). The work of Haggard, Brekstad, and Skard (1960) and Robbins (1963) suggests that it is a problem of differentially accurate recall. In Haggard et al.'s phrase, the interviews "did not reflect the mothers' earlier experiences and attitudes so much as their current picture of the past" (p. 317).

When, through death or refusal, reports of past behavior are unavailable, a proper contingent strategy is to interview others who have had access to the same information, or who can report at second hand. This is very shaky information, but useful if other intelligence is available as a check. For many investigations, of course, the nature of the distortion is itself an important datum and can become a central topic of study when a reliable baseline is possible.[4] If other materials are present, and they usually are in a record-keeping society, the best way to estimate past behavior is to combine methods of study of archival records, available traces, and verbal reports, even if second-hand. Clearly, direct observational methods are useless for past events.

With studies of social change, the most practical method is to rely on available records, supplemented by verbal recall. If one wanted more control over the data, it would be possible to conduct a continuing series of field experiments extending over a long period of years. But the difficulty of such an approach is evidenced by the scarcity of such longitudinal, original-data studies in social science. Forgetting the number of years required, there is the problem of unstable populations over time, a growing problem as the society becomes more mobile. Potential errors lie in both directions as one moves forward or backward in time, and the more practical approach of the two is to analyze data already collected—making the ever present assumption that such are available.

A more integrative approach for studying change is to develop two discrete time series—one based on available records, the other freshly developed by the investigator. With this strategy, it is necessary to have an overlap period in which the relationships between the two series are established. Given knowledge of the relationships, the available records can be studied retrospectively, thereby providing more intelligence than would be possible if they existed alone. Again, there is a necessary assumption: one must be able to reject the plausibility of an interaction between time and the method. If there is any content or population fluctuation beyond change, such a method is invalid. Diagrammatically, where O is an observation and the subscript n equals new data and a available data:

$$O_{a1}O_{a2}O_{a3}O_{a4}O_{a5}O_{a6}O_{a7}O_{a8}O_{a9}O_{a10}$$

$$O_{n6}O_{n7}O_{n8}O_{n9}O_{n10}$$

A final gain from the less reactive methods is frequently the lower cost of data collection. Many scholars know how to conduct massive surveys which effectively control major sources of error; few do so. This knowledge is an underdeveloped resource. With survey interviews often costing $10 or more apiece, the failure is understandable, however regrettable. When the interview or questionnaire is viewed as the only method, the researcher is doomed to either frustration or a studied avoidance of thoughts on external validity. Peace of mind will come if the investigator breaks the single-method mold and examines the extent to which other measurement classes can substitute for verbal reports. The price of collecting each unit of data is low for most of the methods we have stressed. In some cases, the dross rate is high, and it may be necessary to observe a hundred cases before one meets the research specifications. Nonetheless, even under these high dross-rate conditions, the cost per usable response is often lower than that of a completed interview or returned questionnaire. The lower cost permits flexibility to expand into content and population areas otherwise precluded, and the result of this is to increase the confidence one has in generalizing findings. Just as in the case of studying social change, it may be possible to generate different data series—some based on verbal reports, others based on secondary or observational data. Providing for enough cases of the more expensive procedures to yield a broad base for linkage, the larger number of cases can be allocated to the usually less expensive observational or secondary methods. It is important to note that we add "usually" before "less expensive." The savings are centered in data-collection costs, and it may be that all the savings are vitiated by the elaborate corrections or transformations that a particular data series may require. The cost of materials and analysis is an equivocal area indeed.

In the multimethod pattern of testing, the primary gains coming from the less popular methods are protection against reactive measurement threats, auxiliary data in content areas where verbal reports are unreliable, an easier method of determining long-term change, and a potentially lower-cost substitute for some standard survey practices.

Offsetting these gains, there are associated problems for each of the less popular measurement classes—indeed, if they were less problematic, we would be writing an argument in favor of an increased use of the interview.

The most powerful aspect of the verbal methods—their ability to reach into all content areas—is a soft spot in the hidden-observation, trace, and archival analysis procedures. We have noted remarkably adept and nonobvious applications of data from these sources, but for some content areas, the most imaginative of investigator will have trouble finding pertinent material. Individually, those methods are simply not as broad gauged.

Often missing, too, is complete knowledge of the conditions under which the data were collected, the definitions of important terms used in classification, and the control or lack of it over error risks that may be salient. This is particularly disturbing when dealing with comparisons of public records from different areas or from widely different times. The variation in definitions of "suicide" versus "accidental death," or the differential thoroughness with which marriages are entered in official records are examples of this issue. In general, for trace evidence and archival records, a dominant concern is the possibility of selective deposit and selective survival of the research data. Through supporting research designed to learn of these errors, it is sometimes possible to apply corrections to what is available. At other times, the researcher must remain in ignorance and make assumptions. If he restricts himself to working with *only* such data, he remains helpless before their vagaries. If he uses other measurement classes, the process of triangulating all the different data may provide a test of his assumptions and reveal the presence or extent of error. The comparison of data from the different classes can always add intelligence unavailable from comparisons of data from within the single class.

Because of the risks of error and the danger of unknown biases, we have stressed the importance of careful data sampling. Wherever feasible, locational sampling should be employed, extending over regions as well as areas within a single locality. Similarly, time sampling should be considered not only as a device employed within a single day or week, but applied over months and years. By such effort, we are able to protect against both population and content restrictions, and very often produce interesting data from comparisons of results from different locations or times.[5] The need for time and location sampling is no less for observational or archival data than it is for interviews or questionnaires, for sampling is a problem that transcends the class of measurement.

Another common demand, this one not so applicable to the verbal-report approaches, is that for data adjustment and conversion. The need comes from the experimenter's decreased control over the production of his materials. The exception to this is the contrived field experiment, where the investigator can have full control, but the data from archives, trace sources, and observations are frequently too raw to be used as is. The need is underlined because of one of the major advantages of the secondary data—their ability to produce fine time-series information. In time series, it is usually necessary to account for extraneous sources of variation, such as secular trends or cyclical patterns. Thus, the "score" which is the basis of comparison is some transformed measure which is a residual of the total "score." In other studies, the absolute number of cases varies from unit time to unit time, and the only reasonable comparison score is one which is related in some way, through an average or percentage, for example, to the variable baseline. The investigator may have no control over the flow of an observed population, but he can obtain a count of that flow and use this intelligence as the basis for modifying his comparison score.

The more sophisticated forms of transformation, such as index numbers based on multiple components, demand more information, particularly as one assigns relative weights to components collected into a single score. This is not as awesome as it sounds, and if the investigator is sensitive to the potential usefulness of index numbers, he often finds enough secondary data available for the task, or may obtain new information without extraordinarily high marginal costs. Insofar as these transformations demand time and labor to make the raw data more precise, they are disadvantageous compared with standard questionnaire procedures. There are, however, as we have suggested in various points in the text, indications that index numbers and more simple transformations could be used properly in all classes of measurement. The

Zeitgeist may as yet be inappropriate, but an important work will someday link index-number theory and literature to social-science measurement theory and practice.

These, then, are the gains; these the losses. There are no rewards for ingenuity as such, and the payoff comes only when ingenuity leads to new means of making more valid comparisons. In the available grab bag of imperfect research methods, there is room for new uses of the old.

Max Eastman once suggested that books should start with a first section consisting of a few sentences, the second section a few pages, and so on. He even wrote one like that—*The Enjoyment of Laughter*. Since this has been an unconventional monograph on unconventional research procedures, it is proper that it should have an unconventional close. We reverse Eastman's formula and offer a one-phrase final chapter and a one-paragraph penultimate chapter.

NOTES

1. "Almost all experience on the effects of persuasion communications, including those reported in the present volume, have been limited to investigating changes in opinion. The reason, of course, is that such changes can readily be assessed in a highly reliable way, whereas other components of verbalizable attitudes, although of considerable theoretical interest, are much more difficult to measure" (Janis & Hovland, 1959, p. 3).

2. In a similar note on observers, Heyns and Lippitt (1954) ask if the "observer lacks the sensitivity or the vocabulary which the particular observation requires" (p. 372).

3. For an extended discussion of this issue, see Hyman, Cobb, Feldman, Hart, and Stember (1954) and Kahn and Cannell (1957).

4. The courts have handled secondary information by excluding it under the "hearsay" rule (Morgan, 1963; Wigmore, 1935). Epically put, "Pouring rumored scandal into the bent ear of blabbering busybodies in a pool room or gambling house is no more disreputable than pronouncing it with clipped accents in a courtroom" (Donnelly, Goldstein, & Schwartz, 1962, p. 277). The case from which this is cited is *Holmes,* 379 Pa. 599 (1954).

5. See, for example, Caplow and McGee's (1958) discussion of variation in salaries in American universities—particularly the relationship between beginning salaries and the prestige of the institution. In a related report, the head of an employment agency reported, "The Chicago advertising man on the average makes 10 per cent more than his New York counterpart, 25 per cent more than he would make on the West Coast, and 40 per cent more than he would make in a small town or in the south" (Baxter, 1962, p. 65).

EIGHT

A STATISTICIAN ON METHOD

—————•◆•—————

We must use all available weapons of attack, face our problems realistically and not retreat to the land of fashionable sterility, learn to sweat over our data with an admixture of judgment and intuitive rumination, and accept the usefulness of particular data even when the level of analysis available for them is markedly below that available for other data in the empirical area.

—(Binder, 1964, p. 294)

NINE

CARDINAL NEWMAN'S EPITAPH

From symbols and shadows to the truth

REFERENCES

—————•◆•—————

Adams, J. S. (1963a). Toward an understanding of inequity. *Journal of Abnormal and Social Psychology, 67,* 422-436.

Adams, J. S. (1963b). Wage inequities, productivity, and work quality. In *Psychological research on pay* (Reprint No. 220, pp. 9-16). Berkeley: University of California, Institute of Industrial Relations.

Advertising Service Guild. (1949). *The press and its readers.* London: Art & Technics.

Alger, C. F. (1965). Interaction in a committee of the United Nations General Assembly. In J. D. Singer (Ed.), *International yearbook of behavior research* (Vol. 6). New York: Free Press.

Allport, G. W. (1942). *The use of personal documents in psychological science.* New York: Social Science Research Council.

Amrine, M., & Sanford, F. (1956). In the matter of juries, democracy, science, truth, senators, and bugs. *American Psychologist, 11,* 54-60.

Amthauer, R. (1963). Ergebnisse einer studie über krankheitsbedingte Fehlzeiten. *Psychologische Rundschau, 14,* 1-12.

Anastasi, A. (1958). *Differential psychology.* New York: Macmillan.

Andrew, R. J. (1963). The origin and evolution of the calls and facial expressions of the primates. *Behavior, 20,* 1-109.

Angell, R. C. (1951). The moral integration of American cities. *American Journal of Sociology, 57,* 123-126.

Anonymoi. (1953-1960). *Hair style as a function of hard-headedness vs. long-hairedness in psychological research: A study in the personology of science.* Unprepared manuscript, Northwestern University & University of Chicago.

Ardrey, R. (1961). *African genesis.* New York: Delta.

Arrington, R. (1943). Time sampling in studies of social behavior: A critical review of techniques and results with research suggestions. *Psychological Bulletin, 40,* 81-124.

Arsenian, J. M. (1943). Young children in an insecure situation. *Journal of Abnormal and Social Psychology, 38,* 225-249.

Ashley, J. W. (1962). Stock prices and changes in earnings and dividends: Some empirical results. *Journal of Political Economy, 70,* 82-85.

Athey, K. R., Coleman, J. E., Reitman, A. P., & Tang, J. (1960). Two experiments showing the effect of the interviewer's racial background on responses to questionnaires concerning racial issues. *Journal of Applied Psychology, 44,* 244-246.

Babchuk, N., & Bates, A. P. (1962). Professor or producer: The two faces of academic man. *Social Forces, 40,* 341-348.

Back, K. W. (1960). The well-informed informant. In R. N. Adams & J. J. Preiss (Eds.), *Human organization research* (pp. 179-187). Homewood, IL: Dorsey.

Bain, H. M., & Hecock, D. S. (1957). *Ballot position and voter's choice: The arrangement of names on the ballot and its effect on the voter.* Detroit, MI: Wayne State University Press.

Bain, R. K. (1960). The researcher's role: A case study. In R. N. Adams & J. J. Preiss (Eds.), *Human organization research* (pp. 140-152). Homewood, IL: Dorsey.

Bales, R. F. (1950). *Interaction process analysis.* Cambridge, MA: Addison-Wesley.

Bandura, A. (1962). Lecture on imitation learning at Northwestern University.

Bandura, A., & Walters, R. (1963). *Social learning and personality development.* New York: Holt, Rinehart & Winston.

Barch, A. M., Trumbo, D., & Nangle, J. (1957). Social setting and conformity to a legal requirement. *Journal of Abnormal and Social Psychology, 55,* 396-398.

Barker, R. G., & Wright, H. F. (1951). *One boy's day: A specimen record of behavior.* New York: Harper & Bros.

Barker, R. G., & Wright, H. F. (1954). *Midwest and its children: The psychological ecology of an American town.* Evanston, IL: Row, Peterson.

Barry, H. (1957). Relationships between child training and the pictorial arts. *Journal of Abnormal and Social Psychology, 54,* 380-383.

Barzun, J. (1961). *The delights of detection.* New York: Criterion.

Bass, B. M. (1952). Ultimate criteria of organizational worth. *Personnel Psychology, 5,* 157-173.

Baumrind, D. (1964). Some thoughts on ethics or research: After reading Milgram's "Behavioral Study of Obedience." *American Psychologist, 19,* 421-423.

Baxter, J. (1962, May 28). Chicago shops pay better than N. Y.: Big agencies pay more too. *Advertising Age, 33,* 65.

Beloff, J., & Beloff, H. (1961). The influence of valence on distance judgments of human faces. *Journal of Abnormal and Social Psychology, 62,* 720-722.

Benney, M., Riesman, D., & Star, S. (1956). Age and sex in the interview. *American Journal of Sociology, 62,* 143-152.

Berelson, B. (1952). *Content analysis in communication research.* Glencoe, IL: Free Press.

Berger, C. S. (1954). An experimental study of doodles. *Psychological Newsletter, 6,* 138-141.

Berkson, G., & Fitz-Gerald, F. L. (1963). Eye fixation aspect of attention to visual stimuli in infant chimpanzees. *Science, 139,* 586-587.

Berlyne, D. E. (1964). Emotional aspects of learning. In P. R. Farnsworth, O. McNemar, & Q. McNemar (Eds.), *Annual review of psychology* (Vol. 15, pp. 115-142). Palo Alto, CA: Annual Reviews.

Bernberg, R. E. (1952). Socio-psychological factors in industrial morale: I. The prediction of specific indicators. *Journal of Social Psychology, 36,* 73-82.

Bernstein, E. M. (1935). *Money and the economic system.* Chapel Hill: University of North Carolina Press.

Berreman, J. V. M. (1940). *Factors affecting the sale of modern books of fiction: A study of social psychology.* Unpublished doctoral dissertation, Stanford University.

Binder, A. (1964). Statistical theory. In P. R. Farnsworth, O. McNemar, & Q. McNemar (Eds.), *Annual review of psychology* (Vol. 15, pp. 277-310). Palo Alto, CA: Annual Reviews.

Birdwhistell, R. (1960). Kinesics and communication. In E. Carpenter (Ed.), *Exploration in communication* (pp. 54-64). Boston: Beacon Hill.

Birdwhistell, R. (1963). The kinesic level in the investigations of emotions. In P. Knapp (Ed.), *The expression of emotions in man* (pp. 123-140). New York: International Universities Press.

Blake, R. R., Berkowitz, H., Bellamy, R. Q., & Mouton, J. S. (1956). Volunteering as an avoidance act. *Journal of Abnormal and Social Psychology, 53,* 154-156.

Blake, R. R., Mouton, J. S., & Hain, J. D. (1956). Social forces in petition signing. *Southwest Social Science Quarterly, 36,* 385-390.

Blau, P. M. (1955). *The dynamics of bureaucracy.* Chicago: University of Chicago Press.

Bloch, V. (1952). L'étude objective du comportement des spectateurs. *Reveu Internationale de Filmologie, 3,* 221-222.

Blomgren, G. W., & Scheuneman, T. W. (1961). *Psychological resistance to seat belts.* Research Project RR-115, Northwestern University, Traffic Institute.

Blomgren, G. W., Scheuneman, T. W., & Wilkins, J. L. (1963). Effects of exposure to a safety poster on the frequency of turn signalling. *Traffic Safety, 7,* 15-22.

Boring, E. G. (1953/1963). The role of theory in experimental psychology. *American Journal of Psychology, 66,* 169-184. Reprinted in E. G. Boring (1963). *History, psychology, and science* (R. I. Watson & D. T. Campbell, Eds., pp. 210-225). New York: John Wiley.

Boring, E. G. (1961/1963). The beginning and growth of measurement in psychology. *Isis, 52,* 238-257. Reprinted in E. G. Boring (1963). *History, psychology, and science* (R. I. Watson & D. T. Campbell, Eds., pp. 140-158). New York: John Wiley.

Boring, E. G. (1963). *History, psychology and science* (R. I. Watson & D. T. Campbell, Eds.). New York: John Wiley.

Boring, E. G., & Boring, M. D. (1948). Masters and pupils among the American psychologists. *American Journal of Psychology, 61,* 527-534. Reprinted in E. G. Boring (1963). *History, psychology, and science* (R. I. Watson & D. T. Campbell, Eds., pp. 132-139). New York: John Wiley.

Brayfield, A. H., & Crockett, W. H. (1955). Employee attitudes and employee performance. *Psychological Bulletin, 52,* 396-424.

Brock, T. C. (1965). Communicator-recipient similarity and decision change. *Journal of Personality and Social Psychology, 1,* 650-654.

Brock, T. C., & Guidice, C. D. (1963). Stealing and temporal orientation. *Journal of Abnormal and Social Psychology, 66,* 91-94.

Brogden, H., & Taylor, E. (1950). The dollar criterion—Applying the cost accounting concept to criterion construction. *Personnel Psychology, 3,* 133-154.

Brookover, L. A., & Back, K. W. (1966, Spring). Time sampling as a field technique. *Human Organization,* pp. 64-70.

Brown, J. W. (1960). *A new approach to the assessment of psychiatric therapies.* Unpublished manuscript.

Brozek, J. (1964). Recent developments in Soviet psychology. In P. R. Farnsworth, O. McNemar, & Q. McNemar (Eds.), *Annual review of psychology* (Vol. 15, pp. 493-594). Palo Alto, CA: Annual Reviews.

Bugental, J. F. T. (1948). *An investigation of the relationship of the conceptual matrix to the self-concept.* Unpublished doctoral dissertation, Ohio State University.

Burchard, W. W. (1957). A study of attitudes towards the use of concealed devices in social science research. *Social Forces, 36,* 111.

Burchinal, L. G., & Chancellor, L. E. (1962). Ages at marriage, occupations of grooms and interreligious marriage rates. *Social Forces, 40,* 348-354.

Burchinal, L. G., & Chancellor, L. E. (1963). Survival rates among religiously homogamous and interreligious marriages. *Social Forces, 41,* 353-362.

Burchinal, L. G., & Kenkel, W. F. (1962). Religious identification and occupational status of Iowa grooms. *American Sociological Review, 27,* 526-532.

Burma, J. H. (1959). Self-tattooing among delinquents: A research note. *Sociology and Social Research, 43,* 341-345.

Burwen, L., & Campbell, D. T. (1957). The generality of attitudes toward authority and nonauthority figures. *Journal of Abnormal and Social Psychology, 54,* 24-31.

Callahan, J. D., Morris, J. C., Seifried, S., Ulett, G. A., & Heusler, A. F. (1960). Objective measures in psychopharmacology: Baseline observations. *Missouri Medicine, 57,* 714-718.

Campbell, D. T. (1955). The informant in quantitative research. *American Journal of Sociology, 60,* 339-342.

Campbell, D. T. (1956). Leadership and its effects upon the group. *Ohio Studies in Personnel* (Research Monograph 83). Columbus: Ohio State University, Bureau of Business Research.

Campbell, D. T. (1957). Factors relevant to the validity of experiments in social settings. *Psychological Bulletin, 54,* 297-312.

Campbell, D. T. (1959). Systematic error on the part of human links in communication systems. *Information and Control, 1,* 334-369.

Campbell, D. T. (1960). Recommendations for APA test standards regarding construct trait or discriminant validity. *American Psychologist, 15,* 546-553.

Campbell, D. T. (1961). The mutual methodological relevance of anthropology and psychology. In F. L. K. Hsu (Ed.), *Psychological anthropology approaches to culture and personality* (pp. 333-352). Homewood, IL: Dorsey.

Campbell, D. T. (1963). Administrative experimentation, institutional records and nonreactive measures. In B. G. Chandler, E. F. Carlson, F. Bertolaet, C. Byerly, J. Lee, & R. Sperber (Eds.), *Research seminar on teacher education* (pp. 75-120). Report on Cooperative Research Project No. G-011 supported by the Cooperative Research Program of the Office of Education, U. S. Department of Health, Education, and Welfare, Northwestern University.

Campbell, D. T. (1965a). Pattern matching as an essential in distal knowing. In K. R. Hammond (Ed.), *The psychology of Egon Brunswik.* New York: Holt, Rinehart & Winston.

Campbell, D. T. (1965b). *On the use of both pro and con items in attitude scales.* Unpublished manuscript.

Campbell, D. T., & Fiske, D. W. (1959). Convergent and discriminant validation by the multitrait-multimethod matrix. *Psychological Bulletin, 56,* 81-105.

Campbell, D. T., Kruskal, W. H., & Wallace, W. P. (1966). Seating aggregation as an index of attitude. *Sociometry, 29,* 1-15.

Campbell, D. T., & Mack, R. W. (1966). *The steepness of interracial boundaries as a function of the locus of social interaction.* Manuscript in preparation.

Campbell, D. T., & McCormack, T. H. (1957). Military experience and attitudes toward authority. *American Journal of Sociology, 62,* 482-490.

Campbell, D. T., & Stanley, J. C. (1963). Experimental and quasi-experimental designs for research on teaching. In N. L. Gage (Ed.), *Handbook of research on teaching* (pp. 171-246). Chicago: Rand McNally.

Cane, V. R., & Heim, A. W. (1950). The effects of repeated testing: III. Further experiments and general conclusions. *Quarterly Journal of Experimental Psychology, 2,* 182-195.

Cantril, H. (1944). *Gauging public opinion.* Princeton, NJ: Princeton University Press.

Caplow, T., & McGee, R. (1958). *The academic marketplace.* New York: Basic Books.

Capra, P. C., & Dittes, J. E. (1962). Birth order as a selective factor among volunteer subjects. *Journal of Abnormal and Social Psychology, 64,* 302.

Carhart, R. (1967). The binaural reception of meaningful materials. In A. B. Graham (Ed.), *Sensorineural hearing processes and disorders*. Boston: Little, Brown.

Carlson, J., Cook, S. W., & Stromberg, E. L. (1936). Sex differences in conversation. *Journal of Applied Psychology, 20*, 727-735.

Chapman, L. J., & Bock, R. D. (1958). Components of variance due to acquiescence and content in the F-scale measure of authoritarianism. *Psychological Bulletin, 55*, 328-333.

Chapple, E. D. (1962). Quantitative analysis of complex organizational systems. *Human Organization, 21*, 67-80.

Christensen, H. T. (1960). Cultural relativism and premarital sex norms. *American Sociological Review, 25*, 31-39.

Civil rights: By the book. (1965, March 1). *Newsweek, 65*, 37.

Clark, K. (1957). *America's psychologists*. Washington, DC: American Psychological Association.

Clark, W. H. (1955). A study of some of the factors leading to achievement and creativity with special reference to religious skepticism and belief. *Journal of Social Psychology, 41*, 57-69. Abstracted in M. I. Stein & S. J. Heinze (Eds.). (1960). *Creativity and the individual* (pp. 147-148). Glencoe, IL: Free Press.

Coleman, J., Katz, E., & Menzel, H. (1957). The diffusion of an innovation among physicians. *Sociometry, 20*, 253-270.

Coleman, R. P., & Neugarten, B. (1971). *Social status in the city*. San Francisco: Jossey-Bass.

Conrad, B. (1958). *The death of Manolete*. Cambridge, MA: Houghton Mifflin.

Cook, S. W., & Selltiz, C. (1964). A multiple-indicator approach to attitude measurement. *Psychological Bulletin, 62*, 36-55.

Coombs, C. (1963). *A theory of data*. New York: John Wiley.

Cooper, S. L. (1964). Random sampling by telephone: A new and improved method. *Journal of Marketing Research, 1*, 45-48.

Cox, C. M. (1926). *The early mental traits of three hundred geniuses*. Stanford, CA: Stanford University Press. Abstracted in M. I. Stein & S. J. Heinze (Eds.). *Creativity and the individual* (pp. 128-133). Glencoe, IL: Free Press.

Cox, G. H., & Marley, E. (1959). The estimation of motility during rest or sleep. *Journal of Neurology, Neurosurgery and Psychiatry, 22*, 57-60.

Craddick, R. A. (1961). Size of Santa Claus drawings as a function of time before and after Christmas. *Journal of Psychological Studies, 12*, 121-125.

Craddick, R. A. (1962). Size of witch drawings as a function of time before, on and after Halloween. *American Psychologist, 17*, 307. (Abstract)

Cratty, J. (1962). *Conformity behavior as a function of dress and race*. Unpublished manuscript, Northwestern University.

Crespi, L. P. (1948). The interview effect on polling. *Public Opinion Quarterly, 12*, 99-111.

Cronbach, L. J. (1946). Response sets and test validity. *Educational and Psychological Measurement, 6*, 475-494.

Cronbach, L. J. (1958). Proposals leading to analytic treatment of social perception scores. In R. Tagiuri & L. Petrullo (Eds.), *Person perception and interpersonal behavior* (pp. 353-379). Stanford, CA: Stanford University Press.

Crowald, R. H. (1964, August 15). Soviet grave markers indicate how buried rated with regime. *El Universal* (Mexico City), *196*, 12.

Dalton, M. (1964). Preconceptions and methods in *Men Who Manage*. In P. E. Hammond (Ed.), *Sociologists at work* (pp. 50-95). New York: Basic Books.

Darwin, C. (1872). *The expression of the emotions in man and animals*. London: Murray.

DeCharms, R., & Moeller, G. (1962). Values expressed in American children's readers: 1800–1950. *Journal of Abnormal and Social Psychology, 64*, 136-142.

DeFleur, M. L., & Petranoff, R. M. (1959). A televised test of subliminal persuasion. *Public Opinion Quarterly, 23,* 168-180.

Dempsey, P. (1962). Liberalism-conservatism and party loyalty in the U.S. Senate. *Journal of Social Psychology, 56,* 159-170.

Deutsch, M. (1949). An experimental study of the effects of cooperation and competition upon group process. *Human Relations, 2,* 199-231.

Dexter, L. A. (1963). What do congressmen hear? In N. Polsby, R. Dentler, & P. Smith (Eds.), *Politics and social life* (pp. 485-495). Boston: Houghton Mifflin.

Dexter, L. A. (1964). Communications—Pressure, influence or education? In L. A. Dexter & D. M. White (Eds.), *People, society and mass communications* (pp. 394-409). New York: Free Press.

Digman, J., & Tuttle, D. (1961). An interpretation of an election by means of obverse factor analysis. *Journal of Social Psychology, 53,* 183-194.

Dittman, A. T., & Wynne, L. C. (1961). Linguistic techniques and the analysis of emotionality in interviews. *Journal of Abnormal and Social Psychology, 63,* 201-204.

Doig, I. (1962). *Kefauver and crime: The rise of television news and a senator.* Unpublished master's thesis, Northwestern University.

Dollard, J., & Mowrer, O. H. (1947). A method for measuring tension in written documents. *Journal of Abnormal and Social Psychology, 42,* 3-32.

Donnelly, R. C., Goldstein, J., & Schwartz, R. D. (1962). *Criminal law.* New York: Free Press.

Doob, L. W. (1961). *Communication in Africa.* New Haven, CT: Yale University Press.

Dornbusch, S., & Hickman, L. (1959). Other-directedness in consumer goods advertising: A test of Riesman's historical theory. *Social Forces, 38,* 99-102.

DuBois, C. N. (1963). Time Magazine's fingerprints' study. *Proceedings: 9th Conference, Advertising Research Foundation.* New York: Advertising Research Foundation.

Durand, J. (1960). Mortality estimates from Roman tombstone inscriptions. *American Journal of Sociology, 65,* 365-373.

Durkheim, E. (1951). *Suicide* (J. A. Spaulding & G. Simpson, Trans.). Glencoe, IL: Free Press.

Ehrle, R. A., & Johnson, B. G. (1961). Psychologists and cartoonists. *American Psychologists, 16,* 693-695.

Ekelblad, F. A. (1962). *The statistical method in business.* New York: John Wiley.

Ellis, N. R., & Pryer, R. S. (1959). Quantification of gross bodily activity in children with severe neuropathology. *American Journal of Mental Deficiency, 63,* 1034-1037.

Enciso, J. (1953). *Design motifs of ancient Mexico.* New York: Dover.

Evan, W. M. (1963). Peer-group interaction and organizational socialization: A study of employee turnover. *American Sociological Review, 28,* 429-435.

Exline, R. V. (1963). Explorations in the process of person perception: Visual interaction in relation to competition, sex and affiliation. *Journal of Personality, 31,* 1-20.

Exline, R. V. (1964). *Affective phenomena and the mutual glance: Effects of evaluative feedback and social reinforcement upon visual interaction with an interviewer.* Technical Report No. 12, Office of Naval Research Contract No. Nonr-2285(02).

Exline, R. V., & Winters, L. C. (1964). *Interpersonal preference and the mutual glance.* Technical Report No. 13, Office of Naval Research Contract No. Nonr-2285(02).

Fairbanks, H. (1944). The quantitative differentiation of samples of spoken language. *Psychological Monographs, 56*(2, Whole No. 255), 19-38.

Fantz, R. L. (1961a). A method for studying depth perception in infants under six months of age. *Psychological Record, 11,* 27-32.

Fantz, R. L. (1961b, May). The origin of form perception. *Scientific American, 204,* 66-72.

Fantz, R. L. (1963). Pattern vision in newborn infants. *Science, 140,* 296-297.

Fantz, R. L. (1964). Visual experience in infants: Decreased attention to familiar patterns relative to novel ones. *Science, 146*, 668-670.

Fantz, R. L., Ordy, J. M., & Udelf, M. S. (1962). Maturation of pattern vision in infants during the first six months. *Journal of Comparative and Physiological Psychology, 55*, 907-917.

Farris, C. D. (1958). A method of determining ideological groupings in the Congress. *Journal of Politics, 20*, 308-338.

Feshbach, S., & Feshbach, N. (1963). Influence of the stimulus object upon the complementary and supplementary projection of fear. *Journal of Abnormal and Social Psychology, 66*, 498-502.

Festinger, L., & Katz, D. (1953). *Research methods in the behavioral sciences.* New York: Holt, Rinehart & Winston.

Fiedler, F. E. (1962, February). The nature of teamwork. *Discovery.*

Fiedler, F. E., Dodge, J. S., Jones, R. E., & Hutchins, E. B. (1958). Interrelations among measures of personality adjustment in nonclinical populations. *Journal of Abnormal and Social Psychology, 56*, 345-351.

Field, M. (1954). *Children and films: A study of boys and girls in the cinema.* Dunfermline, Fife: Carnegie United Kingdom Trust.

Fisher, I. (1923). *The making of index numbers.* Boston: Houghton Mifflin.

Fiske, D. W. (1951). Values, theory and the criterion problem. *Personnel Psychology, 4*, 93-98.

Flagler, J. M. (1960, December 10). Profiles: Student of the spontaneous. *New Yorker, 36*, 59-92.

Flugel, J. C. (1930). *Psychology of clothes.* London: Hogarth.

Foote, E. (1962, March 5). Pupil dilation—new measurement of ad's effectiveness. *Advertising Age, 33*, 12.

Forshufvud, S. (1961). *Vem mordade Napoleon?* Stockholm: A. Bonnier.

Foshee, J. G. (1958). Studies in activity level: I. Simple and complex task performances in defectives. *American Journal of Mental Deficiency, 62*, 882-886.

Fowler, E. M. (1962, May 13). Help-wanted ads show sharp rise. *New York Times,* p. 1.

Franzen, R. (1950). Scaling responses to graded opportunities. *Public Opinion Quarterly, 14*, 484-490.

Freed, A., Chandler, P. J., Mouton, J. S., & Blake, R. R. (1955). Stimulus and background factors in sign violation. *Journal of Personality, 23*, 499. (Abstract)

Freeman, L. C., & Ataov, T. (1960). Invalidity of indirect and direct measures of attitude toward cheating. *Journal of Personality, 28*, 443-447.

French, E. G. (1955). Some characteristics of achievement motivation. *Journal of Experimental Psychology, 50*, 232-236.

French, N. R., Carter, C. W., & Koenig, W. (1930). The words and sounds of telephone conversations. *Bell System Technical Journal, 9*, 290-324.

Freud, S. (1920). *Psychopathology of everyday life.* London: Unwin.

Fry, C. L. (1933). The religious affiliations of American leaders. *Scientific Monthly, 36*, 241-249. Abstracted in M. I. Stein & S. J. Heinze (Eds.). (1960). *Creativity and the individual* (pp. 148-149). Glencoe, IL: Free Press.

Gabriele, C. T. (1956). *The recording of audience reactions by infrared photography* (Technical Report, NAVTRADEVCEN 269-7-56).

Gage, N. L., & Shimberg, B. (1949). Measuring senatorial progressivism. *Journal of Abnormal and Social Psychology, 44*, 112-117.

Galton, F. (1870). *Hereditary genius.* New York: D. Appleton. Abstracted in M. I. Stein & S. J. Heinze (Eds.). (1960). *Creativity and the individual* (pp. 85-90). Glencoe, IL: Free Press.

Galton, F. (1872). Statistical inquiries into the efficacy of prayer. *Fortnightly Review, 12*, 125-135.

Galton, F. (1884). Measurement of character. *Fortnightly Review, 36*, 179-185.

Galton, F. (1885). The measure of fidget. *Nature, 32,* 174-175.

Garner, W. R. (1954). Context effects and the validity of loudness scales. *Journal of Experimental Psychology, 48,* 218-224.

Garner, W. R., Hake, H. W., & Eriksen, C. W. (1956). Operationism and the concept of perception. *Psychological Review, 63,* 149-159.

Gearing, F. (1952, June). *The response to a cultural precept among migrants from Bronzeville to Hyde Park.* Unpublished master's thesis, University of Chicago.

Ghiselli, E. E., & Brown, C. W. (1955). *Personnel and industrial psychology* (2nd ed.). New York: McGraw-Hill.

Goncourt, Edmond de. (1937). *The Goncourt Journals: 1851-1870* (L. Galantière, Ed. & Trans.; from *Journal of Edmond & Jules de Goncourt*). New York: Doubleday, Doran.

Good, C. V., & Scates, D. E. (1954). *Methods of research, educational, psychological, sociological.* New York: Appleton-Century-Crofts.

Goode, W. J., & Hatt, P. K. (1952). *Methods in social research.* New York: McGraw-Hill.

Gordon, T. (1950). The development of a method of evaluating flying skill. *Personnel Psychology, 3,* 71-84.

Gore, P. M., & Rotter, J. B. (1963). A personality correlate of social action. *Journal of Personality, 31,* 58-64.

Gosnell, H. F. (1927). *Getting out the vote: An experiment in the stimulation of voting.* Chicago: University of Chicago Press.

Gottschalk, L. A., & Gleser, G. C. (1960). An analysis of the verbal content of suicide notes. *British Journal of Medical Psychology, 33,* 195-204.

Gould, J. (1951, March 4). Costello TV's first headless star: Only his hands entertain audience. *New York Times,* p. 1.

Grace, H., & Tandy, M. (1957). Delegate communication as an index of group tension. *Journal of Social Psychology, 45,* 93-97.

Gratiot-Alphandery, H. (1951a). L'enfant et le film. *Reveu Internationale de Filmologie, 2,* 171-172.

Gratiot-Alphandery, H. (1951b). Jeunes spectateurs. *Reveu Internationale de Filmologie, 2,* 257-263.

Green, E. (1961). *Judicial attitudes in sentencing.* New York: St. Martin's.

Green, H. B., & Knapp, R. H. (1959). Time judgment, aesthetic preference, and need for achievement. *Journal of Abnormal and Social Psychology, 58,* 140-142.

Greenhill, L. P. (1955, September 20). The recording of audience reactions by infrared photography. In *Technical report from Pennsylvania State University to U. S. Navy, Special Devices Center* (SPECDEVCEN 269-7-56, pp. 1-11).

Griffin, J. R. (1964, October 27). Coia "catch," kicking draw much criticism. *Chicago Sun-Times,* p. 76.

Griffith, R. M. (1949). Odds adjustments by American horse race bettors. *American Journal of Psychology, 62,* 290-294.

Grinder, R. E. (1961). New techniques for research in children's temptation behavior. *Child Development, 32,* 679-688.

Grinder, R. E. (1962). Parental child learning practices, conscience, and resistance to temptation of sixth grade children. *Child Development, 33,* 803-820.

Grinder, R. E., & McMichael, R. E. (1963). Cultural influence on conscience development: Resistance to temptation and guilt among Samoans and American Caucasians. *Journal of Abnormal and Social Psychology, 66,* 503-507.

Grusky, O. (1959). Organizational goals and the behavior of informal leaders. *American Journal of Sociology, 65,* 59-67.

Grusky, O. (1963a). The effects of formal structure on managerial recruitment: A study of baseball organization. *Sociometry, 26,* 345-353.

Grusky, O. (1963b). Managerial succession and organizational effectiveness. *American Journal of Sociology, 69,* 21-31.

Guilford, J. P. (1954). *Psychometric methods.* New York: McGraw-Hill.

Guilford, J. P. (1956). The relation of intellectual factors to creative thinking in science. In C. Taylor (Ed.), *The 1955 University of Utah research conference on the identification of creative scientific talent* (pp. 69-95). Salt Lake City: University of Utah Press.

Guion, R. M. (1961). Criterion measurement and personnel judgments. *Personnel Psychology, 14,* 141-149.

Gullahorn, J., & Strauss, G. (1960). The field worker in union research. In R. N. Adams & J. J. Preiss (Eds.), *Human organization research* (pp. 153-165). Homewood, IL: Dorsey.

Gump, R. (1962). *Jade: Stone of heaven.* New York: Doubleday.

Gusfield, J. R. (1960). Field work reciprocities in studying a social movement. In R. N. Adams & J. J. Preiss (Eds.), *Human organization research* (pp. 99-108). Homewood, IL: Dorsey.

Hafner, E. M. & Presswood, S. (1965). Strong inference and weak interactions. *Science, 149,* 503-510.

Haggard, E. A., Brekstad, A., & Skard, A. G. (1960). On the reliability of the anamnestic interview. *Journal of Abnormal and Social Psychology, 61,* 311-318.

Hall, R. L., & Willerman, B. (1963). The educational influence of dormitory roommates. *Sociometry, 26,* 294-318.

Hamburger, P. (1950, January 7). Peeping Funt. *New Yorker, 25,* 72-73.

Hamilton, T. (1942). Social optimism in American Protestantism. *Public Opinion Quarterly, 6,* 280-283.

Hansen, A. H. (1921). *Cycles of prosperity and depression in the United States* (University of Wisconsin Studies in Social Sciences and History), Madison.

Hanson, N. R. (1958). *Patterns of discovery.* Cambridge, UK: Cambridge University Press.

Hardy, H. C. (1959). Cocktail party acoustics. *Journal of the Acoustical Society of America, 31,* 535.

Hartmann, G. W. (1936). A field experiment on the comparative effectiveness of "emotional" and "rational" political leaflets in determining election results. *Journal of Abnormal and Social Psychology, 31,* 99-114.

Hartshorne, H., & May, M. A. (1928). *Studies in the nature of character: Vol. 1. Studies in deceit.* New York: Macmillan.

Hartshorne, H., May, M. A., & Maller, J. B. (1929). *Studies in the nature of character. Vol. 2. Studies in service and self control.* New York: Macmillan.

Harvey, J. (1953). The content characteristics of best-selling novels. *Public Opinion Quarterly, 17,* 91-114.

Helson, H., Blake, R. R., & Mouton, J. S. (1958). Petition-signing as adjustment to situational and personal factors. *Journal of Social Psychology, 48,* 3-10.

Henle, M., & Hubble, M. B. (1938). "Egocentricity" in adult conversation. *Journal of Social Psychology, 9,* 227-234.

Henry, H. (1958). *Motivation research: Its practice and uses for advertising, marketing, and other business purposes.* London: Crosby Lockwood.

Herbinière-Lebert, S. (1951). Pourquoi et comment nous avons fait "Mains Blanches": Premieres experiences avec un film educatif realisé spécialement pour les mins de sept ans. *Revue Internationale de Filmologie, 2,* 247-255.

Hess, E. H., & Polt, J. M. (1960). Pupil size as related to interest value of visual stimuli. *Science, 132,* 349-350.

Heusler, A., Ulett, G., & Blasques, J. (1959). Noise-level index: An objective measurement of the effect of drugs on the psychomotor activity of patients. *Journal of Neuropsychiatry, 1,* 23-25.

Heusler, A. F., Ulett, G. A., & Callahan, J. D. (1960, May). *Comparative EEG studies of tranquilizing drugs. Research Laboratories of the St. Louis State Hospital, St. Louis, Mo.* Paper read at Pan-American Medical Congress, Mexico City.

Heyns, R., & Lippitt, R. (1954). Systematic observational techniques. In G. Lindzey (Ed.), *Handbook of social psychology* (Vol. 1, pp. 370-404). Cambridge, MA: Addison-Wesley.

Hildum, D. C., & Brown, R. W. (1956). Verbal reinforcement and interviewer bias. *Journal of Abnormal and Social Psychology,* 53, 108-111.

Hillebrandt, R. H. (1962). *Panel design and time-series analysis.* Unpublished master's thesis, Northwestern University.

Holmes, L. D. (1958). *Ta'u: Stability and change in a Samoan village* (Reprint No. 7). Wellington, New Zealand: Polynesian Society.

Horst, P. (1953). Correcting the Kuder-Richardson reliability for dispersion of item difficulties. *Psychological Bulletin, 50,* 371-374.

Hovland, C. I., Lumsdaine, A. A., & Sheffield, F. D. (1949). *Experiments on mass communication.* Princeton, NJ: Princeton University Press.

Howells, L. T., & Becker, S. W. (1962). Seating arrangement and leadership emergence. *Journal of Abnormal and Social Psychology, 64,* 148-150.

Hughes, E. C. (1958). *Men and their work.* Glencoe, IL: Free Press.

Humphreys, L. G. (1960). Note on the multitrait-multimethod matrix. *Psychological Bulletin, 57,* 86-88.

Hyman, H. H., Cobb, W. J., Feldman, J. J., Hart, C. W., & Stember, C. H. (1954). *Interviewing in social research.* Chicago: University of Chicago Press.

Ianni, F. A. (1957-1958). Residential and occupational mobility as indices of the acculturation of an ethnic group. *Social Forces, 36,* 65-72.

Imanishi, K. (1960). Social organization of subhuman primates in their natural habitat. *Current Anthropology, 1,* 393-407.

In the eye of the beholder. (1964, December 28). *Sponsor, 18,* 25-29.

Jackson, D. N., & Messick, S. J. (1957). A note on "ethnocentrism" and acquiescent response sets. *Journal of Abnormal and Social Psychology, 54,* 132-134.

Jacques, E. (1956). *Measurement of responsibility.* Cambridge, MA: Harvard University Press.

Jaffe, A. J., & Stewart, C. D. (1951). *Manpower, resources and utilizations.* New York: John Wiley.

Jahoda-Lazarsfeld, M., & Zeisel, H. (1932). *Die Arbeitslösen von Marienbad.* Leipzig: Hirzel.

James, J. (1951). A preliminary study of the size determinant in small group interaction. *American Sociological Review, 16,* 474-477.

James, R. W. (1958). A technique for describing community structure through newspaper analysis. *Social Forces, 37,* 102-109.

James, W. (1890). *The principles of psychology.* New York: Holt.

Janis, I. L., & Hovland, C. I. (1959). An overview of persuasibility research. In I. L. Janis & C. I. Hovland (Eds.), *Personality and persuasibility* (pp. 1-26). New Haven, CT: Yale University Press.

Janowitz, M. (1958). Inferences about propaganda impact from textual and documentary analysis. In W. E. Daugherty & M. Janowitz (Eds.), *A psychological warfare casebook* (pp. 732-735). Baltimore: Johns Hopkins Press.

Jay, R., & Copes, J. (1957). Seniority and criterion measures of job proficiency. *Journal of Applied Psychology, 41,* 58-60.

Jones, R. W. (1960). Progressivism in Illinois communities as measured by library services. *Transactions of the Illinois State Academy of Science, 53,* 166-172.

Jones, V. (1946). Character development in children: An objective approach. In L. Carmichael (Ed.), *Manual of child psychology* (pp. 707-775). New York: John Wiley.

Jung, A. F. (1959). Price variations among automobile dealers in Chicago, Illinois. *Journal of Business, 32,* 315-326.

Jung, A. F. (1960). Prices of Falcon and Corvair cars in Chicago and selected cities. *Journal of Business, 33,* 121-126.

Jung, A. F. (1961). Impact of the compact cars on new-car prices. *Journal of Business, 34,* 167-182.

Jung, A. F. (1962). Impact of the compact cars on new-car prices: As reappraisal. *Journal of Business, 35,* 70-76.

Jung, A. F. (1963). Dealer pricing practices and finance charges for new mobile homes. *Journal of Business, 36,* 430-439.

Jung, A. F. (1964). Mortgage availability and terms in Florida. *Journal of Business, 37,* 274-279.

Kadish, S. (1964). On the tactics of police-prosecution oriented critics of the courts. *Cornell Law Quarterly, 49,* 436-477.

Kahn, R. L., & Cannell, C. F. (1957). *The dynamics of interviewing: Theory, technique and cases.* New York: John Wiley.

Kaminski, G., & Osterkamp, U. (1962). Untersuchungen über die Topologie sozialer Handlungsfelder. *Zeitschrift für experimentelle und angewandte Psychologie, 9,* 417-451.

Kane, F. (1958). Clothing worn by out-patients to interviews. *Psychiatric Communications, 1*(2).

Kane F. (1959). Clothing worn by an out-patient: A case study. *Psychiatric Communications, 2*(2).

Kane, F. (1962). The meaning of the form of clothing. *Psychiatric Communications, 5*(1).

Kappel, J. W. (1948). Book clubs and the evaluation of books. *Public Opinion Quarterly, 12,* 243-252.

Katz, D. (1942). Do interviewers bias poll results? *Public Opinion Quarterly, 6,* 248-268.

Kendall, L. M. (1963). The hidden variance: What does it measure? *American Psychologist, 18,* 452.

Kerlinger, F. N. (1964). *Foundations of behavioral research: Educational and psychological inquiry.* New York: Holt, Rinehart & Winston.

Kinsey, A. C., Pomeroy, W. B., Martin, C. E., & Gebhard, P. H. (1953). *Sexual behavior in the human female.* Philadelphia: W. B. Saunders.

Kintz, B. L., Delprato, D. J., Mettee, D. R., Persons, C. E., & Schappe, R. H. (1965). The experimenter effect. *Psychological Bulletin, 63,* 223-232.

Kitsuse, J. I., & Cicourel, A. V. (1963). A note on the uses of official statistics. *Social Problems, 11,* 131-139.

Knox, J. B. (1961). Absenteeism and turnover in an Argentine factory. *American Sociological Review, 26,* 424-428.

Kort, F. (1957). Predicting Supreme Court decisions mathematically: A quantitative analysis of "right to counsel" cases. *American Political Science Review, 51,* 1-12.

Kort, F. (1958). Reply to Fisher's "Mathematical Analysis of Supreme Court Decisions." *American Political Science Review, 52,* 339-348.

Kramer, E. (1963). Judgment of personal characteristics and emotions from nonverbal properties of speech. *Psychological Bulletin, 60,* 408-420.

Kramer, E. (1964). Elimination of verbal cues in judgments of emotion from voice. *Journal of Abnormal and Social Psychology, 68,* 390-396.

Krasner, L. (1958). Studies of the conditioning of verbal behavior. *Psychological Bulletin, 55,* 148-170.

Kretsinger, E. A. (1952). An experimental study of gross bodily movement as an index to audience interest. *Speech Monographs, 19,* 244-248.

Kretsinger, E. A. (1959). An experimental study of restiveness in preschool educational television audiences. *Speech Monographs, 26,* 72-77.

Krislov, S. (1963). Amicus curiae brief: From friendship to advocacy. *Yale Law Journal, 72,* 694-721.

Krout, M. H. (1933). *Major aspects of personality.* Chicago: College Press.

Krout, M. H. (1937). Further studies on the relation of personality and gestures: A nosological analysis of autistic gestures. *Journal of Experimental Psychology, 20,* 279-287.

Krout, M. H. (1951). *Gestures and attitudes: An experimental study of the verbal equivalents and other characteristics of a selected group of manual autistic gestures.* Unpublished doctoral dissertation, University of Chicago.

Krout, M. H. (1954a). An experimental attempt to determine the significance of unconscious manual symbolic movements. *Journal of General Psychology, 51,* 121-152.

Krout, M. H. (1954b). An experimental attempt to produce unconscious manual symbolic movements. *Journal of General Psychology, 51,* 93-120.

Krueger, L. E., & Ramond, C. K. (1965). References. In M. Mayer (Ed.), *The intelligent man's guide to sales measures of advertising* (pp. 29-71). New York: Advertising Research Foundation.

Krugman, H. E. (1964). Some applications of pupil measurement. *Journal of Marketing Research, 1,* 15-19.

Kuhn, T. (1962). *The structure of scientific revolutions.* Chicago: University of Chicago Press.

Kupcinet, I. (1965, March 9). Kup's column. *Chicago Sun-Times,* p. 46.

Landis, C. (1927). National differences in conversation. *Journal of Abnormal and Social Psychology, 21,* 354-357.

Landis, C., & Hunt, W. A. (1939). *The startle pattern.* New York: Farrar & Rinehart.

Landis, M. H., & Burtt, H. E. (1924). A study of conversations. *Journal of Comparative Psychology, 4,* 81-89.

Lang, K., & Lang, G. E. (1960). Decisions for Christ: Billy Graham in New York City. In M. Stein, A. J. Vidich, & D. M. White (Eds.), *Identity and anxiety* (pp. 415-427). Glencoe, IL: Free Press.

LaPiere, R. T. (1934). Attitudes vs. actions. *Social Forces, 13,* 230-237.

Lasswell, H. D. (1941). The world attention survey. *Public Opinion Quarterly, 5,* 456-462.

Lea, T. (1949). *The brave bulls.* Boston: Little, Brown.

Lefkowitz, M., Blake, R. R., & Mouton, J. S. (1955). Status factors in pedestrian violation of traffic signals. *Journal of Abnormal and Social Psychology, 51,* 704-706.

Legget, R. F., & Northwood, T. D. (1960). Noise surveys of cocktail parties. *Journal of the Acoustical Society of America, 32,* 16-17.

Lehman, H. C., & Witty, P. A. (1931). Scientific eminence and church membership. *Scientific Monthly, 36,* 544-549. (Abstracted in M. I. Stein & S. J. Heinze (1960). *Creativity and the individual* (pp. 149-150). Glencoe, IL: Free Press.

Leipold, W. D. (1963). *Psychological distance in a dyadic interview as a function of introversion-extraversion, anxiety, social desirability and stress.* Unpublished doctoral dissertation, University of North Dakota.

Lenski, G. E., & Leggett, J. C. (1960). Caste, class, and deference in the research interview. *American Journal of Sociology, 65,* 463-467.

Leroy-Boussion, A. (1954). Etude du comportement émotional enfantin au cours de la projection d'un film comique. *Revue Internationale de Filmologie, 5,* 105-123.

Lewin, H. S. (1947). Hitler youth and the Boys Scouts of America. *Human Relations, 1,* 206-227.

Lewis, O. (1961). *The children of Sanchez.* New York: Random House.

Libby, W. I. (1963). Accuracy of radio-carbon dates. *Science, 140,* 278-280.

Lippmann, W. (1955). *The public philosophy.* New York: New American Library.

Litter bugged. (1964, November 2). *Advertising Age, 35,* 74.

Lodge, G. T. (1963). Pilot stature in relation to cockpit size: A hidden factor in Navy jet aircraft accidents. *American Psychologist, 17,* 468. (Abstract)

Lombroso, C. (1891). *The man of genius.* London: Walter Scott. Abstracted in M. I. Stein & S. J. Heinze (1960). *Creativity and the individual* (pp. 350-353). Glencoe, IL: Free Press.

Lucas, D. B., & Britt, S. H. (1950). _Advertising psychology and research._ New York: McGraw-Hill.

Lucas, D. B., & Britt, S. H. (1963). _Measuring advertising effectiveness._ New York: McGraw-Hill.

Lustig, N. I. (1962). The relationships between demographic characteristics and pro-integration vote of white precincts in a metropolitan southern community. _Social Forces, 40,_ 205-208.

Lyle, H. M. (1953). An experimental study of certain aspects of the electromagnetic movement meter as a criterion to audience attention. _Speech Monographs, 20,_ 126. (Abstract)

Mabie, E. (1931). A study of the conversion of first-grade pupils during free play periods. _Journal of Educational Research, 24,_ 135-138.

Mabley, J. (1963, January 22). Mabley's reports. _Chicago American, 62,_ 3.

Maccoby, E. E. (1964). Developmental psychology. In P. R. Farnsworth, O. McNemar, & Q. McNemar (Eds.), _Annual review of psychology_ (Vol. 15, pp. 203-250). Palo Alto, CA: Annual Reviews.

MacKinney, A. C. (1960). What should ratings rate? _Personnel, 37,_ 75-78.

MacLean, W. R. (1959). On the acoustics of cocktail parties. _Journal of the Acoustical Society of America, 31,_ 79-80.

MacRae, D. (1954a). The role of the state legislator in Massachusetts. _American Sociological Review, 19,_ 185-194.

MacRae, D. (1954b). Some underlying variables in legislative roll call votes. _Public Opinion Quarterly, 18,_ 191-196.

MacRae, D., & MacRae, E. (1961). Legislators' social status and their votes. _American Journal of Sociology, 66,_ 599-603.

Madge, J. (1965). _The tools of social science._ New York: Doubleday Anchor.

Mahl, G. (1956). Disturbances and silences in the patient's speech in psychotherapy. _Journal of Abnormal and Social Psychology, 53,_ 1-15.

Manago, B. R. (1962). Mad: Out of the comics rack and into satire. _Add One, 1,_ 41-46.

Marsh, R. M. (1961). Formal organization and promotion in a pre-industrial society. _American Sociological Review, 26,_ 547-556.

Martin, P. (1961, May 27). I call on the Candid Camera man. _Saturday Evening Post, 234,_ 26-27.

Matarazzo, J. D. (1962a, September). _Control of interview behavior._ Paper read at American Psychological Association, St. Louis.

Matarazzo, J. D. (1962b). Prescribed behavior therapy: Suggestions from noncontent interview research. In A. J. Bachrach (Ed.), _Experimental foundations of clinical psychology_ (pp. 471-509). New York: Basic Books.

Matarazzo, J. D., Weitman, M., Saslow, G., & Wiens, A. N. (1963). Interviewer influence on duration of interviewee speech. _Journal of Verbal Learning and Verbal Behavior, 1,_ 451-458.

Matarazzo, J. D., Wiens, A. N., Saslow, G., Dunham, R. M., & Voas, R. B. (1964). Speech durations of astronaut and ground communicator. _Science, 143,_ 148-150.

Matthews, T. S. (1957). _The sugar pill._ New York: Simon & Schuster.

May, M. A., & Hartshorne, H. (1927). First steps toward a scale for measuring attitude. _Journal of Educational Psychology, 17,_ 145-162.

McCahill, D. (1963, June 8). Parleys to evaluate Catholic status. _Chicago Sun-Times,_ p. 12.

McCarroll, J. R., & Haddon, W. A. (1961). Controlled study of fatal accidents in New York City. _Journal of Chronic Diseases, 15,_ 811-826.

McCarthy, D. A. (1929). Comparison of children's language in different situations and its relation to personality traits. _Journal of Genetic Psychology, 36,_ 538-591.

McClelland, D. C. (1961). _The achieving society._ Princeton, NJ: Van Nostrand.

McGranahan, D., & Wayne, I. (1948). German and American traits reflected in popular drama. _Human Relations, 1,_ 429-455.

McGrath, J. E. (1962). The influence of positive interpersonal relations on adjustment and effectiveness in rifle teams. *Journal of Abnormal and Social Psychology, 65,* 365-375.

McGraw, M., & Molloy, L. B. (1941). The pediatric anamnesis: Inaccuracies in eliciting developmental data. *Child Development, 12,* 255-265.

Mechanic, D., & Volkart, E. H. (1961). Stress, illness behavior and the sick role. *American Sociological Review, 26,* 51-58.

Melbin, M. (1961). Organization practice and individual behavior: Absenteeism among psychiatric aides. *American Sociological Review, 26,* 14-23.

Melton, A. W. (1933a). Some behavior characteristics of museum visitors. *Psychological Bulletin, 30,* 720-721.

Melton, A. W. (1933b). Studies of installation at the Pennsylvania Museum of Art. *Museum News, 11,* 508.

Melton, A. W. (1935). Problems of installation in museums of art. *Studies in museum education.* Washington, DC: American Association of Museums.

Melton, A. W. (1936). Distribution of attention in galleries in a museum of science and industry. *Museum News, 13,* 3, 5-8.

Melton, A. W., Feldman, N. G., & Mason, C. W. (1936). *Experimental studies of the education of children in a museum of science* (Publications of the American Association of Museums, New Series, No. 15). Washington, DC: American Association of Museums.

Merritt, C. B., & Fowler, R. G. (1948). The pecuniary honesty of the public at large. *Journal of Abnormal and Social Psychology, 43,* 90-93.

Middleton, R. (1960). Fertility values in American magazine fiction: 1916-1956. *Public Opinion Quarterly. 24,* 139-143.

Miller, G. A. (1947). Population, distance and the circulation of information. *American Journal of Psychology, 60,* 276-284.

Mills, F. C. (1927). *The behavior of prices.* New York: National Bureau of Economic Research.

Mindak, W. A., Neibergs, A., & Anderson, A. (1963). Economic effects of the Minneapolis newspaper strike. *Journalism Quarterly, 40,* 213-218.

Mitchell, W. C. (1921). *Index numbers of wholesale prices in the U. S. and foreign countries: I. the making and using of index numbers* (Bulletin No. 284). Washington, DC: U.S. Department of Labor, Bureau of Labor Statistics.

Moore, H. T. (1917). Laboratory test of anger, fear, and sex interest. *American Journal of Psychology, 28,* 390-395.

Moore, H. T. (1922). Further data concerning sex differences. *Journal of Abnormal and Social Psychology, 17,* 210-214.

Moore, U., & Callahan, C. (1943). *Law and learning theory: A study in legal control.* New Haven, CT: Yale Law Journal Company.

Moore, W. E. (1953). The exploitability of the "labor force" concept. *American Sociological Review, 18,* 68-72.

Morgan, E. M. (1963). *Basic problems of evidence.* New York: Joint Committee on Continuing Legal Education of the American Law Institute and the American Bar Association.

Morgenstern, O. (1963). *On the accuracy of economic observations* (2nd ed.). Princeton, NJ: Princeton University Press.

Mosteller, F. (1955). Use as evidenced by an examination of wear and tear on selected sets of ESS. In K. Davis et al. (Eds.), *A study of the need for a new encyclopedic treatment of the social sciences* (pp. 167-174). Unpublished manuscripts.

Mosteller, F., & Wallace, O. L. (1963). Inference in an authorship problem: A comparative study of discrimination methods applied to the authorship of *The Federalist Papers. Journal of the American Statistical Association, 58,* 275-309.

Mudgett, B. D. (1951). *Index numbers.* New York: John Wiley.

Murphy, G., & Murphy, S. L. (1931). *Experimental social psychology.* New York: Harper.

Murphy, G., & Murphy, L. (1962). Soviet life and Soviet psychology. In R. A. Bauer (Ed.), *Some views on Soviet psychology* (pp. 253-276). Washington, DC: American Psychological Association.

Nagel, S. (1962). Ethic affiliations and judicial propensities. *Journal of Politics, 24,* 92.

Naroll, R. (1956). The preliminary index of social development. *American Anthropologist, 58,* 687-715.

Naroll, R. (1960, September). Controlling data quality. In Series Research in Social Psychology. *Symposia Studies Series, 4,* 7-12.

Naroll, R. (1961). Two solutions to Galton's problems. *Philosophy of Science, 28,* 15-39.

Naroll, R. (1962). *Data quality control.* Glencoe, IL: Free Press.

Naroll, R., & Naroll, F. (1963). On bias of exotic data. *Man, 25,* 24-26.

NASA Manned Spacecraft Center. (1962a). *Results of the first United States manned orbital space flight.* Washington, DC: Government Printing Office.

NASA Manned Spacecraft Center. (1962b). *Results of the second United States manned orbital space flight.* Washington, DC: Government Printing Office.

National Advertising Company. (1963). *Shopping center research study.* Bedford Park, IL: Author.

North, R. C., Holsti, O. R., Zaninovich, M. G., & Zinnes, D. A. (1963). *Content analysis.* Evanston, IL: Northwestern University Press.

Olson, W. C. (1929). *The measurement of nervous habits in normal children.* Minneapolis: University of Minnesota Press.

Orne, M. T. (1959). The nature of hypnosis: Artifact and essence. *Journal of Abnormal and Social Psychology, 58,* 277-299.

Orne, M. T. (1962). On the social psychology of the psychological experiment: With particular reference to demand characteristics and their implications. *American Psychologist, 17,* 776-783.

Orne, M. T., & Evans, F. J. (1965). Social control in the psychological experiment: Antisocial behavior and hypnosis. *Journal of Personality and Social Psychology, 1,* 189-200.

Orne, M. T., & Scheibe, K. E. (1964). The contribution of nondeprivation factors in the production of sensory deprivation effects: The psychology of the "panic button." *Journal of Abnormal and Social Psychology, 68,* 3-12.

Osgood, C. E. (1953). *Method and theory in experimental psychology.* New York: Oxford University Press.

Osgood, C. E., & Walker, E. (1959). Motivation and language behavior: A content analysis of suicide notes. *Journal of Abnormal and Social Psychology, 59,* 58-67.

OSS Assessment Staff. (1948). *Assessment of men.* New York: Rinehart.

Paisley, W. J. (1964). Identifying the unknown communicator in painting, literature and music: The significance of minor encoding habits. *Journal of Communication, 14,* 219-237.

Parker, E. B. (1963). The effects of television on public library circulation. *Public Opinion Quarterly, 27,* 578-589.

Parker, E. B. (1964). The impact of a radio book review program on public library circulation. *Journal of Broadcasting, 8,* 353-361.

Pearson, K. (1914). *The life, letters and labours of Francis Galton* (Vol. 1). Cambridge, UK: Cambridge University Press.

Perrine, M., & Wessman, A. W. (1954). Disguised public opinion interviewing with small samples. *Public Opinion Quarterly, 18,* 92-96.

Phillips, R. H. (1962, March 18). Miami goes Latin under Cuban tide. *New York Times,* p. 85.

Platt, J. R. (1964). Strong inference. *Science, 146,* 347-353.

Polansky, N., Freeman, W., Horowitz, M., Irwin, L., Paponia, N., Rapaport, D., & Whaley, F. (1949). Problems of interpersonal relations in research on groups. *Human Relations, 2,* 281-291.

Politz Media Studies. (1958). *The readers of "The Saturday Evening Post."* Philadelphia: Curtis.

Politz Media Studies. (1959). *A study of outside transit poster exposure.* New York: Alfred Politz.

Pollack, I., & Pickett, J. M. (1957). Cocktail party effect. *Journal of the Acoustical Society of America, 29,* 1262.

Pool, I. de Sola (Ed.). (1959). *Trends in content analysis.* Urbana: University of Illinois Press.

Popper, K. (1935). *Logic der Forschung.* Wien: Springer.

Popper, K. (1959). *The logic of scientific discovery.* New York: Basic Books.

Popper, K. (1962). *Conjectures and refutations.* New York: Basic Books.

Prosser, W. L. (1964). *Handbook of the law of torts.* (3rd ed.). St. Paul: West.

Pyles, M. L., Stolz, H. R., & Macfarlane, J. W. (1935). The accuracy of mothers' reports on birth and developmental data. *Child Development, 6,* 165-176.

Quine, W. V. (1953). *From a logical point of view.* Cambridge, MA: Harvard University Press.

Rashkis, H., & Wallace, A. F. C. (1959). The reciprocal effect. *Archives of General Psychiatry, 1,* 489-498.

Ray, M. L. (1965). *Cross-cultural content analysis: Its promise and its problems.* Unpublished manuscript, Northwestern University.

Reddy, J. (1965. February 28). Heady thieves find Wheeling their Waterloo. *Chicago Sun-Times,* p. 66.

Riesman, D. (1956). Orbits of tolerance, interviewers and elites. *Public Opinion Quarterly, 20,* 49-73.

Riesman, D. (1959). Comment on "The State of Communication Research." *Public Opinion Quarterly, 23,* 10-13.

Riesman, D., & Ehrlich, J. (1961). Age and authority in the interview. *Public Opinion Quarterly, 25,* 39-56.

Riesman, D., & Watson, J. (1964). The sociability project: A chronicle of frustration and achievement. In P. E. Hammond (Ed.), *Sociologists at work* (pp. 235-321). New York: Basic Books.

Riker, W., & Niemi, D. (1962). The stability of coalitions on roll calls in the House of Representatives. *American Political Science Review, 56,* 58-65.

Riley, M. W. (1963). *Sociological research: I. A case approach.* New York: Harcourt, Brace & World.

Robbins, L. C. (1963). The accuracy of parental recall of aspects of child development and of child rearing practices. *Journal of Abnormal and Social Psychology, 66,* 261-270.

Robinson, D., & Rohde, S. (1946). Two experiments with an anti-Semitism poll. *Journal of Abnormal and Social Psychology, 41,* 136-144.

Robinson, E. S. (1928). *The behavior of the museum visitor* (Publications of the American Association of Museums, New Series, No. 5). Washington, DC: American Association of Museums.

Roens, B. B. (1961). New findings from Scott's special advertising research study. In *Proceedings: 7th Annual Conference, Advertising Research Foundation* (pp. 65-70). New York: Advertising Research Foundation.

Rogow, A. A., & Lasswell, H. D. (1963). *Power, corruption and rectitude.* Englewood Cliffs, NJ: Prentice Hall.

Rorer, L. G. (1965). The great response-style myth. *Psychological Bulletin, 63,* 129-156.

Rosenbaum, M. E. (1956). The effect of stimulus and background factors on the volunteering response. *Journal of Abnormal and Social Psychology, 53,* 118-121.

Rosenbaum, M. E., & Blake, R. R. (1955). Volunteering as a function of field structure. *Journal of Abnormal and Social Psychology, 50,* 193-196.

Rosenthal, A. M. (1962, February 25). Japan, famous for politeness, has a less courteous side, too. *New York Times,* p. 20.

Rosenthal, R. (1963). On the social psychology of the psychological experiment: The experimenter's hypothesis as unintended determinant of experimental results. *American Scientist, 51,* 268-283.

Rosenthal, R. (1964). Experimenter outcome-orientation and the results of the psychological experiment. *Psychological Bulletin, 61,* 405-412.

Rosenthal, R., & Fode, K. L. (1963). Psychology of the scientist: V. Three experiments in experimenter bias. *Psychological Reports, 12,* 491-511.

Rosenthal, R., & Lawson, R. (1963). A longitudinal study of the effects of experimenter bias on the operant learning of laboratory rats. *Journal of Psychiatric Research, 2,* 61-72.

Rosenthal, R., Persinger, G. W., Vikan-Kline, L., & Fode, K. L. (1963). The effect of early data returns on data subsequently obtained by outcome-biased experimenter. *Sociometry, 26,* 487-498.

Ross, H. L. (1963). The inaccessible respondent: A note on privacy in city and country. *Public Opinion Quarterly, 27,* 269-275.

Ross, H. L., & Campbell, D. T. (1965). *Time series data in the quasi-experimental analysis of the Connecticut speeding crackdown.* Unpublished manuscript.

Ruesch, J., & Kees, W. (1956). *Nonverbal communications: Notes on the visual perception of human relations.* Berkeley: University of California Press.

Rush, C. A. (1953). Factorial study of sales criteria. *Personnel Psychology, 6,* 9-24.

Salzinger, K. (1958). A method of analysis of the process of verbal communication between a group of emotionally disturbed adolescents and their friends and relatives. *Journal of Social Psychology, 47,* 39-53.

Sawyer, H. G. (1961). *The meaning of numbers.* Speech before the American Association of Advertising Agencies.

Schachter, S. (1959). *The psychology of affiliation.* Stanford, CA: Stanford University Press.

Schachter, S., & Hall, R. (1952). Group derived restraints and audience persuasion. *Human Relations, 5,* 397-406.

Schanck, R. L., & Goodman, C. (1939). Reactions to propaganda on both sides of a controversial issue. *Public Opinion Quarterly, 3,* 107-112.

Schneidman, E. S., & Farberow, N. L. (1957). Some comparisons between genuine and stimulated suicide notes in terms of Mowrer's concepts of discomfort and relief. *Journal of General Psychology, 56,* 251-256.

Schubert, G. (1959). *Quantitative analysis of judicial behavior.* Glencoe, IL: Free Press.

Schubert, G. (1963). *Judicial decision-making.* New York: Free Press.

Schulman, J. L., Kasper, J. C., & Throne, J. M. (1965). *Brain damage and behavior.* Springfield, IL: W. I. Thomas.

Schulman, J. L., & Reisman, J. M. (1959). An objective measure of hyperactivity. *American Journal of Mental Deficiency, 64,* 455-456.

Schwartz, M. S., & Stanton, A. H. (1950). A social psychological study of incontinence. *Psychiatry, 13,* 399-416.

Schwartz, R. D. (1961). Field experimentation in sociolegal research. *Journal of Legal Education, 13,* 401-410.

Schwartz, R. D., & Skolnick, J. H. (1962a). Television and tax compliance. In L. Arons & M. A. May (Eds.), *Television and human behavior.* New York: Appleton-Century-Crofts.

Schwartz, R. D., & Skolnick, J. H. (1962b). Two studies of legal stigma. *Social Problems, 10,* 133-142.

Sebald, H. (1962). Studying national character through comparative content analysis. *Social Forces, 40,* 318-322.

Sechrest, L. (1965a). *Handwriting on the wall: A view of two cultures.* Unpublished manuscript, Northwestern University.

Sechrest, L. (1965b). *Situational sampling and contrived situations in the assessment of behavior.* Unpublished manuscript, Northwestern University. (Mimeograph ed.)

Sechrest, L., & Flores, L. (1971). The occurrence of a nervous mannerism in two cultures. *Asian Studies, 9,* 55-63.

Sechrest, L., Flores, L., & Arellano, L. (1965). *Social distance and language in bilingual subjects.* Unpublished manuscript, Northwestern University.

Sechrest, L., & Wallace, J. (1964). Figure drawing and naturally occurring events: Elimination of the expansive euphoria hypothesis. *Journal of Educational Psychology, 55,* 42-44.

Selltiz, C., Jahoda, M., Deutsch, M., & Cook, S. W. (1959). *Research methods in social relations.* New York: Holt, Rinehart & Winston.

Senator Salinger? (1964, August 10). *Newsweek, 63,* 28.

Severin, D. (1952). The predictability of various kinds of criteria. *Personnel Psychology, 5,* 93-104.

Shadegg, S. C. (1964). *How to win an election.* New York: Toplinger.

Shepard, H. R., & Blake, R. R. (1962). Changing behavior through cognitive change. *Human Organization, 21,* 88-92.

Shils, E. A. (1959). Social inquiry and the autonomy of the individual. In D. Lerner (Ed.), *The human meaning of the social sciences* (pp. 114-157). Cleveland: Meridian.

Siersted, E., & Hansen, H. L. (1951). Réaction des petits enfants au cinema: Resumé d'une serie d'observations faites au Danemark. *Revue Internationale de Filmologie, 2,* 241-245.

Singh, P. H., & Huang, S. C. (1962). Some socio-cultural and psychological determinants of advertising in India: A comparative study. *Journal of Social Psychology, 57,* 113-121.

Sletto, R. F. (1937). *Construction of personality scales by the criterion of internal consistency.* Hanover, NH: Sociological Press.

Smith, H. T. (1958). A comparison of interview and observation methods of mother behavior. *Journal of Abnormal and Social Psychology, 57,* 278-282.

Snyder, E. C. (1959). Uncertainty and the Supreme Court's decisions. *American Journal of Sociology, 65,* 241-245.

Snyder, R., & Sechrest, L. (1959). An experimental study of directive group therapy with defective delinquents. *American Journal of Mental Deficiency, 63,* 117-123.

Solley, C. M., & Haigh, G. A. (1957). A note to Santa Claus. *Topeka Research Papers, The Menninger Foundation, 18,* 4-5.

Solomon, R. L. (1949). An extension of control group design. *Psychological Bulletin, 46,* 137-150.

Sommer, R. (1959). Studies in personal space. *Sociometry, 22,* 247-260.

Sommer, R. (1960). Personal space. *Canadian Architect,* pp. 76-80.

Sommer, R. (1961). Leadership and group geography. *Sociometry, 24,* 99-110.

Sommer, R. (1962). The distance for comfortable conversations: Further study. *Sociometry, 25,* 111-116.

Spiegel, D. E., & Neuringer, C. (1963). Role of dread in suicidal behavior. *Journal of Abnormal and Social Psychology, 66,* 507-511.

Stechler, G. (1964). Newborn attention as affected by medication during labor. *Science, 144,* 315-317.

Stein, M. I., & Heinze, S. J. (1960). *Creativity and the individual.* Glencoe, IL: Free Press.

Steiner, G. A. (1963). *The people look at television.* New York: Knopf.

Steiner, I. D. (1964). Group dynamics. In P. R. Farnsworth, O. McNemar, & Q. McNemar (Eds.), *Annual review of psychology* (Vol.15, pp. 421-446). Palo Alto, CA: Annual Reviews.

Steiner, I. D., & Field, W. L. (1960). Role assignment and interpersonal influence. *Journal of Abnormal and Social Psychology, 61,* 239-245.

Stephan, F. F., & McCarthy, P. J. (1958). *Sampling opinions.* New York: John Wiley.

Stern, R. (1960). *Golk.* New York: Criterion.

Stewart, J. Q. (1947). Empirical mathematical rules concerning the distinction and equilibrium of population. *Geographical Review, 37,* 461-485.

Stoke, S. M., & West, E. D. (1931). Sex differences in conversational interests. *Journal of Social Psychology, 2,* 120-126.

Stouffer, S. A. (1934). Problems in the application of correlation to sociology. *Journal of the American Statistical Association, 29,* 52-58. Reprinted in S. A. Stouffer (1962). *Social research to test ideas* (pp. 264-270). Glencoe, IL: Free Press.

Stouffer, S. A., Lumsdaine, A. A., Lumsdaine, M. H., Williams, R., Smith, M., Janis, I., Star, S., & Cottrell, L. (1949). *The American soldier: Combat and its aftermath* (Vol. 2). Princeton, NJ: Princeton University Press.

Strodtbeck, F. L., & James, R. M. (1955). *Social process in jury deliberations.* Paper read at the American Sociological Society.

Strodtbeck, F. L., James, R. M, & Hawkins, C. (1957). Social status in jury deliberations. *American Sociological Review, 22,* 713-719.

Strodtbeck, F. L., & Mann, R. D. (1956). Sex role differentiation in jury deliberations. *Sociometry, 19,* 3-11.

Stuart, I. R. (1963). Minorities vs. minorities: Cognitive, affective and conative components of Puerto Rican and Negro acceptance and rejection. *Journal of Social Psychology, 59,* 93-99.

Sussman, L. (1959). Mass political letter writing in America. *Public Opinion Quarterly, 23,* 203-212.

Sussman, L. (1963). *Dear F. D. R.* New York: Bedminster.

Swift, A. L., Jr. (1927). *The survey of the YMCA of the City of New York* (Limited ed.). New York: Association Press.

Tannenbaum, P. H., & Noah, J. E. (1959). Sportugese: A study of sports page communication. *Journalism Quarterly, 36,* 163-170.

Tarde, G. (1901). *L'Opinion et la foule.* Paris: Felix Alcan.

Terman, L. M. (1917). The intelligence quotients of Francis Galton in childhood. *American Journal of Psychology, 28,* 209-215.

Thomas, D. S. (1929). *Some new techniques for studying social behavior.* New York: Columbia University Press.

Thomas, W. I., & Znaniecki, F. (1918). *The Polish peasant in Europe and America: Monograph of an immigrant group* (Vol. 1). Chicago: University of Chicago Press.

Thorndike, E. L. (1939). *Your city.* New York: Harcourt, Brace.

Thorndike, R. L. (1949). *Personnel selection.* New York: John Wiley.

Toulouse, M. M., & Mourgue, R. D. (1948). Es réactions respiratoires au cours de projections cinématographiques. *Revue Internationale de Filmologie, 2,* 77-83.

Trueswell, R. W. A. (1963). *Survey of library users' needs and behavior as related to the application of data processing and computer technique.* Unpublished doctoral dissertation, Northwestern University.

Turner, W. (1960). Dimensions of foreman performance: A factor analysis of criterion measures. *Journal of Applied Psychology, 44,* 216-223.

Udy, S. H. (1964). Cross-cultural analysis: A case study. In P. E. Hammond (Ed.), *Sociologists at work* (pp. 161-183). New York: Basic Books.

Ulett, G. A., Heusler, A., & Callahan, J. (1961). Objective measures in psycho-pharmacology (methodology). In E. Rothlin (Ed.), *Neuro-psychopharmacology: Vol. 2. Proceedings of the second meeting of the Collegium Internationale Neuropsychopharmacologicum, Basle, July 1960* (pp. 401-409). New York: Elsevier.

Ulett, G. A., Heusler, A., Ives-Word, V., Word, T., & Quick, R. (1961). Influence of chlordiozepoxide on drug-altered EEG patterns and behavior. *Medicina Experimentalis, 5,* 386-390.

Ulmer, S. S. (1963). Quantitative processes: Some practical and theoretical applications. In H. W. Baade (Ed.), *Jurimetrics*. New York: Basic Books.

Underwood, B. J. (1957). *Psychological research*. New York: Appleton-Century-Crofts.

Vernon, D. T. A., & Brown, J. (1963). *The utilization of secondary or less preferred sources of information by persons in potentially stressful situations*. Unpublished manuscript.

Vidich, A. J., & Shapiro, G. A. A. (1955). Comparison of participant observation and survey data. *American Sociological Review, 20,* 28-33.

Vincent, C. E. (1964). Socioeconomic status and familial variables in mail questionnaire responses. *American Journal of Sociology, 69,* 647-653.

Vose, C. E. (1959). *Caucasians only*. Berkeley: University of California Press.

Warner, W. L. (1959). *The living and the dead*. New Haven, CT: Yale University Press.

Warner, W. L., Meeker, M., & Eells, K. (1949). *Social class in America*. Chicago: Science Research Associates.

Washburne, C. (1928). The good and bad in Russian education. *New Era, 9,* 8-12.

Watson, J., Breed, W., & Posman, H. A. (1948). Study in urban conversation: Sample of 1001 remarks overheard in Manhattan. *Journal of Social Psychology, 28,* 121-123.

Watson, R. I. (1959). Historical review of objective personality testing: The search for objectivity. In B. M. Bass & I. A. Berg (Eds.), *Objective approaches to personality assessment* (pp. 1-23). Princeton, NJ: Van Nostrand.

Wax, R. H. (1960). Reciprocity in field work. In R. N. Adams & J. J. Preiss (Eds.), *Human organization research* (pp. 90-98). Homewood, IL: Dorsey.

Webb, E. J. (1957). *Men's clothing study*. Chicago: Chicago Tribune Company.

Webb, E. J. (1961). *The orthographies of seven African languages*. Manuscript in preparation.

Webb, E. J. (1962a). How to tell a columnist: I. *Columbia Journalism Review, 1,* 23-25.

Webb, E. J. (1962b). *Television programming and the effect of ratings*. Paper read at Association for Education in Journalism, Chapel Hill, NC.

Webb, E. J. (1963). How to tell a columnist: II. *Columbia Journalism Review, 2,* 20.

Wechsler, H. (1961). Community growth, depressive disorders and suicide. *American Journal of Sociology, 67,* 9-16.

Weir, R. H. (1963). *Language in the crib*. The Hague, The Netherlands: Mouton.

Weiss, D. J., & Dawis, R. V. (1960). An objective validation of factual interview data. *Journal of Applied Psychology, 44,* 381-385.

Weitz, J. (1958). Selecting supervisors with peer ratings. *Personnel Psychology, 11,* 25-35.

Werner, H., & Wapner, S. (1953). Changes in psychological distance under conditions of danger. *Journal of Personality, 24,* 153-167.

West, D. V. (1962). In the eye of the beholder. *Television Magazine, 19,* 60-63.

Whisler, T. L., & Harper, S. F. (1962). *Performance appraisal: Research and practice*. New York: Holt, Rinehart & Winston.

White, R. K. (1949). Hitler, Roosevelt and the nature of war propaganda. *Journal of Abnormal and Social Psychology, 44,* 157-174.

Whyte, W. H. (1956). *The organization man*. New York: Simon & Schuster.

Wigmore, J. H. (1935). *A student's textbook of the law of evidence*. Brooklyn, NY: Foundation Press.

Wigmore, J. H. (1937). *The science of judicial proof as given by logic, psychology, and general experience and illustrated in judicial trials* (3rd ed.). Boston: Little, Brown.

Williams, R. (1950). Probability sampling in the field: A case history. *Public Opinion Quarterly, 14,* 316-330.

Wilson, E. B. (1952). *An introduction to scientific research*. New York: McGraw-Hill.

Windle, C. (1954). Test-retest effect on personality questionnaires. *Educational and Psychological Measurement, 14,* 617-633.

Winick, C. (1962). Thoughts and feelings of the general population as expressed in free association typing. *The American Imago, 19,* 67-84.

Winship, E. C., & Allport, G. W. (1943). Do rosy headlines sell newspapers? *Public Opinion Quarterly, 7,* 205-210.

Winston, S. (1932). Birth control and the sex-ratio at birth. *American Journal of Sociology, 38,* 225-231.

Wolff, C. (1948). *A psychology of gesture.* London: Methuen.

Wolff, C. (1951). *The hand in psychological diagnosis.* London: Methuen.

Wolff, W., & Precker, J. A. (1951). Expressive movement and the methods of experimental depth psychology. In H. H. Anderson & G. L. Anderson (Eds.), *An introduction to projection techniques* (pp. 457-497). New York: Prentice-Hall.

Yule, G. U., & Kendall, M. G. (1950). *An introduction to the theory of statistics* (14th ed.). New York: Hafner.

Zamansky, H. S. (1956). A technique for assessing homosexual tendencies. *Journal of Personality, 24,* 436-448.

Zamansky, H. S. (1958). An investigation of the psychoanalytic theory of paranoid delusions. *Journal of Personality, 26,* 410-425.

Zeisel, H. (1957). *Say it with figures* (4th ed.). New York: Harper.

Z-Frank stresses radio to build big Chevy dealership. (1962). *Advertising Age, 33,* 83.

Zipf, G. K. (1946). Some determinants of the circulation of information. *American Journal of Psychology, 59,* 401-421.

Zipf, G. K. (1949). *Human behavior and the principle of least effort.* Cambridge, MA: Addison-Wesley.

FURTHER READING

———————•◆•———————

The following references were included in the original bibliography but are not cited in the text.

Aronson, E. (1958). The need for achievement as measured by graphic expression. In J. W. Atkinson (Ed.), *Motives in fantasy, action, and society* (pp. 249-265). Princeton, NJ: Van Nostrand.

Becker, H. S. (1958). Problems of inference and proof in participant observation. *American Sociological Review, 23,* 652-660.

Belknap, G. M. (1958). A method for analyzing legislative behavior. *Midwest Journal of Political Science, 2,* 377-402.

Blau, P. (1964). The research process in the study of *The dynamics of bureaucracy.* In P. E. Hammond (Ed.), *Sociologists at work* (pp. 16-49). New York: Basic Books.

Bridgman, P. W. (1927). *The logic of modern physics.* New York: Macmillan.

Brown, J. W. (1961). *The use of the single case study with actuarial and indirect indices in psychiatric research.* Unpublished manuscript.

Campbell, D. T. (1963). From description to experimentation: Interpreting trends as quasi-experiments. In C. W. Harris (Ed.), *Problems in measuring change* (pp. 212-242). Madison: University of Wisconsin Press.

Campbell, D. T. (1963). Social attitudes and other acquired behavioral dispositions. In S. Koch (Ed.), *Psychology: A study of a science: Vol. 6. Investigations of man as socius* (pp. 94-176). New York: McGraw-Hill.

Couch, A., & Keniston, K. (1960). Yeasayers and naysayers: Agreeing response set as a personality variable. *Journal of Abnormal and Social Psychology, 60,* 151-174.

Couch, A., & Keniston, K. (1961). Agreeing response set and social desirability. *Journal of Abnormal and Social Psychology, 62,* 175-179.

Davis, R. C. (1961). Physiological responses as a means of evaluating information. In A. D. Biderman & H. Zimmer (Eds.), *The manipulation of human behavior* (pp. 142-168). New York: John Wiley.

Dearborn, D. C., & Simon, H. A. (1958). Selective perception: A note on the departmental identification of executive. *Sociometry, 21,* 140-144.

Diamond, S. (1963). Some early uses of the questionnaire. *Public Opinion Quarterly, 27,* 528-542.

Edwards, A. L. (1957). *The social desirability variable in personality assessment and research.* New York: Dryden.

Edwards, A. L., & Walker, J. N. (1961). A note on the Couch and Keniston measure of agreement response set. *Journal of Abnormal and Social Psychology, 62,* 173-174.

Exline, R. V., Gray, D., & Schuette, D. (1965). Visual behavior in a dyad as affected by interview content and sex of respondent. *Journal of Personality and Social Psychology, 1,* 201-209.

Hall, E. T. (1964). Silent assumption in social communication. *Disorders of Communication, 42,* 41-55.

Hartshorne, H., May, M. A., & Shuttleworth, F. K. (1930). *Studies in the nature of character: Vol. 3. Studies in the organization of character.* New York: Macmillan.

Haworth, M. R. (1956). *An exploratory study to determine the effectiveness of a filmed puppet show as a group projective technique for use with children.* Doctoral dissertation, Pennsylvania State University. (University Microfilms No. 19305)

Help wanted ads in September hit new high, NICB reports. (1964, November 2). *Advertising Age, 35,* 74.

Hemphill, J. K., & Sechrest, L. B. (1952). A comparison of three criteria of aircrew effectiveness in combat over Korea. *Journal of Applied Psychology, 36,* 323-327.

Houseman, E. E., & Lipstein, B. (1969). Observation and audit techniques for measuring retail sales. *Agricultural Economics, 12,* 61-72.

Jecker, J., Maccoby, N., Breitrose, H. S., & Rose, E. D. (1964). Teacher accuracy in assessing cognitive visual feedback from students. *Journal of Applied Psychology, 48,* 393-397.

Kanfer, F. H. (1960). Verbal rate, eyeblink and content in structured psychiatric interviews. *Journal of Abnormal and Social Psychology, 61,* 341-347.

Kavanau, J. L. (1964). Behavior: Confinement, adaptation, and compulsory regimes in laboratory studies. *Science, 143,* 490.

Kimbrell, D. L., & Blake, R. R. (1958). Motivational factors in the violation of a prohibition. *Journal of Abnormal and Social Psychology, 56,* 132-133.

Kirk, P. L. (1963). Criminalistics. *Science, 140,* 367-370.

Lander, B. (1954). *Towards an understanding of juvenile delinquency.* New York: Columbia University Press.

Loomis, C. P. (1946). Political and occupational changes in a Hanoverian village, Germany. *Sociometry, 9,* 316-333.

Maller, J. B. (1930). The effect of signing one's name. *School and Society, 31,* 882-884.

Murray, E. J., & Cohen, M. (1959). Mental illness, milieu therapy, and social organization in ward groups. *Journal of Abnormal and Social Psychology, 58,* 48-54.

Nixon, H. K. (1924). Attention and interest in advertising. *Archives of Psychology, 11,* 1-68.

Pettigrew, T. (1964). *A profile of the Negro American.* Princeton, NJ: Van Nostrand.

Robins, L. N., Hyman, H., & O'Neal, P. (1962). The interaction of social class and deviant behavior. *American Sociological Review, 27,* 480-492.

Rotter, J. B., Liverant, S., & Crowne, D. P. (1961). The growth and extinction of expectancies in chance, controlled and skilled tasks. *Journal of Psychology, 52,* 161-177.

Smedslund, J. (1964). Educational psychology. In P. R. Farnsworth, O. McNemar, & Q. McNemar (Eds.), *Annual review of psychology* (Vol. 15, pp. 251-276). Palo Alto, CA: Annual Reviews.

Stouffer, S. A. (1962). *Social research to test ideas*. Glencoe, IL: Free Press. Reprinted from P. F. Lazarsfeld (1940). *Radio and the printed page* (pp. 266-272). New York: Duell, Sloan & Pearce.

Wolfson, R. (1951). Graphology. In H. H. Anderson & G. L. Anderson (Eds.), *An introduction to projection techniques* (pp. 416-456). New York: Prentice Hall.

Yates, F. (1949). *Sampling methods for censuses and surveys*. New York: Hafner.

INDEX

————•◆•————

ABOUT THE AUTHORS

he four authors of this book came together at Northwestern University during the early 1960s. Their project began with brown-bag lunches in which each of the authors contributed his knowledge of "oddball measures." As their collection of unusual measurement techniques grew, they decided to embody them in some systematic way in a book. This "Sage Classic" was the result.

Eugene J. Webb received a Ph.D. in educational psychology from the University of Chicago, after which he did market research for the *Chicago Tribune*. He then taught at Northwestern's Medill School of Journalism from 1960 to 1966, where he became, in Campbell's phrase, "the major wit and author" in developing this book. In the late 1960s, he worked at the Institute for Defense Analysis in the Department of Defense and then moved on to a position in Stanford University's Graduate School of Business.

Donald T. Campbell began his higher education at San Bernardino Valley Junior College (a reminder of the value of community colleges), and went on to the University of California at Berkeley where he studied with Erik Erikson, Nevitt Sanford, and Edward Chace Tolman. After teaching at Ohio State University and the University of Chicago, he joined the Department of Psychology at Northwestern, where he spent much of his career. Later on, he taught at Syracuse and Lehigh Universities. He is widely acknowledged to be the major founder of evaluation research in the social sciences.

Richard D. Schwartz did his undergraduate and graduate work in sociology at Yale and stayed on as a postdoctoral fellow in interdisciplinary studies at Yale's Institute of Human Relations. A sociologist of law, he has taught social sciences and law at Yale, Northwestern, State University of New York at Buffalo (where he was the law school dean), and Syracuse. He is currently the Ernest I. White Research Professor at Syracuse University's College of Law and a member of the Maxwell School's Departments of Sociology and Social Science.

Lee Sechrest is Professor of Psychology at the University of Arizona and founder of the Evaluation Group for Analysis of Data (EGAD), a methodological interest group that has been meeting on a continuing basis for 12 years. A large portion of his current work is aimed at the development of more effective methods of research and data analysis, including dealing with large data sets, longitudinal designs and their analysis, and calibration of measures. In addition, he is working to develop better conceptualizations of culture and cultural variables, including those related to rural experience, and to derive useful measures of those variables. EGAD, under his direction, is involved in a wide range of evaluation projects and activities. He is to receive the Year 2000 Lifetime Achievement Award from Division 5 Evaluation, Measurement, and Statistics of the American Psychological Association. Prior to his arrival at the University of Arizona, where he has been for 15 years, Sechrest taught at the University of Michigan, Florida State University, Northwestern University, and Pennsylvania State University. He is the author, coauthor, or editor of 20 books and monographs and author of nearly 250 journal articles and book chapters.